The Woman
on the Windowsill

The Woman on the Windowsill

A Tale of Mystery in Several Parts

SYLVIA SELLERS-GARCÍA

Yale UNIVERSITY PRESS

New Haven and London

Published with assistance from the Annie Burr Lewis Fund.

Yale University Press books may be purchased in quantity for educational, business, or promotional use. For information, please e-mail sales.press@yale.edu (U.S. office) or sales@yaleup.co.uk (U.K. office).

Set in Minion type by Integrated Publishing Solutions.

Printed in the United States of America.

Library of Congress Control Number: 2019934885

ISBN 978-0-300-23428-2 (hardcover : alk. paper)

A catalogue record for this book is available from the British Library.

This paper meets the requirements of ANSI/NISO Z39.48-1992 (Permanence of Paper).

10 9 8 7 6 5 4 3 2 1

This book is dedicated to the women of my family who came before me and paved the way with encouragement, affection, ferocity, narrative prowess, and a necessary disregard for convention: to my mother, Martha Julia; to her sisters, Silvia and Aura Marina; to their mother, Marta; to her mother, Chusita; and to my father's mother, Anita Hope.

Contents

Note to Readers

This narrative history of Guatemala builds on the work of many other scholars and historians. In order to converse with a broad reading audience, I've mostly kept discussion of these sources and the debates among them to the endnotes. Please consult these notes, which are also aimed broadly, for reading recommendations and scholarly acknowledgments.

Acknowledgments

This is a small book with big debts. Historians sometimes suffer under the illusion that they work in isolation, but in fact the work unfolds over hundreds of interactions, on the page or in person. The single narrator's voice here belies the collaborative nature of historical work, and I had a lot to learn in the course of this project.

The Archivo General de Centroamérica is peopled by archivists and administrators who do heroic work to maintain precious documents in adverse circumstances. I am inestimably grateful to the staff of the archive for their work and for the welcome they extend to scholars.

I am likewise grateful to the many museums, archives, and private collections that generously made their holdings available. My thanks to Saulo Bambi for his breathtaking photographs of wax figures at La Specola in Florence, to the John Carter Brown Library, to the Davis Museum at Wellesley College, to the Blanton Museum of Art, to the National Galleries of Scotland, to the Museo de Américas, to Breamore House, to the Archivo General de Indias in Seville and in particular to Andrew McDonald for sharing his drawing of the water lily variations. A heartfelt thanks to Erin Greb for creating a fabulous map on short notice.

The research and writing benefited from many audiences and contexts. Listeners and readers are as hard to come by as space and time to write. My sincere thanks to audiences at the American Historical Association, the USC-Huntington Early Modern Studies Institute, the Radical Readings workshop at Boston College, the New England Council of Latin American Studies, the Rocky Mountain Council for Latin American Studies, the American Association for the History of Medicine, the Latin American Studies Program at Cornell, the University of Lisbon, the David Rockefeller Center for Latin American Studies, and the participants of the Paper Technologies conference jointly hosted by Yale University and Wesleyan University. I am especially grateful to Matt O'Hara, Susan Deans-Smith, Corinna Zeltsman, Nancy Quintanilla, Raymond Craib, Edwin Ortiz, Erin Goodman, Arthur Corvelo, and Mayra Guapindaia for generative comments and follow-up suggestions. I am just as guilty as other scholars of talking about my work out of context, very much when not formally presenting, and often those conversations have been crucial. Many people at different stages have patiently listened to the gruesome details, the zany connections, and the many doubts, then generously shared their thoughts: Kirsten Weld, Jessica Delgado, Karen Melvin, Alexandre Antonelli, Taylor Boas, Veronica Herrera, Yolanda Martínez–San Miguel, Luciano Naka, Sean McEnroe, Sharyn November, Alejandra Dubcovsky, Zeb Tortorici, and Brinton Lykes. I am grateful to my colleagues in the history department at Boston College for supporting this work in myriad ways.

Brianna Leavitt-Alcántara kindly shared archival documents and suggestions for how to track down leads. Arianne Chernock, Julian Bourg, and Arissa Oh read early versions of the draft and did not cringe, but urged me onward. Prasannan Parthasarathi offered timely and much-needed publishing advice. Zack Matus offered more than one valuable reference. Deborah Levenson-Estrada shared an apartment with me in Guatemala City and then, when I came home with a horrifying criminal case, said, "You have to write about *that*," with an invigorating sense of conviction that would have hardened even the weakest stomach. Sophie Brockmann, Dorian Karchmar, and Kenneth Mills all supported this project generously and early, when the pieces barely hung together. Sacha Ramjit and Kaitlyn Wilson, both the kind of students who teach more than they learn from their professors, spent hours reading obscure criminal cases and sharing their insights (and well-placed outrage).

My thanks to the many hosts, individual and institutional, who made space and time for me to write: José Manuel Mayorga; Adelaide Cromwell; my parents in Antigua; the David Rockefeller Center for Latin American Studies, where I was the Central America Visiting Scholar in the spring of 2018; the Boston College Intersections writing retreat of 2017. Much of this book was written in public libraries. I am grateful to the libraries of Brookline, Beverly, and Hamilton-Wenham, as well as to the wonderful Salem Athenaeum, which transported me to the nineteenth century for brief, immersive moments.

The anonymous reviewers of this book's proposal and manuscript went above and beyond, offering both encouraging feedback and invaluable suggestions. I'm especially grateful for their willingness to accept this book on its own terms and for their ability to recommend revisions in ways consistent with the core ambitions of the project.

Thank you to Jaya Chatterjee, who has shepherded this book to publication with diligence and care. I am grateful to

Dan Heaton for editing and to Alexa Selph for completing this book with an index.

A few people read this book from start to finish, and their comments shaped my thinking in countless ways. I am tremendously grateful to William B. Taylor, Paul Ramírez, Peter Haskin, Sarah Ross, Carolyn Twomey, Andrea Wenz, and Virginia Reinberg for their incisive and patient readership. I really would not have finished this book without the WWC, whose members read drafts of this book not once but *twice*. Apart from all the chocolate, good humor, brilliant comments, and fellowship, you gave me something priceless: deadlines!

My family members have supported this project unstintingly. My mother, Martha Julia, has expressed unshakable faith at every turn. My father, Stephen, not only read the whole manuscript and sent detailed comments, he also accompanied me to the AGCA and pored through archival documents; and *then* he tracked down an article at CIRMA that I couldn't find anywhere else! Tom has cheered tirelessly. Oliver has asked questions about things I'd never considered. Alton and Rowan gave me time, the most precious gift of all. My deepest thanks to Alton, Rowan, Oliver, Tom, and my parents for supporting this work.

Introduction
In Which Don Cayetano Díaz
Opens His Window

The first illusion that must be cast aside is that of the definitive truthful narrative. A historical narrative is a construction, not a truthful discourse that can be verified on all of its points.

—ARLETTE FARGE, *THE ALLURE OF THE ARCHIVES*

Every murder mystery begins with a body. Or it begins with calm, an impression of serenity that promises to shatter at any moment, when the wreckage of a human life is finally revealed. A corpse. A long enmity. A sudden flash of brutality. The disruption of that initial serenity, manifested in death.

Since the body that begins this story is never found, the mystery must begin with calm.

It is the first of July in 1800, shortly after six in the morning. Despite the early hour, there is already movement. Servants have risen to make breakfast. The clap of hands against wet maize dough and the crackle of stove fires mix with slow morning conversations: gossip, last night's dreams recounted and interpreted, plans made for the day. Some have already left the house to run early errands, and their bare feet patter on the street stones. The zanate birds are loud at this hour, clicking and croaking into the humid air.

Don Cayetano Díaz, a reputable surveyor and mapmaker, opens the study window of his well-appointed home in Guatemala City. The shutters, as with all buildings in this colonial capital, open onto the street, where wide stone sills offer perfect vantage points for watching passersby. Díaz does this every day. He opens the shutters and then settles down to work at the desk that sits just below the window. On this morning, he realizes at once that something is different. There is a strange object on his sill. He calls to his brother, for already the object seems ominous. There are drops of blood on the sill's cold gray stone.

Díaz's brother hurries from the house to seek a surgeon, Don Josef Thomas Caseros, and as they return, coincidentally, Díaz sees another acquaintance passing by the window and calls him into the house. Don Narciso Esparragosa, one of the most renowned surgeons in Guatemala—indeed, a leading figure of enlightenment medicine in Spanish America—is making his way to the nearby hospital. Together, the four men examine the object on the windowsill, and now there can be no doubt: placed on a lily pad, as if served on a plate, is a woman's breast.

Narciso Esparragosa examines it with a surgeon's eye. In fact, it is not one breast, but two. They are attached, cut from the body in the shape of an hourglass; the one with less skin has been folded beneath the other. At the other end, the skin extends all the way to the underarm, with its scrap of dark hair.

Esparragosa believes that the cut reveals no expert skill, and he states that he cannot fathom what has prompted someone to do such a thing. None of them can fathom it. They do not understand it; but they do understand that this is a criminal act. A deeply offensive and disturbing criminal act. The evidence must be recorded, and the authorities must be called.

The court *escribano* (scribe and notary), Vicente Antonio de Villatoro, makes his own examination of the breasts, describing them in as much detail as possible. He notes four drops of blood on the sill. He notes a severed nerve and small discolorations of the skin. And he speculates, because of the darkened areolas, that the woman had been pregnant.[1]

It is only because of the coincidence of Cayetano's skill as a mapmaker that we, readers in the present day, have a visual impression of what he saw on the morning of July 1, 1800. Illustrations in criminal cases of this period are very rare.[2] But Díaz had the colored pencils he used for his meticulous drawings of land parcels close at hand, and one of the officials in attendance must have realized that he was uniquely suited to depicting this most unimaginable piece of evidence. His illustration of the severed breasts appears on the second page of the voluminous records for the criminal trial that ensued once the authorities were called and the investigation had begun (Figure 1).[3]

Díaz made a careful drawing, with such precision in the depiction of the rounded breast, the tuft of hair, the incongruous lily pad, that the subject becomes unrecognizable in its verisimilitude. We never see the body this way: mutilated, *dis*embodied. And viewed aerially, like terrain on a map. When I first saw this drawing in the archive in Guatemala City, I was flipping through the pages, not reading, and then I stopped: staring at the inscrutable cluster of shapes for several seconds

1. Drawing in the margin of the criminal case

without comprehending. In fact, not until I had begun reading the case—lured in by the enigmatic drawing in the margin—did I understand what it depicted, and the horror dawned on me retrospectively. *This is what it looked like.*

The horror we experience, realizing the fact of these body parts on the windowsill, is in some ways similar to but in most ways different from what people in Guatemala experienced at the time. The fact that Guatemalans were horrified is clear. Action was taken immediately to identify the "owner"—as they put it—of the breasts. More than a dozen people were jailed over the course of the investigation and dozens of testimonies were taken. More than a hundred folios were filled with depositions, orders, correspondence, and speculations on the part of the presiding judges. Bodies were exhumed. The investigation spilled over into nearby towns and villages. A special police patrol was created to lie in wait for the perpetrator. Guatemala City was horrified. But not in the way we are horrified.

We are horrified in a manner trained by long exposure to crimes of this nature—fictional and factual. We have well-established habits of reading and viewing horrific crime, and we have well-established genres on the subject, which are at least partly devoted to spectacularly gruesome acts of violence against women. Through these habits and genres and their depictions of such acts we are trained to be both morally outraged at the misogyny and simultaneously titillated. Sometimes the latter is an explicit aim, but mostly it is concealed, wrapped in the moral outrage as something provoked so that the reader or viewer can understand—and even enjoy—what is being condemned.[4]

We are also trained, culturally, through exposure to legal codes and expectations about human rights. We have a particular understanding of the idea of the "victim." However unpleasant it was for Cayetano Díaz to be singled out, clearly the party most wronged in this case was the woman: that missing woman so terribly separated from a part of herself. To us, she is equally a victim regardless of age, class, or race.

And less obviously, we are also trained to understand specific acts of violence as meaning certain things. Machine-gun fire sprayed across a city street is not the same as a single stab to the back in a suburban kitchen, which is not the same as an elaborate death by many cuts under a freeway. We have our own language, with its precise vocabulary, of violence.

In all these ways, Guatemalans perceived this event and experienced horror differently. To begin with, not everyone could be construed equally as a victim. Only certain people could be the victims of certain kinds of crimes. While in some cases the laws did make formal distinctions, the most powerful distinctions were cultural. It was understood that an Indian servant woman could not really be raped. It was understood that a low-class *mulato* man could not really be insulted. These severed breasts, identified as nonwhite, spoke immediately to viewers about the potential wrongs the woman was eligible to suffer.

Guatemalans' vocabulary of violence and their acculturation through legal norms were also different.[5] This becomes apparent when we look closely at criminal cases from the period. Secular courts heard plenty of cases involving violence against women, including homicide, but in the majority of cases officials did not care to pursue them. And this in an era of dramatically rising criminal prosecutions for social violence. Between 1500 and 1700, 135 cases relating to different kinds of violence were heard by Guatemalan secular courts. And then in the following century, these courts heard 2,700 cases. A twenty-fold increase in the number of cases. Most of this dramatic increase is focused in the last quarter of the eighteenth century, when courts heard some 200 to 300 cases every year.[6]

What caused this dramatic increase in the number of cases relating to social violence? Population growth? Changing economic conditions? A radically more violent culture?

Probably none of these. The city's population did grow dramatically, but it had stabilized by the end of the eighteenth century. Economic conditions were changing, but not in a way that suddenly deprived many people of basic needs. And the notion that a culture—any culture—is radically more violent than another should be met with skepticism. There's a long history of characterizing Latin America—and Guatemala, particularly—as inherently violent. Chalking this up to culture not only entails a dubious approach to human behavior, it overlooks the process by which historians themselves contribute to loose characterizations of "culture."

The increase in cases almost certainly reflects an increased prosecutorial zeal on the part of colonial officials rather than an increase in actual crime per capita. In other words, the rise in the number of cases reflects what was happening in the courts, not what was happening on the streets. A deliberate tightening of social control during this period formed a central piece of the broad agenda for reform. The Bourbon crown, which ruled Spain after the War of Succession in the early eighteenth century, instituted a gradual set of reforms that influenced many aspects of social, economic, and political life in the Spanish empire. Economic reforms reshaped trade and taxation. Political reforms reparceled areas of governance and buttressed this governance with a dramatically expanded military. Social reforms modified when, on whose authority, and whom one could marry. And other reforms unifying the crown's social, economic, and political aspirations aimed to create an orderly and productive population. Patrols in urban areas kept a close eye on public drunkenness and public behavior in general; taverns had to improve and brighten their lighting; and people were limited in what kinds of weapons they could carry. And, as a result, the number of criminal cases rose dramatically. In its sweeping attempt to consolidate the means of violence in the hands of the state—that is, in the military and police—the Spanish crown and its courts correspondingly aimed to constrain and control the means of violence among civilians. Spanish Americans needed to be reined in.[7]

This makes it all the more striking that officials cared so little about cases of violence against women. Cases of rape against children elicited visible scorn and disgust, but rape against grown women left court officials unmoved, and by the end of the century the Spanish crown took the startling step of declaring punishment unnecessary in cases of rape. Similarly, homicides of women—particularly homicides of wives by husbands—often ended at the complaint stage. Savage domestic assaults that threatened women's lives in most cases caused officials little concern.

These crimes do cause us concern, and in some cases horror. The case of the breasts on Cayetano Díaz's window causes us horror in the same way: we see it as an extreme version of the crimes described above. But if Guatemalans—in particular officials—did not feel revulsion, or even concern, when faced with terrible crimes against women, why then did they react with horror in this case?

The horror of Guatemalan officials, in contrast to ours, sprang from the very public statement made by the perpetrator: the violation of public space and public peace; and, most of all, the deliberate and almost extravagant flaunting of impunity. It was a clear rebuff of that carefully orchestrated social control with which Bourbon reformers planned to make people orderly, obedient, and useful. Consider that once the breasts were discovered, officials carried them to a public place so that they might be seen and "identified" by everyone in the city. The sight of the breasts themselves was not the problem, in their view. The problem was their placement by someone else and the charged message such placement conveyed.

In some ways, understanding this message is the central problem of this book. Let me refer again to our present day in order to demonstrate the way we so easily understand similar messages without realizing that we do. Newspapers of the past few years are tragically peppered with articles about drug cartels that leave mutilated bodies as warnings for rivals and uncooperative officials. In Guatemala, a relative described to me the difficulty she had one morning getting her children to school without letting them see the severed body parts that had been left, scattered like debris, around the house of a neighbor. These messages are obvious to the point of idiocy. They are obvious because we know, through long and painful intimacy, the context of the drug trade.[8]

In a similar way, infamously in Guatemala but more obscurely in the United States, mutilation was an eloquent tool of communication during the thirty-six-year armed conflict. Best known is the case of Rogelia Cruz, the Guatemalan beauty queen whose discarded body, raped and dismembered, breasts cut off, was discovered under an overpass in Guatemala City in 1968. There, too, the message sent by the state's security forces to the urban student movement (of which Cruz's boyfriend was a member) was glaringly clear. Cruz's boyfriend and his friends retaliated with suicidal vehemence, and the armed conflict in the city turned a corner, entering long decades of disappearances punctuated by such gruesome communiqués.[9]

Each of these crimes has a perpetrator: a drug cartel, the Guatemalan police force. But knowing who committed the crimes is less satisfying than comprehending the context in which they happened. Drug cartels operate in a complex web linking international trade, local economies, and modern conceptions of health and morality (to name only a few). Cruz's horrible murder was one piece of a terrible armed conflict, in which the United States' Central Intelligence Agency, the early-twentieth-century banana trade, Marxism, land reform, and indigenous activism all form necessary contexts. Similarly, we may wonder about who left the breasts on the windowsill. The most immediate mystery is "What happened?" But while many historical narratives are built around this question, there are better—more interesting, more revealing—questions to ask. In this case, too, understanding the context is more satisfying than pinning the perpetrator. Rather than "who did it?" we should ask, in this case, "what did it mean?" What are the contexts that make it intelligible? What did this case signify to Guatemalans? What does it reveal to us about Guatemalans of the time? What can we learn about violence and the culture of violence by understanding how this case unfolded?

Just as both of the contemporary instances of violence could be used to unveil the histories of the drug trade in the twenty-first century or the Guatemalan armed conflict in the twentieth, this book unveils the history of Guatemala in 1800 through this instance of violence. I intend to tease out the meanings of this crime piece by piece, unfolding one critical context in each chapter.[10] The case of the woman on the windowsill is not about some unknown, deranged person acting out a perverse passion. It is about more lasting elements: the shape of a new urban landscape, religious symbols, enlightenment medicine, conceptions of gender, a misguided sense of justice, and the reengineering of violence by the state.

1

Strangers in the Valley
In Which Brígida Arana Seeks
Her Missing Daughter

The archives do not necessarily tell the truth, but, as Michel Foucault would say, they tell of the truth.

—ARLETTE FARGE, *THE ALLURE OF THE ARCHIVES*

I n the early hours of July 1, 1800, the authorities took a number of steps in swift succession. The breasts were transported to the *cabildo,* the city council's offices, so that anyone in the city might view them and perhaps identify them. Next, authorities in every section of the city and in the nearby towns were notified to be on the lookout for a woman's corpse. Further, permission was requested from the archbishop to exhume any bodies buried on sacred ground since June 30. And last of all, the authorities went in person— accompanied by "a great multitude of people" to search the area deemed most likely to yield the body with its missing breasts.

These proceedings give us a sense of how significant this incident seemed. The city paused. Its attention shifted. People stopped what they were doing, and they attended to this remarkable event. They wanted to be a part of it.

The *barranco del incienso,* a ravine that forms a natural barrier on the western edge of the city, was marginal in more ways than one. Its steep sides trap mist and rainclouds, creating the "incense" for which it is named, and resulting, at times, in a perilous descent into its depths. Some of the city's less appealing functions took place there, at the edges: sewage, decomposition, and death.[1] The ravine abutted the San Juan de Dios Hospital and its attached cemetery, where those who died at the hospital might be buried. Small manufactories, such as brickworks, took advantage of the setting, as did people who could not afford the more established residences of the city center. They erected instead more rudimentary housing—*ranchos* and *solares.* The ravine attracted stray dogs and vagabonds, the most marginal inhabitants of the city's physical margins. And the ravine was the site of a horrific murder that had occurred sixteen years earlier: the body of a young man, Norberto Contreras, had been found there in March 1784. Contreras had been brutally tortured, and his killer was never found.[2] Given all of these associations, it is not so surprising that the officials leading the search assumed, as a starting point, that the barranco del incienso was a likely place to find a mutilated corpse.

The first search through the ravine turned up nothing. But on July 2, a more persistent examiner returned with a striking report. Miguel Rodrigo de Lorenzana, one of the city's *alcaldes de barrio,* investigated the ravine independently. Alcaldes were district magistrates with diverse responsibilities and powers; they apprehended criminals, they led patrols, to some degree they investigated crimes, and they brought cases directly to the city courts. Miguel Rodrigo began at the hospital, which in his mind, as in many, was already linked to the gruesome crime.

One of the administrators at the hospital reported to Miguel Rodrigo that near dawn on July 1 he had been drawn out to the open corridor of the hospital by a troubling noise, and he had seen there a man whose face and features were obscured by a poncho. The man was maneuvering a descent into the ravine through the hospital's drainage, accompanied by a white dog. He was gone some time and when he returned he departed in the direction of the city center. The dog, which had been barking incessantly on the descent, had suddenly quieted. Miguel Rodrigo understood the grisly implication: the ravenous dog had been fed with something found in the depths of the ravine.

The hospital administrator also had seen, somewhat later in the morning, two men stretched out at the ravine's edge, resting in the sun, but as their heads were covered with ponchos, they had not been identifiable.

Stimulated by this discovery, Miguel Rodrigo scoured the entire slope of the ravine as far as he was able, stopping to speak with a pair of men at a brickworks. They told him that the night in question had been a noisy one; from matins all the way until dawn they had heard continuous disturbances coming from the direction of the hospital cemetery. The feral dogs of the ravine, they said, would not stop their furious barking.

And at dawn the dogs had more evidence to offer, for they all returned from the depths of the gorge with fresh meat, their mouths bloodied. One dog with a litter of pups, they said, had come back with food for her offspring, but they could not tell what kind of meat she carried in her jaws.

Miguel Rodrigo took this disturbing testimony with him

into the barranco del incienso, hoping to find some evidence of what the dogs had eaten in the early hours of July 1. He speculated, perhaps optimistically, that he might find some wild animal carcass or other such remains. But his search in the ravine produced nothing more.

As Rodrigo once again climbed the slope toward the rough houses at the ravine's edge, he spotted two women walking together. They appeared to be searching for something, but when they saw the alcalde they stopped and conferred, seemingly undecided as to whether they should continue or turn back.

Suspicious, Rodrigo approached them and asked their business. One of the women confessed that her name was Brígida Arana and that she was searching for her daughter, Liberata Bejarano. Liberata had run away from home the night before, around the hour of matins, in the company of two strange men. No one had seen her alive since then.

Rodrigo questioned her further, and he asked her—one hopes with some delicacy—whether she had seen the breasts displayed at the city council offices. Brígida responded that she had indeed seen the breasts, and that in size and color they were identical to her daughter's.

We are lucky that the case of the severed breasts is readable. There are frustrating silences and maddening dead ends, but the words themselves are mostly legible. Documents at the Archivo General de Centroamérica, the AGCA in Guatemala City, are kept in bundles—*legajos*—tied with string. You find the string, like the documents, in varying stages of decay. Sometimes the documents have all their edges, and they have been sewn together carefully, and they make fairly tidy stacks inside the bundles. More often, the documents show evidence of the journey they have taken through the centuries: rats and worms have left strange holes and ragged indentations; water stains bloom across the pages like persistent clouds; humidity and rot leave enigmatic discolorations beneath the words.

A document favored by the fates of archival preservation might look like Figure 2.[3] A less fortunate document might look like Figure 3.[4]

Colonial documents are transporting in a way that contemporary documents are not. Yes, the writing itself looks unfamiliar, and the words describe circumstances far removed from our own. But it is their physical difference that makes you realize, in a manner impossible to ignore, that they belong to an entirely different world.

Confronted with documents like these, you are compelled to think about how they have reached you: how uncertain the path by which the words arrive in the present; how difficult the passage taken by each piece of paper, at once so fragile and so astonishingly durable. Some archivist has brought it out of the vast, dark warren of the stacks (for the AGCA cannot afford bulbs for every aisle of its nine floors), where it has been since Joaquín Pardo, the indefatigable document curator who created the archive's card catalogue, paged through it in the early twentieth century to record an entry. Before that, the document lived in a kind of limbo as it was shuttled from one location to another, perhaps bundled with others of its kind, perhaps loose and half forgotten. And before that, it might have spent time with a local official who kept the crown's papers at home (as many officials did), stuffed into a corner or a desk drawer or a family wardrobe.[5]

Then it is a small leap to imagining the original circumstances in which the document was made. A room filled with light from a courtyard door. A scribe bent over the paper; the

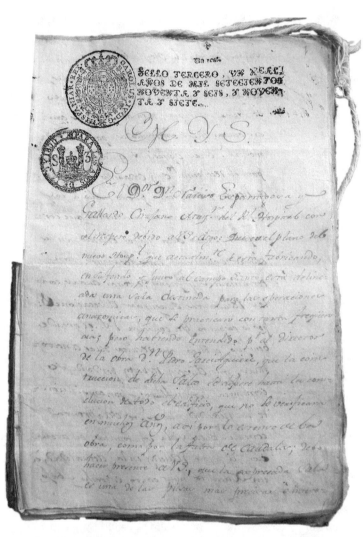

2. A legible document from the Archivo General de Centroamérica

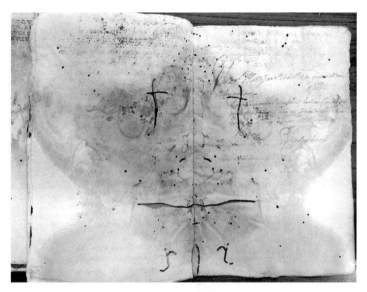

3. A document at the AGCA damaged by water and vermin

impassive face of a listening judge; a man or woman seated before them, trying to put into words the way it happened, the way everything suddenly fell apart. Long silences. Touching the paper makes the archive and everything around you seem temporarily insubstantial, as if it is only one more ephemeral stopping point in the document's journey.

Arlette Farge, in her marvelous exploration of French archival documents from this same period, recounts finding a purse full of seeds among the pages of the case she was consulting. A letter written by a country doctor explained that they came from a young woman who, once a month, discharged the seeds from her breasts. (Yes, I know—breasts seem to be everywhere in the eighteenth century.) Farge recounts debating whether to open the purse and finally making up her mind, then marveling as the seeds poured "down on the yellowed document, as golden as they were on their first day, a brief burst of sunshine."[6] I have never found such an extraordinary object, but I do recall finding, in a legal dispute from this period, two love letters confiscated over the course of the proceedings. They were still sealed. Their intended recipients never received them, never read what was inside. I did not open them, but I stared at them a long while, wondering at what had been lost in those closed packets of paper.

The documents I was reading at the AGCA contained a great deal of loss. All were criminal cases from the colonial period, and all connected somehow to acts of violence. After a time, reading such cases carries you past the disorienting surprise of encountering a material fragment of the past. The paper is still shocking in its physicality, but you begin to think about the words and the lives described by the words. You begin to wonder what it means that so many people suffered these losses. Parents losing children, women losing their honor, husbands losing their wives—most often by their own hand.

These are only the most obvious losses, the ones directly addressed by the courts' deliberations. There are others, hazy as the faded water stains, that seem to lie behind the words and are more difficult to discern. A loss of trust between neighbors. A loss of clarity about who belongs. An eroding sense of safety.

Partly for reasons of safety, I used to stay in Antigua, the colonial capital, when I did research at the archive.

A beautiful grid of ruins in the shadow of volcanoes, the old capital is a strange jewel these days, an ornate labyrinth with passages that seem to spill onto any number of lost pasts. One passage leads to lavish convents, renovated as luxury hotels, and galleries where the only sound is the murmuring of stone fountains. This is a past in which servants still pad quietly through the tile corridors on bare feet, and everyone is there *para servirle*—to serve you—and the grotesque disproportion of means between the server and the served is concealed by the elegance of their mutual conduct. It hardly seems possible that such circumstances should have survived beyond the nineteenth-century plantations in which they flourished, but they have. Another passage leads to the neighboring mansions occupied by the *narcos,* who with their quiet comings and goings, their massive guard dogs, their opulence, their obviousness, and their staged imitation of old money seem caricatures drawn from the 1980s. Yet another finds the foreign hippies, young and old, who though they seem to have vanished from most major cities of the world still appear in places like Antigua, dreadlocked and sandaled, dreamy or bitter according to their luck, their dreams and bitterness transported intact from the 1960s. There is the passage leading to a hazy, indefinite past where Guatemalans from the city seek an elusive balm of nostalgia in the piping sound of the marimba, a comforting sense of provincial containment in the narrow, cobblestone streets. And there is a passage leading to the remote place where women market vendors speak rapidly to one another in Kaqchikel, carrying baskets that have been made in the same way for hundreds of years, wearing *huipiles* with patterns that would have been familiar to eyes that had never seen Europeans.

Antigua has the air of a place inhabited by people who wish to hold on to the past. Perhaps it feels this way because it is a city of ruins, and those who have stayed are those who deliberately chose wreckage of the past over the alternative. On July 29, 1773, the city was convulsed by a series of earthquakes that destroyed many of the buildings and left much of the population homeless. Some stayed to rebuild. Others favored moving to a new location. It had already been done before. Antigua itself, then Santiago de los Caballeros de Guatemala, was the relocation of a capital that had been ruined even earlier in the colonial period by earthquakes and mudslides. This time, once more, the prevailing current took the capital to a new site. Santiago became Antigua, and a bucolic valley some thirty miles northeast became Nueva Guatemala—the new Guatemala City.

Guatemala City, now as then, makes a marked contrast with Antigua. When I would travel into the city to research at the archive, I would take a shuttle into Zone 1, where the Archivo General de Centroamérica confronts the city with its impassive gray face. Just on the other side of the national library, the archive is part of a cluster of buildings surrounding the central plaza. Municipal buses roar down the street, crowding the air with their blaring horns, blackening the pages of the archive's documents with their exhaust smoke.

The house where Cayetano Díaz lived, centuries ago, is only a short walk from the archive. Though much of the block has been remodeled, leaving nothing of Díaz's home, one portion of probable colonial origins remains (Figure 4).

The condition of the building speaks for itself. Relatives and archivists told me constantly that Zone 1 was terribly dangerous, and horror stories abounded. I tried to follow my advisers' stern instructions, walking quickly from the shuttle to the archive, carrying anything of value well hidden. At lunchtime, I would eat in the kitchen for archive staff, who kindly lent me their ancient microwave so that I could eat beside them at the spotless formica tables. Then a half hour before closing time, I'd start to wonder. Would the shuttle be on time, or

4. A portion of what was probably Cayetano Díaz's house
in Guatemala City

would it be one of those days that would find me waiting by
the closed door, counting down the minutes to my inevitable
demise?

I had every reason to believe the rumors were true. The
police officer who guarded the archive's entrance changed into
plainclothes at the end of work each day because she considered it too dangerous to step out onto the street in her uni-
form. A relative of mine who sometimes did research at the
archive, Ramiro Ordóñez Jonama, would wait with me for
the shuttle whenever he happened to be there. Diminutive and
impeccably dressed, he would clutch my elbow protectively
and make gentlemanly jokes with the air of a man who knows
how to laugh in the face of death. All around us, in the passing

buses and darting cars, on the teeming sidewalks and the busy corners, I could see nothing but strangers. People I did not know; people who could be dangerous; people who were there for reasons I could not guess at or presume.

It is difficult to imagine, now, in a Guatemala City that roars and bellows and screeches, a time when the fear of strangers was quiet. The fear was still there—as palpable and wildly speculative as ours in the present—but it arrived silently and often under cover of darkness.

For one thing, the pace was different. Be it a task or a vice, a single enterprise would unfold unhurriedly, occupying many hours of the long day. An Indian servant spent an entire slow morning at a neighbor's house, watching the mute girl do her sewing. A pair of siblings went to matins in the early morning and then stopped by a *chichería*, drinking the hours away until three in the afternoon. An impromptu gathering in the afternoon was prolonged when someone brought a guitar, and others joined the party, and afternoon stretched into evening.

It is not that things always moved slowly, but that things as they happened were spacious: they could take up the day. Gossip, a pair of errands, a visit to see a new baby, calling on a customer to collect payment, visiting a cousin who borrowed a shawl; they filled the hours until they were all gone. And nothing filled the hours more easily than conversation. The entire life of the neighborhood, of the city, was turned over and over by word of mouth, passing from the alcalde to his wife, from the wife to the servant, from the servant to the neighbor's servant, from the neighbor's servant to the market vendor.

People stood in their doorways and leaned out through their windows. It was how greetings and gossip, provocations and flirtations, challenges and insults were exchanged. People lingered in thresholds knowing that these were the nodes through which the real activity of the city passed.

So when the breasts were found on the windowsill of Don Cayetano Díaz, the word was passed from door to door. The doctor, perhaps, dropped a word or two on his way to the hospital. A servant from Díaz's household might have given her whispered account to the baker when she went out to buy bread. However it happened, word of the severed breasts moved from house to house as if carried on a current of water, and it was not long before the multitude had heard the news.

Two strange men. The phrase, first dropped by Brígida Arana in response to the alcalde's questions, went on to have a long echo in the case proceedings. It is evident from the very early orders for exhumation that the authorities were inclined to suspect a certain kind of crime. But Brígida Arana's declaration of her daughter's disappearance catapulted the investigation in a new direction. This was now no longer the pursuit of a woman's corpse; it was the pursuit of a murderer.

When you read a criminal case of this kind, some pieces of it make their significance immediately apparent. The severed breasts: there they are, shocking and unignorable in all their incomprehensibility. But most significant pieces conceal their significance at first: they slip into the record without comment. Without exclamation marks—or illustrations—in the margins. Only upon rereading (and rereading) do they stand out, and then what were plain threads in the fabric of the case suddenly seem bright.

On one of these rereadings, I realized the importance of the man with the white dog and the two men who had been resting at the edge of the ravine, their faces obscured by ponchos. The first might even have been one of the two seen later.

Regardless, there they were. *Two strange men.* Miguel Rodrigo had even seen them by the ravine. His mention of them in the testimony suggests that he, too, made the connection retrospectively. Though he does not say so, we can imagine that he wondered what they were doing at that hour at the ravine's edge, so close to where the dogs had made their grisly meal. Were these the same men who had taken Liberata?

Miguel Rodrigo and the other officials who would soon question everyone related to the missing Liberata Bejarano began to focus on the two men: those mysterious figures who had seemingly, from Brígida's description, whisked her away into the night.

Two strange men, knocking on a young woman's door in the darkness, might sound menacing in any context. But in Guatemala City at this time, strangers—unknown, unfamiliar, not of the neighborhood—carried a particular connotation. Guatemala City was booming: in less than twenty years, its population had nearly quadrupled; in 1776 there were only 5,917 inhabitants, and by 1793 there were 23,434 persons counted in the census.[7] The rebuilding of the city after the earthquake had required, as it had in the past, an influx of labor for new construction. This time, the labor was drawn from communities far and wide, not just from nearby.[8] Guatemala City had changed its population when it changed its location: previously a collection of fairly small neighborhoods in which most people knew each other well, it had become a city of small neighborhoods filled with many unfamiliar faces. Unfamiliar and also transient, for the construction projects going on in and around the city offered ideal short-term employment for men en route elsewhere or men who came and went with the season.[9]

And, as the line of inquiry around the two men demonstrates, unfamiliar faces could be dangerous. The two men at the edge of the ravine seem sinister in their description not because they were sleeping in such an unsavory spot but because their faces were covered. Concealed thus, they could not be identified as people of the neighborhood, people known to be incapable of such a crime as this one. Concealed thus, they could be anyone and capable of anything.

Of course, from a different perspective, almost everyone in Guatemala City was a stranger. There is something ironic or galling, depending on how you see it, about the alarm over strange men, given Guatemala's longer history.

For thousands of years, Mesoamerica, a region stretching roughly from central Mexico to Nicaragua, was home to peoples described by scholars today as the Nahua, the Olmec, the Mixtec, the Zapotec, and the Maya.[10] Some of these are so ancient that we are not even certain what they called themselves. Others have endured into the present; in Guatemala today, more than half the population is Maya.

The accounts of Christopher Columbus reaching the Caribbean and Hernán Cortés reaching Mexico are well known, if persistently distorted. In the popular imagination there is still far too much emphasis on warfare and far too little recognition of the role disease played in wiping out, by some estimates, 95 percent of the native population of the Americas. Scholars have made blindingly clear that Spanish military successes were far more infrequent than claimed in traditional histories, and that even in cases of military victory, disease had already taken a significant toll on the native population.

This is the case for Guatemala, whose story of Spanish and Maya encounter is less well known outside of the region. We might think of Pedro de Alvarado as one of the first strangers in the valley, arriving in 1524 with more strangers from

Spain and Mexico. (Another persistent distortion is that the
conquests were all by Spaniards. In Guatemala, as elsewhere,
native allies were just as evident in numbers, just as vital for
military defeat when it occurred.)[11] While recent treatments of
Cortés have revised the popular conception of a brilliant military commander—Inga Clendinnen's memorable description
is "personally brave" but "unremarkable as a combat leader"—
similar studies of Alvarado have done little to challenge the
characterization of an impulsive, reckless, and rapacious Spaniard bent on personal acquisition and careless of Indian lives.[12]
This is the man who, in Cortés's absence, ordered the massacre
of unarmed Mexica during a religious ritual in Tenochtitlán,
the Aztec capital. His presence in the record suggests, tellingly,
where some elements of the conquistador caricature come from.

At this distance, with few and severely skewed sources, it
is difficult to know exactly what occurred after Alvarado arrived in Guatemala in February of 1524. It is certain that some
military engagements occurred with Maya K'iche' foot soldiers,
and it is certain that by some means—the terms are unclear—
the rival Kaqchikel Maya came to ally with the Spaniards. How,
why, and for how long are still debated. There is more clarity
about the fading alliance, the constant and uncompromising
demands for gold from Alvarado, and the eventual rebellion
that lasted much longer than any allegiance.[13]

We should be skeptical of any Spanish descriptions of
"ruling" Guatemala beginning in the 1520s. What does it even
mean to "rule" when the native population has fled to the hills
and the Spaniards who are present have not comprehended
even the most basic contours of the region they claim to com-
mand? From the point of view of the K'iche' and Kaqchikel,
not to mention the many other Maya groups who had not as
much contact with Spaniards in these early days, their pres-

ence must have looked very different. It makes more sense to think of Spaniards controlling and perhaps ruling a fairly limited outpost that expanded, in the decades that followed, to claim other contained outposts.

Even as they expanded their reach, Spaniards never inhabited the entire territory. Much of it they had never seen. Instead, they populated nodes along a network, like clumps on a spider's web, and their dependence on Indians was extreme. The labor that made agriculture thrive, the tribute payments that oiled the machinery of the Spanish state, and the guided navigation across the web of unknown terrain were all provided by Indians. Spaniards did branch out, and they did grow more numerous. But even with the stark demographic collapse of the Indian population, which plateaued and then gradually began to recover in the seventeenth century, Spaniards never outnumbered native Maya. So it must have continued to seem in the eyes of the majority of the population that the strangers were the people of Spanish descent living among them, the people of Mexican descent who had assisted in the conquest, and the people of African descent who were forcibly brought to the Americas by the slave trade beginning in the sixteenth century.

After the first generation of Spaniards died off, others would have seen this differently. The children born in Guatemala of Spaniard and Indian, Spaniard and African, African and Indian, would have thought of the places they lived in as defining of their identities. People of all races, mixed or otherwise, tended to identify themselves not only in terms of race but also in terms of place. This continued into the nineteenth century, some would say to the present. Official documents of the colonial period almost always account for age, race, marital status, and place of origin. To say one is a *natural,* or native, of Guatemala City is to say that one was born there and lives there. To be a natural of Ciudad Real or Ciudad Vieja living in Guatemala City is to say that one is from elsewhere.

At once outsiders and neighbors, people from elsewhere occupied a space of uncertainty. How long had they lived in the neighborhood? How did they treat people? What were their habits? Were they generous and circumspect or unreliable and meddling? Did they attend church devoutly, or did their drunken shouts wake the neighbors in the middle of the night? All of these qualities would have been folded effortlessly into a conception of the person who resided next door, natural or not, constituting more than reputation—constituting her position, her character, her good or bad name.

The stranger is dangerous precisely because these qualities are unknown.

The disappearance of Liberata Bejarano should be considered in this light—an awareness of what it meant to be visited by strangers, a sensibility to the importance of neighbors, good and bad.

For it turns out Brígida had not seen her daughter leaving the house. She had not seen the strange men, either. When the persistent magistrate, Miguel Rodrigo, followed Brígida home to inspect the premises and gather information, he discovered that their next-door neighbor, Bartolo Arana, was the one who had seen everything. And his account complicates the story. Yes, Bartolo had seen two men ask after Liberata around the hour of matins; but they had not stolen her away. Rather, Bartolo himself had told them on her behalf that she was sleeping. Later in the night, he had seen the girl leave home alone.

And how did she leave? The magistrate was shown the spot where Liberata had left—a hole beneath her bed. A hole in the wall or a hole in the dirt floor: it is impossible to say for certain from the brief description. But the result is the same.

Perhaps Miguel Rodrigo, seeing the hole beneath the young woman's bed, experienced the same shifting awareness I did when reading about it. Until that point, I was imagining a distraught mother, desperately seeking a beloved daughter who had been whisked away by two sinister strangers. But a hole beneath the bed is not the usual point of entry for a sinister pair of strangers. A hole beneath the bed is made from the inside. It is something secret, something stealthy. It is an escape route.

What was Liberata escaping from?

2

History of Violence
In Which Liberata Bejarano's Cause
for Flight Is Revealed

If we aim to "defend stories" and bring them into history, we must commit ourselves to demonstrating in a compelling manner the ways in which each individual constructed her own agency out of what history and society put at her disposal.

—ARLETTE FARGE, *THE ALLURE OF THE ARCHIVES*

Brígida Arana gave testimony on July 3, 1800, about the events surrounding her daughter's disappearance, repeating the story she had given to Miguel Rodrigo. She said Liberata had "fled" (*huido*) at eleven in the evening on June 30. Hearing the next morning about the severed breasts, she went at once to look at them. The court asked whether anyone in particular was in the habit of asking after her daughter, and Brígida said that an Indian named Marcos had been coming by, seeking Liberata's hand in marriage. He was sixteen years old and from the nearby town of Mixco. (The mention of his hometown signaled clearly that he was identifiable, placeable—not a stranger.) The court asked what had happened during the day before Liberata's disappearance, and Brígida recounted that she and her daughter had gone to a wedding at someone's home. But far from engaging any young men at the party, Liberata had spent most of the time with her mother in the kitchen. For a short time they joined the company and watched the celebrations. Brígida had little more to add, and the judge could extract nothing else of significance from her testimony.

For some time before the disappearance, Liberata and Brígida had been sharing their home with two others, Narcisa Vargas and Simon Archila. Twenty-eight-year-old Narcisa had been staying with them for two weeks. She was questioned next, and she explained that she had stayed at the rancho to keep an eye on it while the mother and daughter attended the wedding. No, she had not seen Liberata flee the house. No, she had not seen Liberata keep company with any strange men. In fact, no young men at all had called for her ever.

Simon Archila, a sixty-year-old widower from Guatemala City, had rather more to say. At eleven in the evening on the night in question, he had woken to the sound of dogs barking and had gotten up. Doing so, he discovered Liberata in the act of fleeing through the kitchen—a space that would have been out of doors in such a house. He asked her what she was doing. Liberata replied that she was going out for a while—*un rumbo*—and she asked him not to tell her mother. Heading back to the house, Simon encountered Brígida, and he told her at once that her daughter was leaving. "I don't believe you," she said, affirming that Liberata was still in her bed. But when they went in to check, the bed was, of course, empty. Simon had warned her, saying, "She's jumping the fence now." But Brígida had paid no attention and had not gone after her daughter.

They asked Archila whether he had known Liberata to flee before, and he said that in the three months he had lived with them, nothing of the kind had happened. But Brígida herself had mentioned to him that Liberata had attempted to run away on another occasion.

At this point, having spoken with all the people most intimately connected with Liberata, the court widened its scope. It called in several people who had been at the wedding mentioned by Brígida. It heard testimony about a young man who had supposedly harassed Liberata on the street—a dead end. It interrogated the Indian named Marcos, who supposedly wanted to marry Liberata but who protested that, on the contrary, Liberata and her mother had been scheming to ensnare him in marriage—another dead end. And in a manner obscured to us because it is not described, they began to hear more about other possible connections: people who might have known Liberata in other ways or whose relationships with her emerged through rumor.

Most people testified that they knew little about the disappeared girl. She had attended the wedding that day, but nothing remarkable had happened, and certainly Liberata herself had done nothing out of the ordinary. Yet the picture of Liberata begins to change at this point in the case, even as the people testifying knew nothing about the circumstances of her possible murder. A woman named Juana Bejarana, a thirty-three-year-old free *mulata* who was either more talkative or more perceptive than others, described going to visit Brígida the day after the disappearance. Brígida said that her daughter had made a hole under her bed and escaped through it in the night. Liberata had fled "con sus naguas sin fustán con una camisita vieja"—in nothing but a petticoat and an old undershirt. Moreover, Juana knew for a fact that Liberata had fled on a previous occasion, on Saint Anthony's Day. Liberata had run away, and Brígida had found her and brought her home. Liberata's back bore visible injuries from the beating she had received upon her return.

The court did not demonstrate any particular interest in this beating, but nonetheless, as a result of the expanding inquiry, the circumstances around it grew clearer. In order to establish whether Liberata fled the house regularly and whether she was in the habit of going to one place or another, the judge began asking each witness what he or she knew about Liberata's past attempts to run away. On July 10 a woman named Petrona Ordóñez testified that Liberata had taken refuge at her house on "only" three occasions. The same day, Josefa Valeria Arévalo recounted that Liberata sometimes sneaked out of her house—always in her petticoat—but never at night because her mother was in the habit of sleeping in front of the door to make sure the girl did not escape. And then on July 11, María Isabel López told the court that Liberata had been known to run away because sometimes her mother drank too much and hit her with a stick.

By this point, the pattern is clear, and it suggests a very different story. The two strange men may very well have played a part somehow, but they had not absconded with Liberata, luring her away from the safety of her home. On the contrary. Liberata was attempting to flee a violent home. She had tried to run away so many times that her mother had to sleep across the door to stop her. Finally, desperation and ingenuity prompted her to make a hole beneath her bed and escape into the dark, at the most dangerous hour of the night and only in her underclothes. It seems fair to conclude that only a very unhappy, very dire set of circumstances would make such a risk seem worthwhile.

Most proceedings in a criminal case unfold without direct comment, and only through their line of questioning do we get a sense of what court officials were thinking. The remarks from the attorney for the crown (the *asesor*) are the exception.[1] Sometimes terse, sometimes talkative, they are always more direct than the rest of the proceedings. On July 18, the asesor examining Liberata's case considered the investigation to date and offered suggestions for the next course of action. He noted that while many people related to the case were in jail (eleven, at this point), none of them was guilty of any wrongdoing except for Brígida Arana, "who responded with indolence on the occasion of her daughter's flight and who saw the breasts, believing them to be her daughter's, yet these made little or no impression upon her." These reactions were suspicious, the asesor said; they suggested Brígida *no estaba ignorante del suceso*— was not entirely ignorant of what had happened.

So, he argued, it seemed likely that the breasts were not Liberata's at all. Indeed, it seemed probable that Liberata was alive and well. But the problem posed by the severed breasts remained. "What can be in no doubt," he wrote, "is that these belonged to a woman, and whoever she was, she died at the hands of the cruelest torturers."[2]

Both parts of his assessment are interesting. Taken together, they are telling and representative comments on the forms of violence common in Guatemala City and the nature of official response. On the one hand, the violence of the unknown woman's death is clearly recognized. On the other hand, the violence of Liberata's home life is not. It is not just that one act is worse than the other. The abuse Liberata fled from, obvious as it appears to a present-day reader, simply did not register.[3]

One could counter that the case was about a murder, so the abuse of a wayward girl mattered little to the investigators for this reason. This is probably true. But it is also true that the larger pattern of official response in this period reveals a consistent and undeniable indifference to domestic violence. More—it would almost seem that domestic violence *wasn't* violence.[4] Violence was something else, something that officials tried deliberately to identify, prosecute, and condemn.

This case raises obvious questions about the nature and frequency of violence in Guatemala City. Was murder a common occurrence? Was mutilation a frequent accompaniment? Was the city a particularly violent place in other ways?

These questions are surprisingly difficult to answer, despite the wealth of cases relating to social violence. For the period between 1500 and 1811, the AGCA contains thirty-five hundred cases or complaints involving such crimes. The greatest number of these by far, twenty-one hundred, are about *heridas*—injuries or assaults. Indoors or outdoors, with weapons or without, one on one or in crowds, injuries took all forms.

Most injuries revolved around an insult or a provocation between people who knew each other, with slights to personal honor emanating like smoke from every word, glance, and gesture. Such disputes, reflecting long enmities or unspoken jealousies or subtle tensions, can seem trivial or bizarre to the point of incomprehensibility. The case of Manuel Barahona, a forty-year-old mulato knifed by Joseph Ambelis in 1767, is typical. Manuel recounted running into Joseph on the street and asking him the whereabouts of their mutual acquaintance, Pedro de Norra. Joseph said he had no idea where he was. Manuel replied, "How could you not know where he is? I just saw him with you." Joseph grew enraged at this seemingly harmless question, calling on two others nearby who assisted him in pummeling Manuel to the ground. Manuel sustained a knife wound five fingers deep in his lung, barely surviving to tell the tale.

Only with later testimony does this outsize response begin to make sense. Manuel had apparently fought with Pedro de Norra four days earlier, suffering at his hand a first knife injury. When Manuel saw Pedro and Joseph together standing on a street corner, off in the distance, he hurried toward them to confront his assailant. But by the time he arrived Pedro had disappeared, leaving only Joseph, who protected his friend by saying he knew nothing of his whereabouts. Then, no doubt guessing Manuel's motives, he took the offensive and attacked before Manuel could head off to seek revenge. Pointing once again to the significance of strangers and strangeness, Joseph responded to Manuel's questions by saying, "I'm not your friend and I don't know you." Manuel clearly did know him, for he could give his name in testimony, but the disavowal signaled an important distancing: a statement of Manuel's position as someone unknown, potentially hostile—a permissible target.[5]

In private dispute and public brawl alike, alcohol was an almost omnipresent catalyst. Even in cases where the accused had multiple reasons to lash out, alcohol often provided the pretext or opportunity.[6] The results were unpredictable, often leading to unintended consequences. Cayetano de Molina, for example, was tried in 1763 for nearly killing his mother with a stone. Cayetano had been fighting with his wife, Dorotea, before they headed to his mother's house for lunch, and when they reached her house the quarrel continued. As they argued in the patio, Cayetano's mother headed out to make the peace.

The stone Cayetano had seized and hurled toward his wife struck his mother, felling her instantly. In this case, Cayetano had been *ebrio y lisiado*—drunk and disabled by alcohol— particularly condemning words in a culture that commonly described the lesser zones of inebriation as being *alegre,* happy.[7]

Alcohol is especially prominent in homicide cases, which account for more than one thousand of the thirty-five hundred. The line between homicide and assault should be considered a blurry one, at best, since many of the homicides are cases of assault from which the victim did not recover. (Case in point, the investigation concerning Cayetano's mother is actually labeled a homicide. All assumed she would die, and the doctor considered it a miracle that she survived.) Though there are exceptions, this is the general shape of a homicide case in eighteenth-century Guatemala: a dispute among acquaintances or family or friends, a repeated engagement of escalating violence, a miscalculation due to alcohol, and a catastrophic result.[8]

The kind of extravagant display evident in the case of the severed breasts is unusual—almost unique. There are several cases in which unidentified corpses are found by the side of the road, or near the river, or propped up near a church. But these deaths fit other patterns—highway robbery, suicide, a death at home and funeral costs that relatives cannot afford. And there are a few cases of mutilation in which injuries result in the loss of limbs.[9] But these fit other patterns: they are assault cases in which the mutilations are incidental.

The only case I know of deliberate mutilation occurred in 1784—the case mentioned above involving the young Norberto Contreras.[10] It has some similarities with the 1800 case, but also significant differences. Contreras had gone missing on March 9, 1784, after coming home from work, having a meal with his mother, and going out again to do an errand. He was found on the morning of March 10 in the barranco del incienco. Contreras had been beaten severely about the head and torso. His eyes and nose were burned; his nostrils were plugged with sticks. His hands were bound, and the same rope had been wound around his midsection, wrapped around his genitals, and then tied to a nearby tree. It also appeared, from the scrapes found on his back and arms, that he had been dragged a considerable distance. These injuries are difficult for us to contemplate, even at a distance of more than two hundred years; they are aggravated by the knowledge that he suffered them while he was still alive and that his killer was never found. There is some small consolation in the knowledge that there is no other case like it in colonial Guatemala.

So while murder was fairly common, mutilation was uncommon to the point of rarity. Perhaps an additional, more pertinent question pertains to the victim: how common was violence against women? Looking at these 3,500 cases, it appears that violence against women occurred less frequently than violence against men. There are 225 cases of domestic abuse and 125 cases of rape, or what was called estupro. Of the homicides in these files, 960 are killings of men and 93 of women. Of the injuries and assaults, 1,783 were on men and 671 on women (including the cases of domestic abuse). So the statistical portrait suggests that violence was much more often directed toward men than women.

But the statistical portrait, it turns out, is a complete distortion. The incidence of cases says very little about what kind of violence was actually taking place. Consider this: in the sixteenth century, there was 1 case of social violence per decade. In the seventeenth century, there were 6 cases per decade. In the eighteenth there were 152 cases per decade. And the first decade of the nineteenth century saw a staggering 1,799 cases. One wonders how the judges had time. As suggested in the introduction, this incredible rise in the number of cases cannot be taken at face value as evidence of greater violence. Surely crimes of violence occurred more than once every other year in the seventeenth century. But the increase in the number of cases can be interpreted as reflecting a greater focus on the part of Bourbon authorities.[11]

So the better question is about what this distortion means. What can we actually say about violence in this period, given the remarkable intensification of attention to a certain kind of crime? What kinds of crimes drew most attention? Which attracted none at all? Should we think about the cases of violence against women differently, given this distortion?

Yes—without a doubt. It is almost certain that the cases of violence against women greatly underrepresent the actual incidence of violence against women. At first glance, the cases seem deceptively straightforward: violence happens, and women report it. But with close reading, the patterns of neglect begin to emerge.[12]

Many of the cases begin and end at the complaint stage. Many more end in acquittals, and the logic of these acquittals is revealing. Consider the case of Josefa Gonzales, who on the third of March of 1800 was admitted to the hospital with severe lacerations on her back. Josefa testified that the previous day she had gone to the plaza to sell *chicharrones*—pork cracklings—and that her husband, Marcelo Contreras, came by at about ten. Together, they went to the house of the Marquis de Aycinena, where breakfast was being served in the vestibule (another telling indication of how these entryways served as points of exchange). It was too late to attend Mass, so they

walked down along Calvary Street (*la calle del Calvario*) toward Ciudad Vieja. Marcelo asked her for the money she was
carrying, and she handed it over, thinking he needed it for a
purchase.

As they neared the archways that marked the way to Ciudad Vieja, Marcelo ordered her to step down off of the road
into the ravine and to take off her clothes. She asked him, as-
tonished, why she should do such a thing. He told her that she
would find out in a moment and ordered her again into the
ravine. She did as he asked. Then "he ordered her to put her
arms out and tied them and put her on the ground, putting his
foot on her throat so that she could not scream, and then he
whipped her hard about a dozen times with a leather strip tied
in knots, and having rested for a moment he said: that he had
already put up with too much from her because she was having an affair with his brother [-in-law] Josef Corrado." He told
her that he knew this for a fact because on another occasion
when he had beaten her, Josef Corrado had come to her defense. Then he proceeded to whip her another eight times. She
pleaded with him *por la pasión de nuestro señor jesucristo no
le pegase*—for Christ's sake to have pity upon her—and he replied that for Christ's sake he was beating her, whipping her
again another fifteen times. Josefa could no longer protest. He
stopped then, seeing a couple who were up on the road, looking down at the strange scene, but before telling her to get up
he whipped her several more times, now on the head.

Having returned to the main road—one imagines with
some difficulty—Josefa walked along before him. Seeing that
he meant to hit her again, she attempted to run. He caught up
with her and said, "Go ahead then and complain [to the au-
thorities] and she answered that she would not seek justice
[from the law] because the heavens would grant her justice."

Josefa's testimony is unusual for the amount of detail she gives about the words they spoke to each other, and the comment at the end about seeking justice is particularly telling. Despite her assurance that she would seek justice from heaven, Josefa did also seek justice from the authorities. The doctor testified that she had whip marks on her legs, buttocks, arms, and head, but that they would heal. The victim's mother testified that it was true that Marcelo's brother-in-law had come to Josefa's defense at Christmas the previous year when Marcelo tried to beat her, but she said nothing about an affair. After hearing this evidence and seeing that Josefa did, in fact, recover, the court freed Marcelo Contreras and reprimanded him to treat his wife "with the appropriate moderation." He was ordered to pay the costs of the short trial, but there was no other punishment.[13]

Though the arresting alcalde described Josefa as having been "cruelly whipped," the court was less moved. Consistent with custom and law, it determined that Contreras was within his rights as a husband to punish his wife, rights informed if not explicitly premised on conceptions of honor. Here lies one of the explanations for the burgeoning files of criminal courts in the late colonial period: there are far more complaints than full cases, and more dropped cases than completed ones. This is due to the incredible zealousness on the part of alcaldes, and to the relative laxness of the judges. The initiative—scrupulousness, one might even say—of Miguel Rodrigo scouring the ravine after the severed breasts were discovered was evinced by many alcaldes. The case files grew thick because so many alcaldes were out on the street, apprehending people for potential crimes, great and small.

The most revealing cases are those in which people were arrested before a crime had even been committed. Officials observed suspicious circumstances and acted immediately to prevent those circumstances from turning criminal. In 1790, for example, a young woman was walking by herself at 10:30 in the evening. The two officials who spotted her observed that she did not wear a veil. When they questioned her as to her purpose for wandering alone at that hour, her answers were unsatisfactory, and they promptly took her to the women's jail. Only when her mother came (from another city) to take charge of her was the young woman, María Desidora, released.[14]

Bourbon policing was energetic in the extreme, and as this case and others demonstrate, it had a paternalistic inclination that was entirely in keeping with the larger priorities of reformers at the time. This is the period in which reforms gave greater authority to parents over whom their children could marry, extending this authority well beyond adolescence.[15] In the officials' rapid response we can see both a paternalistic protectiveness for a sixteen-year-old girl and a zealous approach to crime prevention.

A similar combination is evident in the case of María Michaela. In 1801, she complained to her alcalde, Rafael García y Goyena, that a man named Domingo Corono had raped her, leaving her pregnant. García y Goyena, though quite willing to arrest Domingo, refrained so that the assailant could be free to work and pay the child's expenses. But when the baby died, García y Goyena promptly placed Domingo in jail. Taking up Domingo's case, the court was less inclined to punish María Michaela's attacker. Before dismissing the case outright, it asked the alcalde to explain his logic in arresting Domingo. He testified that when confronting Domingo with the charges, he had responded at first with silence. Then he said "'that as a weak man he had done it: that no one was free of temptation or of having a bad moment' and other similar statements aimed not to deny or alter the offense but to excuse it in a general way."[16] Despite this persuasive evidence and interpretation, the asesor determined that it was impossible to establish whether violence had taken place, and he suggested that the violence described by María Michaela seemed "inverosimil"—unrealistic or implausible. Domingo was set free.

Several elements are worth noting here. The alcalde and the asesor took different positions. García y Goyena, as he makes clear in his testimony, had no doubt that a crime had been committed, and he thought the perpetrator should pay. His position was a paternalistically protective one toward María Michaela, as demonstrated by his willingness to let Corono free to provide for the child. But the asesor considered the case with a different eye. For him, the whole case hinged on whether violence had occurred. The problem, in this case and others, was that violence, in his terms, could almost never be positively verified.

It would seem otherwise at first glance. Surely violence leaves marks on the body? But the courts held a very high standard in cases of rape. In many, the line of questioning revolved around whether other people witnessed the rape in order to testify that it occurred violently. Of course, in most cases, rape occurred when women were alone—by happenstance or by deliberate maneuvering by the perpetrator. Then, the questioning revolved around other indicators of violence: were the injuries visible? Did the victim scream? Were her screams heard by others? It is maddening to read testimony after testimony in which a woman explains that she could not scream because a knife was being held to her throat or her head or her chest; the court invariably determines in these cases that violence cannot be proven because she did not scream.

Even in cases where the injuries were severe, other explanations were offered and accepted. Michaela de los Santos, an Indian widow in her early twenties, accused Don Josef Melchor de Ugalde of rape, saying that her resulting injuries were so extreme that she could not walk. She sent for her parents, who lived in Ciudad Vieja, and they came to pick her up. After she stumbled repeatedly, they begged a young man on the road to lend them his horse for one *real* so that she might make it home. Michaela had given the name of two witnesses—young servants in the house of Don Josef who had seen her taken into the kitchen and heard everything. Both young servants, for obvious reasons, claimed in court they had heard nothing. Don Josef responded with indignation to the charges, saying that the nursemaid had acquired the injuries by falling off the very horse that carried her home. It is difficult to read such testimony—and the response—with equanimity. One wants to jump into the courtroom and demand of Don Josef why a horse was necessary in the first place if not, as Michaela claims, to transport an injured woman who could not walk. The charges against Don Josef—a person of importance in Guatemala City—were dismissed out of hand despite the visible injuries. In his concluding comments, the asesor speculated that Michaela probably hadn't been married (thus ignoring her declared widowhood) and, "being a nursemaid, is not the type who would even need to be forced."[17]

Such a response is fairly typical, and it speaks to a larger attitude toward nonelite women that is impossible to ignore. It is important to distinguish the paternalistic and sometimes overbearing zealousness of alcaldes—cops on the street, as it were—from the cool indifference of asesores—judges in the courts. While the former cast a wide net, eager to address crimes before they even occurred and willing to include the protection of women in their notion of an ordered society, the latter had a more deliberate and less inclusive definition of violence. Maintaining order was still paramount to judges: but they seem to have believed certain crimes did not threaten that order. Rape and domestic violence, in particular, were not threatening.

This conclusion is evident in the perplexing—and vexing— usage of the term *estupro*. Technically, estupro occurred when a man persuaded a (virgin) woman to have premarital sex on the promise of marriage and then broke his promise. In such cases, a woman's honor (not her body) had arguably been violated. The term leaves aside entirely the question of consensuality, so it does not encompass what we would call *violación*— violation or violent rape, which had no separate legal category.[18] Estupro cases usually ended with the court ordering the two to marry. But in the course of court proceedings, the term grew capacious; *estupro* was used to describe everything from defloration by a lover to violent rape by a stranger. This had the curious effect of arguing, culturally and legally, that rape— forced intercourse—did not exist. Rather, anything that we might call rape was treated as consensual sex in which the woman, for fanciful reasons of her own, alleged that she was unwilling. Naturally, this made it very easy to dismiss cases of rape/estupro.

When a 1796 law in Spain declared that "prisoners arrested for estupro should not be bothered [*molestados*] with prison sentences," it allowed the Guatemalan courts to ignore rape altogether.[19] It is possible that the estupro law, written across the Atlantic, truly intended to target only these cases in which consensual premarital sex went awry. But if the Guatemalan case is any indication, in some places estupro operated as an umbrella term, meaning something like "sex that results in a woman complaining." As a result, violent rapists would, by the turn of the century, no longer be "bothered" with prison sentences. An interesting method of resisting such dismissal is evident in cases like Michaela de los Santos's, which occurred in 1798. At no point do she and her father allege estupro—instead, they use other words like "forced," "damaged," and "bleeding"—thereby implying that the crime should be construed as an injury. A good strategy, but not necessarily successful; the asesor observed that she could have avoided the "violence" of her "misguided dalliance" altogether by simply leaving the house.[20] There is, of course, a telling irony in the unconscious contradiction of "violence" and "dalliance."

So what did judges actually care about? What crimes seemed to warrant punishment? What violence was really considered violence?

The only rape cases I have read that truly provoked a response from the court are cases involving children. For example, in a particularly revealing case from 1771, Cipriano Antonio, a twenty-year-old single mulato, was accused of raping Iginia de Oliveros, a seven-year-old girl. Cipriano allegedly accosted the girl while she was on her way to do an errand. Covering her mouth so that she could not scream, Cipriano took her into one of the rooms of the house where he worked as a servant and there raped her. Iginia did not report the crime, but her mother noticed that her legs and clothes were smeared with blood. The doctor called in to consider the case confirmed that she had been raped.

The response to Cipriano is interesting. The woman he worked for, hearing the accusation, promptly tied him up and flogged him, even though he denied the charges. (He later confessed to them under questioning—one wonders whether this was also under duress.) It seems particularly significant to me that Iginia's mother identified Cipriano in her testimony as a "forastero"—an outsider, a stranger. Iginia, in her testimony, used the same word to describe him.

Also telling is the doctor's account, which describes Iginia's body as "extraordinarily damaged, as a result of the violence that Cipriano Antonio committed to have intercourse with her which was impossible due to their difference in size." The use of the word "violence" here speaks volumes.

Finally, several people in the case—including the asesor— use the word *estupro* to describe the rape. Here there is no question that violence occurred. In response to Cipriano's protests that he had not used force, the judge said it was "unbelievable that a child who appears to be barely seven years old could have consented voluntarily to such a hideous act." The asesor referred to the matter as one "of great gravity" and sentenced Cipriano to fifty lashes along with four years of exile. Yet the word *estupro* was used, signaling the degree to which it was used as an umbrella term.[21]

Judges also responded—sometimes—to cases of domestic abuse that resulted in homicide. In some cases the proceedings fall away midcase. But in several cases men were imprisoned or sentenced to hard labor for killing their wives. In 1779, Timoteo Pirir was sentenced to two months' prison for stabbing his wife in the chest, causing her death.[22] In 1781, Manuel Toribio Granados was sentenced to two hundred lashes and four years of service in public works for stabbing his wife in the back.[23] And Vicente Bolaños was sentenced to six months' hard labor for dragging his lover across the floor soon after she had given birth, killing her and one of the newborn twins. In this case we can probably say that the infant's death influenced the court's decision.[24]

And judges responded to cases of violence—domestic or

otherwise—when they spilled over into the public sphere, threatening disorder. In a surprising case from 1782, Lucía Suncín, a
button maker from Guatemala City, complained to the court
about her husband, Ramón Ortiz. A forty-four-year-old mulato libre, Ramón had already been in prison eight times at his
wife's instigation. Now she renewed her protests, saying that
her husband routinely stole her button-making supplies to buy
aguardiente—a hard liquor made from sugar or maize. If he
was not sent to the *presidio* as punishment, she declared, there
was a danger "that he would violently take her life." Ordinarily
this would not have impressed the judges, but in this case three
men from the neighborhood testified to the damages caused
by this most "disorderly" husband; and two of the men were
addressed as "Don"—men of high standing. Don León Trolivo
testified that Ramón was always drunk, "and that for this reason he scandalizes everyone in his house and all of his neighbors, who thereby are apprised of all the insufferable behavior
to which he subjects [his wife]." He added, crucially, that "when
he plays [cards] he becomes even more insolent to the point
where he is a danger [*pernicioso*] to the whole republic." Similarly, José Manuel Palencia testified that Ramón mistreated
his wife "with injurious words, scandalizing the people of his
house and the neighbors as much with his insolent words as
with his continual shouting and he scandalizes the city." And a
third man, Don Domingo Manuel Pineda, also testified to the
mistreatments and scandal.[25]

    This term—"scandal" or "scandalous"—is a red flag in
criminal cases for this period. The phrasing is "dar escándalo"—
to give scandal—and it suggests something more than what we
imagine. Scandal to us suggests something inappropriate, racy,
and a little fascinating. For colonial Spanish Americans, es-

cándalo was a crime. Legislation from the late colonial period targeted activities deemed to cause escándalo, identifying these as primary sources of social disruption. Repeatedly, magistrates used the word to support their arrest of unruly criminals: they were causing escándalo; their actions provoked great escándalo; so-and-so is known to create escándalo.

What, exactly, was escándalo? Disruption. Violent disorder. Shaming contagion.[26] As Jessica Delgado has argued in the context of scandal and piety, escándalo could be deeply perilous, tipping the contaminated subjects into a dangerous spiritual and moral impurity. "Throughout most of the colonial period," Delgado says, "priests and parishioners talked about sin, scandal, and shame as contagious. The language they used to do so centered around two words: *escándalo,* or 'scandal,' and *escrúpulo,* scrupulousness, but more accurately, a troubled conscience." These two qualities affected the individual, but they also affected the people around her—indeed, they could spread just as contagion spreads. "Private sin was ultimately less of a concern than sin that was known beyond the sinner. Truly private sin endangered only one soul, whereas publicly known sin affected, and perhaps infected, all who came into contact with it."[27] (Delgado also argues, relatedly, that piety could counterbalance this. So scandalous acts in the vicinity of a convent might be somewhat less hazardous, the devoted works of the nearby nuns creating a kind of counterweight.) The vital point is that scandal was deeply injurious, to both the offender and the people in his vicinity. To be touched by scandal meant to enter a precarious state from which one would need to recover. In very real ways, scandal was worse than violence. A violent act threatened the body. A scandalous act threatened moral and spiritual health.

That this is so becomes clear in the testimony of the three men, who admit that Ramón hurt his wife but stress, rather, that his treatment scandalized the neighborhood and the city. *The city is in danger,* their testimony says. *This man is a threat to us.* The asesor was inclined to agree. Though Ramón had, without irony, defended himself by saying that his wife drove him to drink, the asesor wrote a lengthy decision in which he spoke eloquently about the dangers posed "to the good order of the Republic" by men like Ramón. He considered the eight incarcerations, in addition to the one he served through the course of the latest trial, sufficient for a term of imprisonment, but he ordered that Ramón not be released until a suitable master button maker (*Maestro Botonero*) could be found, and that Ramón be released into his care. This man would from now on be in charge of reforming Ramón and ensuring that he toed the line.

The concern with escándalo, paired with the desire for order and the adaptable paternalism of colonial authorities, gives us a more complete picture of how violence was perceived in this period. As Victor Uribe-Uran has highlighted in his study of spousal homicides, violence toward women "had to cause 'serious injuries,' 'severe bleeding,' or 'public outrage'" in order to warrant prosecution.[28] Violence became "violence"—a category of juridical concern—only in certain circumstances. Most clearly, violence in the home was rarely problematic, unless it spilled over, becoming a public problem. Perhaps the more accurate description is that alcaldes and courts alike were not addressing violence. They were addressing public disorder, and sometimes violence happened to cause it. But where other acts caused public disorder, they could be just as dangerous, just as potentially destabilizing.

Liberata's mother kept the violence at home, and so in

this regard she had done nothing wrong. But when Liberata fled from home and her breasts—or someone else's—ended up on a windowsill, something far more serious occurred. It was a very public declaration that the offender could do as he liked. An outbreak of escándalo that threatened the city's peace and good order. A destabilizing act like no other.

3
Iconography
In Which the Perpetrator Offers New Evidence

It is through this giant maze of spoken words and uncovered actions that we can find some partial answers to our poorly formulated questions. But no such answer is definitive, because later in the same document, or in a different document, details will emerge that put into question what we had discovered earlier and events will then cohere differently.

—ARLETTE FARGE, *THE ALLURE OF THE ARCHIVES*

While the breasts on the windowsill were interpreted as a disruption, this is not their only possible meaning. There are others, and it is almost certain that to most people in Guatemala, several of these meanings would have resonated simultaneously—a complex chord with several notes.

It could be that somewhere in these possible meanings

lies the meaning intended by the perpetrator. We cannot be sure what was in his mind, apart from one thing: he was trying to communicate. The placement, arrangement, and presentation of the breasts was deliberate. These were not careless actions, and they were not private actions. They were purposeful and public. *Some* message was intended.

We have confirmation of this in what happened next. On July 26, a thirteen-year-old boy named Josef María Bonifacio Cárdenas was walking home from the city market with two of his teachers. It was about two in the afternoon. Thirteen-year-old boys know about the allure of the awful like no one else, and Josef María was no exception; he was drawn to a swarm of flies on a windowsill, and when he peered over the stone ledge he discovered a pair of severed hands.

"Look at the hands," he said to one of his teachers, or, according to another witness, "There are some corpse's hands here." There were four witnesses to the discovery: the two young ladies who accompanied him, an old woman sitting in a doorway, and one Nicolasa Lara, a servant who had been doing the laundry when her mistress told her to go pick up tortillas in the market. None of them saw who had placed the hands.

Don Ambrosio Rodríguez Taboada, an alcalde of the city, gave official notice to the court, and Doctor Don Narciso Esparragosa was once again called to examine the evidence. He described one right hand and one left hand that were clearly a pair. They had begun to decompose and were infested with worms. They had been severed at the wrist. Their color was "amulatado," a word used to describe people of mixed race. Their size and shape indicated that they were a woman's. And, crucially, the doctor observed that the nails were long, "as if they had belonged to someone with a long illness." Then he made an inference that made sense at the time but that would soon become problematic: he found it plausible that the hands and the breasts had been taken from the same person. The skin color was the same, and the state of decomposition fit the timeline.[1]

A few additional points about the hands bear mention. Other witnesses describe the hands as being placed palm to palm: the fingers slightly enmeshed, one hand resting atop the other. Perhaps the drawing of the severed breasts made by Cayetano Díaz served as inspiration, for an illustration was made of the hands for inclusion in the court records (Figure 5).

The drawing was probably made by someone other than Díaz—perhaps the official notary—since it evinces neither his customary materials nor his skill. A clumsy rough draft is penned on the opposing side of the page, and the final result shows hands that appear more generic than specific. Where are the long nails, for example? Nevertheless, the drawing gives us a sense of how the hands were placed. And there is greater intrigue in *where* they were placed, for the windowsill upon which they were found belonged to Doña Manuela Manzano, a woman living across the street from Don Cayetano Díaz.

Manuela Manzano claimed to know nothing about the hands. She testified that an acquaintance had knocked on her door at noon, and since her door to the street was kept firmly shut, she had opened her window to see who it was. If the hands had been there at noon, she would have seen them. They had, then, been placed on the sill sometime between noon and 2 P.M.

The officials had Brígida Arana summoned from the women's jail, to see whether she could determine whether the hands belonged to her daughter, Liberata. Upon seeing them, Brígida gave the following startling response: her daughter "had

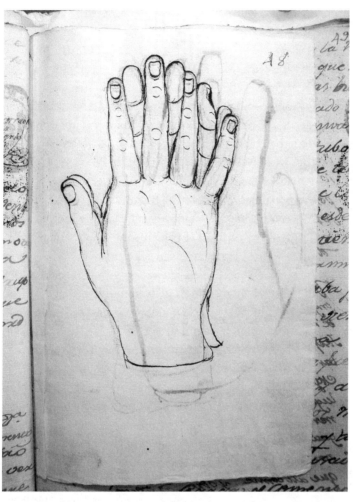

5. Severed hands, as drawn in the criminal proceedings, 1800

been seen [alive] in Antigua Guatemala, so the hands could not be hers."[2]

Was the rumor true? Could Liberata be alive? If she was still alive, then who was the "owner" of the breasts? Had the entire investigation been on the wrong track from the start? Did her reappearance mean that some other woman was missing? And what did it mean that the hands were left on the sill of Manuela Manzano, who lived so close to Cayetano Díaz? What about the fact that the hands were left in the middle of the day, when there was presumably a good deal of foot traffic? The hands, in a much greater state of decomposition than the breasts, were also placed, like the breasts, in a deliberate way. A *staged* way. What did this staging mean?

These are all compelling and rather vexing questions, but let's put most of them aside for a moment to focus on the last—the way the breasts and hands were staged—in order to think about the possible communication intended by the perpetrator and the meanings perceived by the people of the city.

A first possibility:

We must begin by confronting the interpretation that leaps to mind for a present-day reader. According to this interpretation, the breasts and hands are a message left by a person inferred to be sexually violent, assumed to be mentally unstable, as part of an ongoing conversation about the dangers of urban life for young women. The author of such a message is almost certainly a man. It can be read as a statement of misogynist triumph and, simultaneously, as a warning of more horrors to come.

Although this was my initial reading of these messages and it was probably yours, too, it's unlikely that the Guatemalan public jumped to a similar interpretation. The strongest

evidence I can find to support such a view is the asesor's comment that the owner of the breasts had died "at the hands of
the cruelest torturers." These words could be construed as support for an imagined villain along the lines I first envisioned: a
Jack the Ripper–style killer with experience and sadistic flair.
But it could also support other conceptions. A torturer is not
necessarily a misogynist. Cruelty is not necessarily sadistic, or
insatiable, or serial.

We imagine the Ripper-style villain so clearly not because he is so universal but because we are so familiar with his
depiction that we *imagine* him to be universal. This particular
profile is rare. Men like the Ripper appear infrequently in the
historical record. But they make for popular books and film
and television, so we read and watch a disproportionate number of stories about them.[3] And then, before long, it begins to
seem as though they are everywhere. The long history of fic-
tionalization makes this villain—and the type of message he
sends, a sinister code relayed to a terrified public—seem plausible, even common.

In 1800 in Guatemala, there was no such familiarity. Jack
the Ripper would not hit the London tabloids until the late
nineteenth century. Sigmund Freud, the unmentioned foundation for many of these fictionalized tellings, had yet to be
born. Even if the perpetrator of these crimes was a textbook
example of a violent, mentally unstable misogynist (and good
evidence would emerge later that he was), Guatemalans would
not have recognized his message in this way, so clearly, so
instantly.

And yet . . . Guatemalans did understand that the message was
violent. I've suggested the kinds of violence and nonviolence
that were familiar in the city—assault, homicide, rape—and

it's possible that Guatemalans would have read these messages with that vocabulary in mind. But there's more to this lexicon that I haven't yet explored, for beyond home and street and tavern, along the coast and across the ocean, in the recent and distant past, lay another kind of violence. The violence of war. More specifically, given Guatemala's history, the violence of conquest.

A second possibility:

Mutilation of live and dead bodies was an unignorable element of military conquest—perhaps not so frequent as to be ordinary, but recurrent enough to be recognizable as a tactic of terror. Hernán Cortés once replied to a Mexican chief by severing the hands of his messengers, sending them home with their truncated arms to communicate his unwritten response.[4] Bartolomé de Las Casas, the Spanish soldier-turned-Dominican who railed against the empire for the horrors it visited upon Indian victims, also catalogued the instances of brutality in his *Short Account of the Destruction of the Indies,* written in 1542 and published many times over.[5] Mutilation is one of them. His account reads like the very best propaganda—shocking, eye-popping, unbelievable, except for the persistent first-person witness who insists that these things were real, were evidenced, were documented. Spaniards who smashed infants against rocks. Who set their dogs on defenseless Indians. Who competed to see who could do more damage to the Indian body with a single blow of the sword.

My entry into colonial history happened with Las Casas, before I could read well enough to understand what conquest or even history really was. The illustrations to his text created by the engraver Theodor de Bry (who had never been to the Americas) amplified the sensational effects of the text (Figure 6).[6] De Bry, a Protestant, had his own reasons for depicting so

Quadam autem die, circa quartam noctis vigiliam in
multos Cacicos, Satrapas, & alios Indianos irruit, qui tamen se
satis tutos existimabant (fides enim, & securitas illis data erat, se
nullam iniuriam, aut damnum recepturos) qua fide nitentes, ex
motibus, in quibus latebant ad vrbes, sine vlla suspicione, aut ti-
more, reuertebantur, quos omnes cepit, & manus in terram ex-
tendere iubens, ipsemet ense proprio illis abscindebat, se eos
castigare

6. Illustration by Theodor de Bry in Bartolomé de Las Casas's
Short Account of the Destruction of the Indies

lavishly the horrors committed by Catholic conquistadors; his images reflect his talents, but they also reflect a broader antagonism between Protestant and Catholic. They are one brushstroke in the vast portrait of Spanish villainy known as the "black legend." They are powerful images. I have no doubt they stunned the sixteenth-century viewer just as much—if in a different manner—as they stunned my childhood self.[7]

I remember staring at this scene, reproduced in some book about the Americas that sat innocuously on my parents' shelf, trying to make sense of what I was seeing. The hands and noses shorn. The woman attempting to pick up her severed hand. The man at the chopping block, offering up his arm with a staggering combination of willingness and dismay. In the background, just as inexplicably, people plummeting from a hillside and being eaten by dogs. For me the greatest point of anxiety was the woman in the foreground, lying helplessly with her gushing arms extended to either side. Now when I look at her, she seems almost absurd—hopelessly mischaracterized, with her classical nude proportions and flowing hair. But when I was a child, poring through books I was too young to read, her face and posture summarized for me the questions to which I could not fathom answers: *How could this happen? How could someone do this? Who are these people who kill and maim with such efficient ease?*

De Bry's images were widely reproduced, but even if this image and others that illustrated Las Casas's text were not direct references for Guatemalans, the fact of mutilation in warfare would have been easily, intuitively familiar.[8] Indeed, soldiers were everywhere in the city, and while we have no sense of statistical incidence for this period, veterans with scars and missing limbs must have been a visible reminder of how war did happen, *was* happening. In this light, it seems likely that a mutilated body part would have spoken more of warfare than of domestic violence.

There is another kind of conquest, too, that must be considered: the ongoing conquest of Guatemalan people by the state. Some scholars even characterize the Bourbon period as a *re*conquest: an aggressive reining in, an imposition of order.[9] The imposition of order sometimes required punishments, and one of those punishments resonates undeniably with the severed hands. For certain crimes, most notably for carrying prohibited weapons, people were placed in the stocks. Sometimes for a few hours, sometimes for more than a day, sentenced criminals were punished in public, their hands and heads dangling through the holes, suggestive of severing. In 1799, for example, an Indian man named Francisco Xavier Díaz was apprehended by the police patrol carrying a knife that he claimed to need for work. He was given twenty-five lashes with the knife held at his throat, and then for three consecutive days he was brought out and placed in the stocks with the offending knife beside him.[10]

Picture it, and the message is clear. An Indian man. A European device. A public punishment that enacts a visual dismemberment.

A third possibility:

It is tempting to read in these body pieces some message of resistance: a fierce statement about the violence of colonialism; a salvo on the damage done to native bodies; or even an argument about the brutality meted out to women through colonial rule. "The issue is not simply that violence against women happens during colonization but that the colonial process is itself structured by sexual violence," the argument goes, as voiced by Andrea Smith and Luana Ross, present-day writers. "The history of colonization of Native people is interrelated with colonizers' assaults upon Indian bodies. It is through the constant assaults upon our bodily integrity that colonizers have attempted to eradicate our sense of Indian identity."[11]

Could we interpret the perpetrator's message along these lines?

We know that the breasts and hands belonged to someone of mixed race. We know that in late-eighteenth-century Guatemala, people of mixed race were confronting increasingly rigid constraints of social stratification. The *casta* system, a framework for racial categorization that dominated colonial perceptions in urban Spanish America, gradually came to replace baggier categories clumped around five poles: Spanish, Indian, black, *mestizo* (mixed Spanish and Indian), and mulato (mixed Spanish and black). We know more about these categories than we might, not because people suddenly began to self-identify with dozens of new labels but because paintings from the late colonial period illustrate the labels in surprising detail. The so-called casta paintings show nuclear families with mixed-race offspring, sometimes laid out in a grid, like early Punnett squares predicting the outcome of various racial combinations, and sometimes alone on the canvas as part of a series.[12] The casta paintings were produced in Mexico, but as in so much else, Mexico mirrored aspects of New Spain as a whole.[13] Across the region, the logic of the casta system reflected the enlightenment-era conception of race as something influenced by bloodlines, geography, and climate. Historian Magali Carrera, in her list of combinations presented by a typical set of casta paintings, signals their emphasis on mixture, on progeny, and on racial "deterioration":

1. Español and india beget mestizo
2. Mestizo and española beget castizo
3. Castizo and española beget español
4. Española and negro beget mulato
5. Española and mulato beget morisco
6. Morisca and español beget albino
7. Español and albina beget torna-atrás
8. Indio and torna-atrás woman beget lobo
9. Lobo and india beget zambaigo
10. Zambaigo and india beget cambujo
11. Cambujo and mulata beget albarasado
12. Albarasado and mulata beget barcino
13. Barcino and mulata beget coyote
14. Coyote woman and indio beget chamiso
15. Chamisa and mestizo beget coyote mestizo
16. Coyote mestizo and mulata beget ahí te estás[14]

The terms for the various castas point to animals, ethnicity, and station: combination number thirteen results in a "coyote," and number eight yields a "lobo," or wolf. Combination number five results in a "morisco" or Moor, an early modern word for Muslims living in Spanish Iberia. Combination number seven results in a "torna-atrás" or "throwback." It's particularly interesting that in this set presented by Carrera, the combination of Spanish and Indian (number 1) can, through three generations of coupling with Spaniards, result once again in a Spaniard (number 3), whereas a similar coupling between Spaniards and people of African descent (numbers 4 through

7. Juan Rodríguez Juárez, *De español y de india produce mestizo,*
c. 1715

7) do not yield a Spaniard—they yield the aforementioned
"torna-atrás." One could read this as an argument about the
indelible stain of "black blood" or, correspondingly, about the
potential erasure of Indian blood.

And the paintings offer additional arguments about the
consequences of interbreeding. Particularly in the latter part
of the eighteenth century, families with Spaniards are depicted
as harmonious and affluent, while mixed-race families are depicted as struggling. Consider the contrast between the early-
eighteenth-century paintings by Juan Rodríguez Juárez and
José de Ibarra (Figures 7 and 8) and the next two from 1763 by
Miguel Cabrera (Figures 9 and 10).

In the earlier paintings, both families seem contented

8. José de Ibarra, *De mulato y mestiza, lobo tente en el aire,*
c. 1725 (Museo de Américas, Madrid)

9. Miguel Cabrera, *De español y mestiza, castiza*, 1763
(Museo de Américas, Madrid)

10. Miguel Cabrera, *De castizo y mestiza, chamizo*, 1763
(Museo de Américas, Madrid)

and wealthy—extravagantly so, even. Half a century later, in the 1763 paintings, there is a clear contrast between the family headed by a Spanish man and the family headed by a mixed-race man: leisure and happiness attend the first; poverty and a threat of violence attend the second. There is a gendered argument in Cabrera's series, too—the families headed by a Spanish man do well, regardless of the woman's race, whereas families of mixed-race fathers seemed doomed to suffer. But this notion of a protected sphere created by a Spanish head of household is not universal or even consistent. In a 1774 painting by Andrés de Islas (Figure 11), the threat of racial mixture is much starker.

The message hardly requires interpretation. These are the risks of marrying a black woman, the painting argues: violence at home, a terrified child, a loss of safety and dignity. Taken as a whole, the paintings do not present a single argument—they are complex and sometimes contradictory. But more often than not, they seem to warn the viewer about the costs of racial mixture, and even where they do not warn, they certainly reveal sharp and animated racial thinking: they participate in the making of race as something related to color, to lineage, and to status.

Casta paintings cannot be taken as a transparent reflection of colonial reality, of course—these are snapshots of colonial mentalities more than of colonial lives.[15] Historians continue to debate the origins and purpose of the genre: they may have been created as curiosities for export to Spain; they may have been expressions of local pride, demonstrating the richness and variety of the Americas; and they may been constructions of racial taxonomies consistent with European enlightenment values.

Relating all three explanations causally, historian Susan

11. Andrés de Islas, *De español y negra nace: mulata*, 1774
(Museo de Américas, Madrid)

Deans-Smith argues that racial thinking in enlightenment-era
Europe at once influenced and provoked elites in New Spain.
The growing popularity of the genre is at least partly due to the
prevalent "culture of curiosity." This culture relied heavily on
natural history, which in turn relied heavily on systems of classification. Classifying flora and fauna was not enough; "questions of human nature, national characteristics, and debates
over nature versus nurture" encouraged the classification of
human beings, as well. A particular sore spot for Spanish Americans was the Comte de Buffon's 1749 publication on natural
history, which classified people according to region and climate and judged Americans inferior to Europeans.[16] Rather
than despair at such rhetoric, Americans strove to find a place
for themselves within it: the casta paintings, "which may have
been interpreted by viewers as pleasurable, informative, and
even comforting, could also convey a more serious claim that
even racially miscegenated populations might be made productive and orderly under the guiding, civilizing hand of their
Spanish imperial masters."[17]

Productive and orderly. These were two of the crucial
guiding principles for Bourbon reformers, whose efforts to
transform the Spanish empire went far beyond political and
economic change. Curbing drunkenness and vice, converting
sloth into efficiency, promoting decency and hygiene—these
were all as important as oiling the gears of administration and
improving methods of taxation. Scholars have gone back and
forth about the impact of Bourbon interventions, and I have
been most convinced by approaches that acknowledge variety.
That is to say, in some places and in some areas, Bourbon reforms were half-hearted or redundant; but in other places, they
were dramatic. Historian Pamela Voekel, examining reforms in
Mexico City, describes their intent and effect as "social engi-

neering." She describes how the bureaucracy "engineered un-precedented campaigns to extirpate the vices of the people and to inculcate in them the new virtues of hard work, sobri-ety, and proper public propriety." The campaigns were put into effect by neighborhood police who targeted Mexico City's poor. They cared particularly about the poor because these people represented the greatest ills of society—sloth and "moral turpitude." In order to make the city more productive as a whole, these offenders had to be transformed.[18]

In her striking and memorable analysis, Voekel writes that Bourbon rule targeted the body. "Reform efforts were more than just rhetoric," she argues. "The new division between high and low culture cut across not only the social formation, but also the topography of the city, and even the body of the individual, as the lower classes became bracketed with the now shameful functions of the lower body."[19] In other words, the reforms were not just about using terms like "elite" and "poor"—or, we might add, *español, mestizo, negro, torna-atrás;* they were physical. They were bodily. They involved creating separate urban spaces for elite and poor and even associating different parts of the body with elite and poor. Elites engaged the higher faculties of the mind; the poor engaged the lower faculties of digestion and defecation. Yes, perhaps elites had to rely on their alimentary canals along with everyone else, but their dedicated spaces in the city could be cultivated and presented as if they didn't. Clean churches and plazas. Smooth roadways and shining stucco walls. Where the poor inevitably had to be—the market, the roads, the taverns, their homes—they were expected to control and conceal those functions that marked them as low.

Part of this "bracketing," as Voekel terms it, involved the provocation of disgust—the making of disgust—to separate elites, with their ample resources for order and sanitation, from nonelites, with their lack of such resources. Elites could afford the space and staff to effectively suppress bodily waste, for example, while the poor could not. Voekel thereby argues that reformers targeted not poverty but the poor—that is, the behavior of the poor was criminalized, but the causes of poverty were ignored. And to this approach she finds a startling resistance. As Bourbon reformers targeted the body, the people in their crosshairs responded with their bodies. They were not just "passive spectators." Instead, they protested against the viceregal palace, an unignorable symbol of royal power. "Despite the ordinances concerning public lewdness . . . three armed guards had to be posted around the palace . . . to prevent the return of the socially repressed: the army of pueblo bajo who daily urinated and defecated against its walls."[20]

Though Voekel's focus is not on race, and though her documents focus on Mexico City, the leap to Guatemala's socially repressed and impoverished casta population is not too great. Bourbon reforms were just as heavy-handed in Guatemala City, and racial stratification was just as marked.[21] If we imagine the mounting pressure of the social engineering described by Voekel alongside the increasingly rigid constraints of racial taxonomies, the atmosphere seems right for a forceful, belligerent, even violent response. A response made *with the body*. Could we be witnessing a message like the one voiced by piss and shit on the palace walls? Could the message left by the hands and breasts be, "Do not try to constrain my body, because I will take it apart and throw it back at you?" Could it be something even more pointed, along the lines of what Andrea Smith writes? Something like, "This is what you've done to me. Now *look* at it."

There's a moment in the depositions that makes it seem

possible. Remember the five witnesses to the discovery of the hands? A thirteen-year-old boy, two young women who are his teachers, a servant, and "an old woman in a doorway." For the space of a few pages, the court zeroes in on this old woman, whom the witnesses describe variously as "a poor woman" or "the unknown woman who is said to be crazy." They would recognize her were they to see her again, they all claim, but none know her name. And in her signaled poverty, her reputed insanity, she seems a candidate for the kind of response that would be made angrily—perhaps justly—against the civilized people of the city who keep their doorways and windows clean but cannot find a scrap of food or a place of shelter for an elderly woman.

It's possible, but I confess that I find it unlikely. Not because it seems impossible that someone would do such a thing, but because the two instances—the breasts, the hands—give us much less to work with than Voekel's evidence of daily urination and defecation.

And so, a fourth possibility:

Let's step back once more to consider yet another set of meanings potentially perceived by the people of the city. Here the meanings are still about violence, but the violence is glossed in a different manner. The horrors performed upon the body by conquistadors or soldiers or reformers do not end in horror. They go on to be transformed into something luminous, redemptive, even sacred.

What if in these pieces of a woman's body, Guatemalans saw references to God?

This is the possibility that requires the most decoding. To us the references might seem obscure, but we are not steeped in the visual vocabulary of Catholicism as colonial Spanish

Americans were.[22] Consider that residents of Guatemala City would have been familiar with the story and likely some images of the martyrdom of Saint Agatha (231–51) of Sicily.[23] King Quintianus of Sicily was said to have fallen in love with Agatha, "a great beauty of noble birth who had dedicated her virginity to Christ." But when she refused him, Quintianus "subjected her to all types of indignities, including sending her to the house of Aphrodisia, who kept a brothel." Agatha still resisted. Quintianus had her beaten and then, as a crowning punishment, had her breasts shorn.[24] Agatha was healed miraculously by Saint Peter, only to be burned on the coals by an infuriated Quintianus.

Not all martyr saints have enjoyed Saint Agatha's longevity. Popular in the Middle Ages due to Jacobus de Voragine, who included her story in his *Legenda Sanctorum,* Saint Agatha was also widely depicted during the Renaissance and into the early modern period. A wave of "porno-violent hagiography," as one scholar puts it, emerged from a culture of piety that was at once fervent and propagandistic. Nerida Newbigin relates that "devotion required stronger and more sensual stimuli in a society which combined extremes of piety and violence with a taste for the miraculous."[25]

One has only to glance at a few of these images to understand immediately what Newbigin means. I am particularly struck by the seventeenth-century depiction by Francesco Guarino, whose Saint Agatha, surrounded by men, somehow looms larger than all of them (Figure 12). The expressions of the observers suggest not horror or disgust but more a mixture of indifference and ghoulish attentiveness. Notice, too, that her hands are bound (visually severed, at least) at the wrist. These are hands that are limp and soft. They could appear dead. Though her story is one of fierce resistance, here there is

12. Francesco Guarino, *Martirio di sant'Agata (taglio dei seni),*
circa 1640

none, not even the resistance that can be described as pain in
opposition to the blade that cuts her breast. What she seems to
feel is not the severing sword but the gesture of the angel above
her—the bliss of what that contact means. Perhaps it is not
going too far to describe the bliss of her expression as tinged
with eroticism.[26] As art historian Martha Easton writes in her
analysis of earlier Agatha images, we can presume "that the
image of a tortured female body must have theological significance to be presented as a religious image for contemplation."
Nevertheless, viewers might come away with other, very dif-

ferent, impressions. "In visual effect, one can read medieval images of St. Agatha as sensual, sadistic, voyeuristic, and violent; in fact, it may be this combination of the religious and erotic that gave the images much of their power, and made St. Agatha such a popular iconographic subject."[27]

While there are many images that show Agatha in the excruciating moment of martyrdom, there is another kind of depiction, one that shows her afterward—miraculously healed, but with the evidence of her mutilation. It is not uncommon in these images for Saint Agatha to stand beside her breasts or even to hold them upon a plate. Lorenzo Lippi's Saint Agatha, from the mid-seventeenth century, also holds a pair of shears, presumably the ones used to mutilate her (Figure 13).

Or consider the early-sixteenth-century painting by Giovanni Cariani, which similarly shows Saint Agatha—here with a palm frond for sainthood—holding one of the breasts that lies before her on a plate (Figure 14). To us this might seem shocking, morbid, even masochistic. It is here that we must follow the transformation of not just the breasts themselves, but their meaning. The breasts no longer signify the torture done to a female body; they signify the strength of her womanly resistance, the power of her chastity, the miracle of her healing. And through them we can thereby see the triumph of other forces. As Easton observes, writing in 1994, "even in the twentieth century the breast is a multivalent symbol of motherhood, fertility, and femininity as well as sexuality. In the Middle Ages the breast also signified food."[28]

Both these Agathas look directly at the viewer, their expressions placid, to my eye slightly smug. They look content, almost untouchable, slightly remonstrating. The breasts themselves are round, whole, uncorrupted. It is perhaps not too great a leap from these depictions of breasts neatly nestled upon

13. Lorenzo Lippi, *Saint Agatha*, 1638–44

plates to the placement of a severed breast upon a lily pad—
the round leaf a plate of sorts.[29]

What about the lily pad? We know it served a practical
purpose—that is, to carry the breasts from one place to another.
But is the leaf something more than just a handy receptacle?

In fact, the lily pad might be an additional piece of code.
Water lilies do not have consistent symbolism in Christian

14. Cariani (Giovanni Busi), *Portrait of a Young Woman as Saint Agatha*, 1516–17

iconography, but the water lily and its fruit are an integral part of the "lentic aquatic ecosystem" represented in the Maya iconographic tradition. In their analysis of water lily iconography in classical and postclassical Maya images and glyphs, J. Andrew McDonald and Brian Stross discuss how the water lily has generally been interpreted by scholars as a symbol for

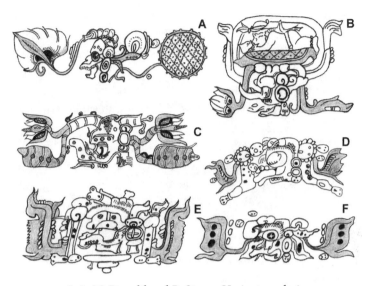

15. J. A. McDonald and B. Stross, *Variant renderings of Water Lily Monster*

the "natural principles that govern birth, the regeneration of life, and the fate of successive dynasts." But in their study, Mc-Donald and Stross also find a close connection between the water lily and the divine serpent, a widely depicted figure in Maya images. They argue that "by virtue of close and recurrent iconographic associations between the divine serpent and water lily, we can only assume that the symbolic significance of this plant form overlaps to a certain extent with that of its reptilian accessory" (Figure 15).[30]

In other words, where we see the water lily, we can infer the presence of the serpent, and vice versa. So what does the serpent mean? McDonald and Stross consider one depiction of a serpent as "a tubular conduit through which mortals and immortals confer with each other." The gods make contact with the world of the living through a serpent's open jaws. And the serpent, in this case, is not just a serpent: it "can also be interpreted as a flowering water lily stalk, given that this plumed serpent is actually a flower serpent, as indicated by the water lily flowers adorning the creature above and below."[31]

McDonald and Stross conclude that water lilies are more significant symbolically than previous scholars have allowed, partly because of what the water lily does. They argue "that the long-held hypothesis that water lilies possess entheogenic properties is supported by these recurrent associations."[32] That is, the water lily was probably used as a drug in Maya rituals, and those rituals were about communicating with the gods.

So—what could this mean? A reference to Saint Agatha, a martyr saint, paired with what is perhaps a reference to communication with the gods. What do these say when taken together?

Let's take another look at the perpetrator's second message. What if we consider the pair of hands, resting against each other, fingers lightly entwined, as a gesture of hands at prayer? Imagine each of the objects as a piece of code with a single meaning. Saints are intercessors with God. The water lily symbolizes the conduit through which mortals and immortals speak. The hands re-create the gesture of prayer, by which the penitent appeals to God directly. Could we take all these pieces as a message about communicating with God? If so, what is the perpetrator saying about communication with God? That the city should do it better? More? That attempts to communicate with God are futile?

That only through such radical ruptures of the body can we hope to make God or the gods hear us?

Perhaps. I find this possibility more persuasive, largely because the lily pad and the hands are so deliberate, and I can find no other single meaning that fits all these pieces of evidence so well. But there is another context to consider, one that may augment or complicate the potential references to religious iconography.

A fifth possibility:

Colonial Guatemalans moved through their city with awareness that both people and places were imbued with qualities of sacredness or profanity, beauty or ugliness, and purity or corruption. These were as nuanced, clear, and tangible as the spectrum of wealth and poverty are to us today. Consider the complexity of histories and associations you skim over, the immediate rush of (stifled?) emotions and sensory experiences you feel, when you walk along a city street that has boarded-up windows, then see a bundled figure in torn clothes beside a dumpster, then catch a whiff of alcohol mixed with mildew and vomit. The experience is sensory, but you might also think about the history of urban spaces, and the systemic causes of homelessness and poverty, and the policies that do or don't address the conditions manifested in the space you've just seen. Or, in another moment, consider what it's like when you walk along a commercial street with broad windows cleaned daily, where the mannequins are wearing what you can tell, at a glance, must be thousands of dollars in cut cloth, where the people who pass by do not meet your eye but only glance briefly over your figure, if they glance at all, assessing your worth in the same way you assessed the mannequin. Once again, the experience is made of smells and sights and sounds, but you might think about the fortunes made and expended in such places, and how the garments that cover your body might mean so much in some contexts and so little in others, and how the pieces of fabric are stitched together on the other side of the globe and brought to the window before you by long, fraught processes. Perhaps you wonder about who cleans the windows and floors and what they wear when they are doing it. You see what I mean. At a glance, we see and inhale an entire world of meanings in these contexts, connecting with histories and meanings we know intimately or imperfectly—but we are deeply aware, regardless of how well we know. Now imagine a similar sense of valence, but along a different spectrum, one in which the scandalous and the sacred are as powerful as poverty and wealth.

Let me try to convey a sense of how I imagine such a place. In the previous chapter I described scandal and scandalousness as elements more charged, more significant, than we are used to seeing them. Here let us delve deeper into this worldview. Jessica Delgado's conception of escándalo is worth exploring in more depth, as it establishes not only the nature of these elements but also their importance: when people testified before ecclesiastical judges in New Spain, they "spoke of other people's sins as causing strong feelings of pain and shame." That's the sense of escándalo. Feeling this way was "a spiritually harmful experience in which one became implicated in and tainted by what they had observed." The sentiments did not stop there. "Once 'scandalized' people spoke of entering into or forming 'escrúpulo.' Theologically, this tainting brought concrete spiritual danger, as God could not be in the presence of sin. Whether shame took root in the mind and heart as a result of one's own misdeeds or those of another, it meant separation from God's grace." As a consequence, a soul in this condition "could not partake in the Eucharist, risked more time in purgatory, and was more vulnerable than usual to sin and spiritual disorder." Here is where the analogy to contagion is clearest. There could be no easy separation of scandal, once it emerged. "Scandal, by its nature, was a public affair; news of sinful behavior, once publicly known, tended to spread, and with it, the personal effects of escrúpulo. A community of individuals embroiled in escándalo and escrúpulo was a community whose defenses were weakened against chaos and disorder."[33]

In this striking conception, sin is a taint—it is something dangerous upon contact, and that contact occurs by knowing and seeing. Imagine what it would mean to Guatemalans, then, to *see* physical evidence of sin—the gruesome manifestations of a horrible crime—in a public place. You see the breasts or hands, and at once you are compromised by what you have seen. The community space has been despoiled. The sin of the crime sits on the sill and spreads, the sight and thought of it probing into hearts and minds striving to remain chaste. Perhaps you think about the horrible deed itself—how it happened, how the skin was cut away from the body, how the body looked as it was destroyed. As you imagine these things, you are dwelling in sin, contemplating and immersing yourself in it. Or perhaps you imagine, inadvertently, the impulses that led the perpetrator to commit such an act. Through your mind drift dark wishes and desires: the pleasure of tearing human skin; the fueling anger that makes such pleasure possible. All these thoughts, however fleeting, sting your conscience and infect it like poison. The thought of the body ripped to pieces worms its way in and grows, like a cancer.

Can we be sure that these were viewed as evidence of sin, after considering so many other ways of seeing them?

I think so. If they were viewed as sadistic cruelties, allusions to conquest, or messages of resistance, this would not preclude their interpretation as sins. Even if they were seen as religious references, I believe they would have read as a despoilment or distortion of religious references. To my eye there is no reverence in the placement of these tokens but a deliberate perversion of sacred meanings. Consider how William Taylor elaborates the relationship between sacredness and beauty: "Beauty was understood to be a perfection of proportion and technique that was pleasing to God, asserting the charisma of the image—the being of the figure represented, the life in it—and inviting divine favor."[34] Beauty was assessed by the feelings that it evoked—"the reception or actions by faithful viewers, the feelings of love, awe, and anguish"; these "counted most in this conception of beauty." It was powerful, but so was its counterpart—"the stench and ugliness of evil in the world."[35] If the breasts and hands did speak of communication with God, they made a mockery of it: they made it ugly and corrupt. The symbols of the divine brutalized and brought low.

Here it might be useful to consider an unrelated case that occurred some fifteen years later; it offers an interesting complement, suggesting a clearer articulation of a similar message.

In 1817, the offices of the Guatemalan inquisition found themselves targeted by a flurry of nasty hate mail—slipped under the door, in one case tacked to the cathedral wall.[36] The perpetrators in this case were less coy, and they even signed their missives with sly pseudonyms like "the philosopher." One of the first messages, painfully direct, reads, "I shit on God/ and on his ministers—/that's the truth, you pricks" (Figure 16).[37]

On the reverse of the small page is a "notice": "TODAY is [the feast day of] Saint James/Upon him/I SHIT." The English translation does not convey the original rhyme, which in its radical succinctness reads like a dirty limerick. But these letter writers could be verbose, too. They also sent an impressively creative set of commandments (Figure 17).

16. Anonymous hate mail sent to the Guatemalan Inquisition, 1817

Commandments:
1. Abhor God above all things: the church and its bishops
2. Do not fear the name of God
3. Profane the festivals and temples
4. Dishonor one's superiors
5. Kill the friars and nuns
6. Fornicate with all kinds of people
7. Take up arms against the infamous inquisition
8. Kill those who consider our true Doctrine anathema
9. Pay no attention to the threats of excommunication; these are mere words
10. Shit on the saints and on the church

3.

Mandamientos.   9.

1.º Aborrecer há Dios, sobretodas las cosas: y a la iglesia y Obispos.

2.º No temer el Nombre de Dios.

3.º Profanar las fiestas, y templos.

4.º Deshonrar a los superiores.

5.º Matar a los frailes, y Monjas.

6.º Fornicar a toda clase de personas.

7.º Tomar las armas contra la infame inquisicion.

8.º Que si echan Anatema por nuestra verdadera Doctrina; matar al que lo mandare.

9.º No asercarse del jugueto de la Excomunion; pues son palabras.

10.º Cagarse en los Santos, y en la iglesia.

11.º Rogar al DIABLO, que el Principe que nasca; sea gran erege.

12.º Desir: Jesus es un tonto: Jesus es un Loco: Jesus es un Cabayo: Jesus es un Burro. &. &.

17. Mock "commandments" sent to church officials
in Guatemala in 1817

11. Plead with the DEVIL that the prince be born
12. Say: Jesus is dumb; Jesus is crazy; Jesus is a horse;
    Jesus is a donkey.

Keeping up an almost daily drip, the dissenters delivered sonnets, philosophical letters, and more than one defaced image. An illustration of Saint Jerome came adorned with insults: "Murderer. Judas. Malevolent. Serpent. Hydra. Basilisk. Stupid. Hypocrite. Traitor. Liar. Villain. Idiot" (Figure 18).

In a separate notice, they informed the inquisitors that they had given a crucifix two hundred lashes, all the while shouting insults at it. Any one of these acts would have given the inquisition substantial grounds for a strong case; in some times and places, such heretical statements could have resulted in a swift trial and a death sentence. The message communicated by this bundle of documents could not be more clear— or loud. Disrespect. Anger alongside bitter humor. A deliberate challenge to the long authority of the inquisition and the Catholic Church. The authors of the 1817 documents display a somewhat different sensibility than the perpetrator of the 1800 crimes: a barbed vengefulness that revels in the uproar being caused but that also advances an intellectual case. There is a coherent argument about the church and its representatives, however foul-mouthed the voice that makes it.

What I suggest these colorful heretics and the perpetrator in the 1800 case have in common is the knack for perverting the sacred so that it becomes profane.[38] The argument sounds different to me, but the method of communicating it has similarities. If the person who left the breasts and the hands *did* intend religious references, we might think of the effect as something similar to what is done in Figure 18: a precise and grotesque inversion that would have struck viewers as sacrile-

18. A defaced print of St. Jerome sent anonymously
to Guatemalan officials, 1817

gious in the extreme. *Your gods are not listening,* such a message might say. *You place all your faith in them. But they do not hear you.*

Even if we put aside the possible references to iconography, I believe that these pieces of a woman's body would have affected many who saw and learned of them as palpable and powerful elements of scandalous contagion. Horrible facts and thoughts and deeds, to be worked through and expunged as stains upon the conscience. We have an additional layer here to the disruptiveness of Bourbon order—a disruption of spiritual order, of spiritual health.

4

Enlightened Medicine
In Which Dr. Narciso Esparragosa
Analyzes the Case

More so than any text or novel, the archive collects characters.

—ARLETTE FARGE, *THE ALLURE OF THE ARCHIVES*

After the discovery of the hands on July 26, the authorities redoubled their efforts. Orders were given for exhumations, and on the twenty-seventh the escribano recorded the official visit to the parish cemetery of Los Remedios, also known as El Calvario because of its placement at the south of the city on a high hill. The officials arrived at four in the afternoon, but the parish priest could not be found. Feeling pressure to proceed with the exhumations, they decided not to wait for the key, but to enter through the bell tower passageway, which was known to be unlocked.

Once in the cemetery the officials set about their inspection. For the unpleasant task of opening graves, they had brought with them several of the city's butchers, and these commenced clearing the mounds of grass and seeing whether any of the graves had been disturbed. None had. But there were two recent gravesites: one smaller, as for a child, and another larger. The escribano ordered the butchers to unearth the larger grave, and, he wrote, "when about one third had been uncovered they struck upon the corpse of a woman with no hands."[1] The escribano called at once for the officials, who ordered the butchers to complete the exhumation.

The corpse exhumed from the cemetery of Los Remedios was in advanced stages of decomposition. Much of it had been cut away, including the breasts and hands. The officials presumed that they had finally found the body from which the hands and breasts had been taken, and they called for Liberata's mother, who was still being held in prison. When the corpse had been fully unearthed, Brígida Arana was brought forward. Perhaps she was spared the full horror of this encounter by her conviction that Liberata was still alive, counting as she did on the testimony of those who had seen her recently in Antigua. But the sight of a corpse so disfigured by decomposition and mutilation must have been difficult, regardless. Brígida declared, as she examined it, that the corpse did not belong to her daughter.

By now it was late afternoon. Intent on identifying the corpse that seemed to lie at the very heart of the mystery, the officials searched for and finally found the sacristan of Los Remedios. Asked about the two fresh graves, the sacristan told the city officials that the two recent burials were of an older woman named Simona and a villager from the town of Guadalupe. The older woman, Simona, had died after a long illness, part of which she had spent at the Hospital San Juan de Dios.

Her relatives had taken her home after her stay at the hospital, and she had died on July 21. And then these relatives, duly called and asked to view the corpse, acknowledged without any doubt that the woman who lay before them was Simona Villagrán, whom they had nursed in her final days and who had died only a week earlier.

Due to the late hour and the darkness, further examination of the corpse was postponed until the morning. But the discovery of Simona had, the officials realized, both partly solved and partly complicated the mystery. On the one hand, the decomposed hands almost certainly came from Simona's corpse. But Simona had still been alive on the first of the month, when the breasts appeared on Cayetano's windowsill. What did this mean? Did it mean that these were cases of corpse mutilation, rather than homicide? And was it possible to avoid the conclusion that not one but multiple bodies had been damaged by the perpetrator? Where had the first pair of breasts come from, since they could not be Simona's? And where were Simona's breasts, since these were cut away?

Doctor Narciso Esparragosa rose early on July 28 in order to examine the exhumed corpse as soon as possible. Soon after six in the morning, he had the corpse moved to an examination room, where it was cleaned and aired. His first observation was that the corpse's internal organs were escaping through her lower body. He thought at first that this was due to cuts made to the corpse's genitalia. Events occurring in the following months would corroborate this troubling observation, but at the time it must have seemed an implausible explanation. Upon further examination, Esparragosa decided that the rupture of the internal organs was more likely due to decomposition. The corpse had no other injuries apart from the mutilations. He observed that the hands had been severed at the wrists and that the ears had been cut off at their roots. With precision, he detailed that the shape of the missing breasts matched the breasts found on July 1: the skin of the left breast had been torn all the way to the armpit, while the skin of the right breast had been cut closer to its center. He admitted that the swath of skin cut away from the corpse was probably larger than that which had been found on Cayetano's windowsill, but he reasoned that decomposition had changed the shape of the cuts. The body had been wrapped in several old cloths, including a rough garment worn by the Recoleto Order. The corpse's head had little hair other than on the very front and top of the skull. Finally, he declared that he believed no further evidence would be gleaned from the corpse of Simona Villagrán. The body's decomposition was already so great that even a block away residents complained of the stench. Indeed, he argued, the vapors of the body imperiled not only him and his assistants but the neighborhood at large. The greatest risk, in his view, was that the corpse's vapors would engender an infection that might then spread to the whole city.

Strangely, given the timeline of events, Dr. Narciso Esparragosa seemed intent on demonstrating that the pair of breasts found on July 1 did, indeed, belong to Simona's corpse. The logic of his conclusion is inscrutable, but also typical of him: on the one hand, methodical and precise; on the other hand, stubborn and self-confident to a fault.

Concealed inside Esparragosa's enigmatic conclusion are some interesting possibilities for our case, and they revolve around the practice of dissection. It wasn't exactly revolutionary in 1800, but Esparragosa's use of dissection *was* novel in Guatemala City. To understand the significance of Esparra-

gosa's actions, we need to understand both him and his medical moment.

Dr. Narciso Esparragosa was a central figure for turn-of-the-
century medicine in Guatemala, even for the larger New Spain.[2]
He testified in many, if not most, secular court cases that required medical expertise; he was at the forefront of the early
inoculation efforts in Guatemala; and he changed many sur-
gical practices among contemporaries. He wrote frequently
for the influential Guatemalan *Gazeta* and developed groundbreaking techniques for ocular surgery and for safe breech
births. Esparragosa was also arrogant, filled with a sense of his
own importance, and poorly equipped to handle personal re-
jection. The former made him well known, and the latter made
him not universally liked. Even in the official documentation,
a degree of impatience with Esparragosa's foibles is evident.

Esparragosa left his native Venezuela soon after completing his medical degree because he wished to join a wealthy
uncle in Guatemala who might offer resources and contacts.[3]
Once there, he worked with José Felipe Flores, already a renowned figure of experimental medicine in Guatemala, trained
in the former capital of Antigua Guatemala. Flores, for his part,
was delighted to find a worthy mentee. Enthusiastic about the
possibility of pursuing research in the growing field of European medicine, Flores left the country in 1797 and happily
handed over his responsibilities at the San Juan de Dios to Esparragosa, then only thirty-six years old.

Perhaps he was a little young for the post. Or, more accurately, perhaps some aspects of his character were simply not
suited to a position that required high visibility and some degree of public criticism. He was, for example, adamant about
how he was addressed, insisting on "Don" and "Doctor" and

aspiring to more. John Tate Lanning, a pioneering scholar of Spanish America whose works on medicine, the enlightenment, and intellectual history defined the early field, describes Esparragosa's obsession with his form of address as "representative of his generation." This was evident in his "attachment to high-flown forms of address, his anxiety about being accorded the 'title of *Señor*' when, in 1802, he was presented with his title as 'His Majesty's Royal Surgeon.' In 1813, after an unrelenting insistence and after pestering the *Capitán General* of the *audiencia,* he was accorded the title '*Señor*'—eleven years after requesting the honor."[4] To my eye, the anxiety, insistence, and pestering may be representative, but they're also particular. Without denying that some other men of high standing in Spanish America aggressively pursued such honorifics, it must be understood that not all of them did.

It might help us understand Esparragosa's role in this investigation better if we consider a different kind of criminal case, one that Lanning probably did not have on hand when he studied the eminent surgeon's career. Esparragosa's name is everywhere in criminal cases, but usually he is giving expert testimony. In one case from 1797, however, Esparragosa is the defendant. A woman named Doña Josefa Paniagua, a young widow in Guatemala City, accused him of what in our day would probably be some combination of stalking, forced entry, and sexual assault. She complained that the treatment had been ongoing for eight years.

The purpose in what follows is not character assassination but character illumination. What can we learn about Esparragosa by observing how he behaved in private, how he behaved under pressure, and how he thought about women? Can we learn something that either ties him to the corpse mutilations in an unexpected way or, more likely, explains his approach as he participated in the investigation? And broadly speaking, can we learn something from his behavior about the place of women in colonial society?

Josefa Paniagua began the complaint by explaining, through an escribano, that she had first tried to speak privately with Narciso Esparragosa. "Using the gentlest possible terms and guided by courtesy, [she] pleaded and begged him" not to come to her house any longer.[5] This had proved ineffective, and now she hoped the court would ask him "to abstain from entering into the house of the expressed Doña Josefa, even if he does so with the pretext of exercising his judgment in Medicine and Surgery, with the understanding that if this gentle and polite corrective [does] not prove sufficient to contain him," harsher measures would be taken. When the document was delivered and its contents made known to Esparragosa, he objected that it was "gravely prejudicial and improper." He claimed that her statements were false and that she had never formally asked him to stay away from her house. Then he asked to see the documentary proof so that he could form a response. Abruptly, what had been a delicate private matter became a legal one.

The court asked for statements, and on June 27, 1797, it heard testimony from Yrene Guzmán, who had been a servant for Doña Josefa. Yrene lamented that Esparragosa had been the cause of her dismissal, for once when Doña Josefa was out, Don Narciso had sent a boy delivering a platter of sweets—the eighteenth-century equivalent of an extravagant box of chocolates—and Yrene had accepted them, thinking her mistress would want them. But when Doña Josefa returned, she exclaimed that "only the Devil could have urged her to accept such a present without her permission," and Yrene was ordered to return the sweets immediately. Doña Josefa scolded her severely and ultimately dismissed her.

Just as with extravagant chocolate nowadays, the sweets were meant to open other doors. Yrene had gone to Doña Josefa's house another ten times to do laundry, and on one of these occasions Doña Josefa had been bathing herself in the *pila* (the pool of an inner patio) when Don Narciso knocked on the door. Doña Josefa said to Yrene that if it was her son, Josef Antonio, knocking at the door, then she should let him in. And then,

> having opened the door and believing it to be Josef Antonio and finding herself faced with Esparragosa, she wished to block his entry, telling him that the Señora was bathing, but he ignored her objections and pushed his way in to the very pila, where he found Doña Josefa, and since the declarant was hurrying behind Esparragosa, her mistress said to her, "Look how you sell me out, *India*," to which the declarant answered "how could you say I'm selling you out when the moment I opened the door this man hit me in the face with it?"

Imagine the charged air in the courtroom. The indecencies of poor, mixed-race women were one thing, but bursting in on a Spanish woman of high standing in the midst of her bath . . . that was something else altogether. That was beyond the pale. What did Esparragosa do next? He stood at the open stove—the *cocina*—next to the pila so that he could gaze upon Doña Josefa for a good long while. Doña Josefa began throwing buckets of water at him from the bath, and Yrene, proving herself no help at all, suggested that she stop because Esparragosa was already very wet, "to which her mistress responded, 'I'll soak him all the way through and maybe that way the Devil will take him, which is what I want. I want him to get out of here.'"

This may sound more like flirtation than real anger, but we need to tune our ears to the pitch of eighteenth-century insults. Doña Josefa would not have invoked the devil if she were playing, and she would not have reiterated to Esparragosa later, once he had left and returned to complain about the soaking, that she never wished to see him in her house again. Yrene testified that in her other nine visits to Doña Josefa's house, Esparragosa had always found a reason to be there, and that on every occasion Doña Josefa had said "that she in no way wished to be in communication and begged him not to cross her threshold and on other occasions admonished him with complete seriousness that he ought not to give her gifts because people would come to certain conclusions." And then, finally, the confrontations had become violent. One afternoon of the previous year, Doña Josefa had injured Esparragosa with a pair of scissors "because he attempted to caress her face." On another occasion, he had pressed a present upon her and she had burst out angrily, "What a disgusting, shameless man you are," throwing a pair of scissors in his direction.

Esparragosa was not the first or the last man unable to understand the meaning of "no." Perhaps it's unsurprising that to a certain kind of man with certain sentiments, even a pair of well-aimed scissors can mean "maybe." As the testimony of Yrene and other servants, who confirmed her reports, made clear, Doña Josefa had said "no" many times, in many ways. Doña Josefa herself, when she came before the court, said that Don Narciso's unwanted attentions had been going on for eight years. For the first three, he came to her house only once in a while, but that in the previous five years he had "pursued her incessantly." After being warned by the authorities, Don Narciso had only escalated his efforts, arriving twice each day to seek her out. Notably, she signed her own testimony with a solid, practiced hand.

The court's response is a little dizzying from our vantage point, when we consider that in other cases it looked upon rape and domestic abuse with little more than a shrug. The criminal justices concluded on June 30 in Doña Josefa's favor, declaring that "there is no place for the statement interposed by Dr. Don Narciso Esparragosa, nor is there place for the proceedings he requests, and he should be informed of this with the appropriate respect without allowing him an opportunity to respond in the moment of notification." In other words, Esparragosa was not even allowed to reply. He was ordered to pay all the legal fees and never to enter Doña Josefa Paniagua's house for any reason whatsoever. If he did, she was to notify the court immediately, and it would take action against him.

There is much to learn from these brief, intense, rather painful proceedings—about the mindset of the justices, about the place of women in colonial society, and about the character of Esparragosa. What seems at first a shocking hypocrisy on the court's part makes more sense if we think about colonial conceptions of race, class, and honor. While scholars have demonstrated that honor, that all-encompassing and (to us) runic quality so central to colonial identity, was important to high and low classes alike, colonial elites and their representative official structures—like the criminal court—would not have recognized the honor of a woman of low standing.[6]

Recall, from Chapter 2, the Indian nursemaid who was incapable of being raped. Consider Paniagua's own furious insult, hurled as both epithet and condemnation, to her maid: *India*. People on the bottom rungs of the hierarchy might have used the same currency as elites, but honor was like capital: not everyone had the same amount. Indias had mere pennies. And Josefa Paniagua, a doña of Spanish background with her own property and grown son, had a fortune.

When, in the midst of her court testimony, a woman like Paniagua dropped a reference to her honor and her brothers' efforts to protect it, the statement had weight. Legal scholar William Miller, describing honor-based cultures generally, argues that we should see honor less as a set of rules than as a condition that permeated every aspect of a person's consciousness: "how you thought about yourself and others, how you held your body, the expectations you could reasonably have and the demands you could make on others; it determined the quality of your marriage and the marriage partners of your children. It was your very being."[7] Crucially, this quality was not individual but collective. How you behaved impinged upon those close to you.

Honor was felt as a "keen sensitivity to the experience of humiliation," and it was enacted through the impulse to exchange one shaming act for another, the impulse to correct a perceived account imbalance. This conception captures the importance of shame and humiliation, and it expresses how the quality was predicated on relationships with others. But it doesn't acknowledge the degree to which honor could be acquired in Spanish America by means other than the humiliation of others. It's more accurate to imagine "honor" as two different, intertwined qualities in Spanish America: honor-status and honor-virtue.[8]

Honor-status was acquired at birth. People entered the world with different levels of honor-status, depending on family background and legitimacy. This foundation, which gave elites a decided advantage, could rarely be acquired by someone who hadn't been born into privilege. But "*honra,* or honor-virtue, could be won or lost, accumulated or squandered through the actions of an individual or family." Your choices and conduct determined your honor-virtue. Naturally, these could be negotiated through rumor and reputation far more than the fixed values of social background. That's why good behavior mattered greatly. Chastity, physical courage, honesty, integrity, generosity, as well as avoidance of negative qualities—drunkenness, gambling, disrespectful behavior, and vice of all kinds—mattered for honor-virtue.[9] A highborn don might drink and duel his way into ill repute. Meanwhile, a lowborn mestizo might accumulate wealth and respect and education, live decently and with consideration toward his neighbors, and find himself a grown man with more social standing than the drunken don.

This twofold manner of understanding honor was Iberian, and many aspects of it transferred to the Americas, but with time, conceptions of honor became differentiated, varying from region to region. That said, the conflict between Esparragosa and Paniagua could have unfolded in the same way almost anywhere. For women, many kinds of sexual conduct were dishonoring. We would expect adultery to be dishonoring, but for widows, even starting a relationship too soon after a husband's death was seen as dishonorable. Moreover, "any allusion to the promiscuity or immorality of a mother, wife, or daughter was potentially devastating to the reputation of an individual man or a family."[10] So while Paniagua's exclamations on the record seem to point to her own honor—she berates her servant for selling her out or, more crudely in the Spanish, actually selling (pimping) her—she may well have been worried for her brothers and her son as well. Crucially, the absence of long collective memory in the Americas meant that questions of honor that might have been resolved socially, reputationally, were often instead arbitrated in courtrooms.[11] Many women elsewhere in colonial Latin America resorted to both legal means and to violence (remember the scissors) in order to defend their honor.

These preoccupations may seem a little quixotic, if not quaint, but trying to see honor from the colonial vantage point is worth the effort. Just as understanding scandal can help explain the intended and perceived nature of the crime, understanding honor can help explain what was at stake for some of the principals. The two are not unconnected. While escrúpulo sprang from a sense of spiritual malaise, an awareness of God's gaze, dishonor sprang from a sense of social malaise, an awareness of the neighbors' gaze. A single incident might easily trigger both. The severed body parts would have provoked escrúpulo in some who saw them, and there is also a whiff of dishonor in being chosen as their recipients: to Guatemala City residents, why the breasts and hands were left on *those people's* windowsills must have been an urgent question.

Most of us don't live in communities in which everyone knows one another—and their parents, and grandparents—but most of us do belong to communities, professional or otherwise, in which we know a majority of the members, at least by name. In those communities, reputation matters. We can understand the embarrassment of being suspected of plagiarism, or sexual assault, or substance abuse. And we are also familiar with how, even in a society that purports to cultivate class mobility, birth privilege confers or withdraws benefits. Having certain parents, attending certain educational institutions, having a certain skin color or a certain surname, speaking with a certain accent or deploying a certain vocabulary can all open and close doors. Combine these two aspects—the importance of reputation (honor-virtue) and the power of implied social standing (honor-status)—and we begin to inch our way toward conceptions of Spanish American honor.

For Paniagua, these visits from Esparragosa were a smear on her good name. They called into question her ability to keep her own home, her ability to restrain her own impulses. They impugned her status as a good mother and a good widow. And it is significant that Esparragosa was so willing to trample on the honor of a woman he claimed to admire. He was, in essence, despoiling the very prize he pursued. What does this tell us about him? We know he had his own preoccupations with honor, as his persistent quest for the title of *Señor* indicates. But apparently concern for his own honor did not engender a sensitivity to the honor of others, or at least of women. If he could not find it in him to respect the honor of this woman, this lovely widow whom he showered with gifts and possibly wished to marry (no other route was permissible for a couple of this social standing), how much could he have respected women of the kind who came to his hospital? Are we witnessing in his behavior a sinister inability to see women other than as objects to be analyzed, pursued, and acquired? Or are we witnessing something else? Did he want Paniagua so much that he could not behave rationally in her company? Did he simply get carried away by "passion," time and again?

Perhaps he explained it that way to himself. Esparragosa had a particular view of how passionate emotions worked and what they could do. In a fascinating case from March 1797 (a lot was going on for Esparragosa that year), the eminent surgeon was called to give testimony regarding the death of one Don José Ramírez, who died soon after an altercation with a

neighbor, María Mallén. Ramírez was a master bricklayer, a
married man with children, whose home shared an outer wall
with Mallén's. At seven-thirty on the morning of March 22,
Ramírez and Mallén had exchanged words over a portion of
the wall that had collapsed into Ramírez's property. A heated
argument ensued, and not long afterward the neighborhood
heard the shouts of Ramírez's wife; she was found holding her
husband in her arms. He had collapsed from "cólera"—a fit of
rage. Several witnesses confirmed the cause and the consequences. The surprise is that Esparragosa confirmed it, too. His
intriguing analysis is worth quoting in full:

> Having acknowledged the corpse of José Ramírez,
> and having no reason to believe that he was struck
> or poisoned, he found it necessary to dissect the
> body—upon which it became clear that the very
> grave cause for the sudden death was the violent
> onset of rage that he experienced: this is one of the
> Passions that attacks the system with greatest ease
> and greatest force and so it is no surprise that it took
> his life as it has done to others—there is no scarcity
> of verified precedents in the History of Medicine.
> And so he [Esparragosa] does declare and ratify
> that rage was the cause of his death.[12]

José Ramírez's wife, Doña Rafaela Cilieza, also referred
to the "passion" that had taken hold of him before he walked
eight paces and collapsed in her arms. Meanwhile, the unre-
pentant Mallén had shouted, "Leave him there and may the
Devil take him!" Perhaps this contributed to the widow's conviction that Mallén had not just happened to provoke her husband's death but had in fact murdered him—she "dedicated

herself to quickening the rage with bitter statements and ridi-
cule." For several pages Cilieza went on about the injustices
done to her husband. It is not surprising, given what we know
about honor and the court's protection of it, as well as its long-
standing loyalty to men titled *Don,* that Mallén was called in
for questioning. She never appeared, having likely fled, and it
was probably a wise choice.

    As is often the case, the personal and the professional
cannot be neatly separated. These two very different cases, the
one personal and the other professional, offer us some insights
into both the man and the medical moment. What does it tell
us about Narciso Esparragosa, the man? Inferring a general
portrait from the particulars, I think we see a man who was
representative in more ways than one. He cared about his own
honor deeply, but he did not care much for the honor of women.
His work was premised on the use of logic and rationality, but
he believed in the power of irrational, violent passions and was
deeply driven by them himself. He understood, as the Ramírez
case indicates, that those passions could override even the life
forces of the human body—how much easier, then, for those
passions to override the strictures of colonial courtesies.

    We might say, if we wished to write a maxim for Narciso
Esparragosa, that reason was the rule but passion was paramount.

Treating cólera, rage, as a cause of death was also representative
of the moment. To us it may seem a strange contradiction for
someone supposedly on the cutting edge of modern medical
science. But modern medical science in 1800 was an evolving
field, and it incorporated aspects of earlier belief in surprising
ways. In particular, the relationship between the body and what
we think of as "emotion" drew on long traditions that would

not emphatically change until later in the nineteenth century. As Fay Bound Alberti argues in her work on the history of medicine, the period in which Esparragosa worked was characterized by change, but that change was "neither linear nor straightforward," so that "the principle of mind/body holism" allowing Esparragosa to theorize about passion and death was "retained in medical practice well into the modern period."[13]

The long tradition Esparragosa drew upon had its roots in humoral medicine, an approach to psychology and physiology that held sway in most of Europe for several hundred years.[14] Humoral medicine maintained that the human body was a microcosm of the universe, and that as such it contained the four qualities—hot, cold, moist, and dry—that corresponded to elements in the natural world: fire, air, water, and earth. Balancing these humors was essential to human health, but the precise balance required varied from person to person and was determined both by hereditary traits and by environment. Central to this paradigm was the interrelatedness of mind, body, and soul. Humors, produced in the liver, made their way into the blood and affected not just the physical body but the psychic and emotional body as well. So disproportions of humors could manifest as physical illness or as unfavorable emotional outbursts. Moreover, the imbalance and its emotional expression could create a kind of feedback loop, so that "passions engender humors and humors breed passions."[15]

A burst of anger—or some other passion—could easily imbalance the body to a fatal point. A sixteenth-century account of anger, which described it as "an affection, whereby the bloud about the heart being heated, by the apprehension of some injury offered to a man's self or his friends," could easily have found its way into Esparragosa's own explanation of Ramírez's death.[16] An English *Treatise of Anger* from the early seventeenth century similarly described "bloud ready to burst out of the vaines, as though it were affraide to stay in so furious a body. The brest to swell, as being not large enough to containe their anger."[17] As Alberti demonstrates in her study of the human heart and its conception over time, these ideas had remarkable longevity, and in the period Esparragosa worked, they still held sway. Other theories had come to compete with humoral medicine, in particular what Alberti calls "hydrodynamical" theories that imagined the body mechanistically and, in complement to them, nerve theory. "As the human frame became a composite of fluids and solids," she writes, "it was the solids (nerves and fibres) that were conceived as the 'true basis of the body.' Rather than being related to the apprehension of the soul *as* mind, emotions were redefined as a product of sensory perception and material processes."[18] But such theories did not entirely displace the explanations of traditional humoral medicine, and only in the mid-nineteenth century (in Europe at least, which is Alberti's focus) did the more material explanations effectively dominate.

So what seems at first an antiquated way of thinking—that one could die in a fit of rage—is both antiquated and, in fact, representative of Esparragosa's moment. There is no doubt that in other ways, Esparragosa was avant-garde. For example, in 1804 he published in the Guatemalan *Gazeta* what must have seemed a rather risqué analysis of a supposed "hermaphrodite," Juana Aguilar. As Martha Few has demonstrated in her study of the case, Esparragosa sought to invalidate the very use of the term, setting himself apart as the bearer of newer, more modern medical knowledge. He claimed that the supposed hermaphrodite was a fiction, a "monster of nature" invented by misguided scholars and physicians, and a painful demonstration of how common ignorance could triumph over science. By blowing the myth to pieces, Esparragosa wanted to assert both the dominance of modern Western medicine and his own place in it.[19]

With a characteristic mixture of self-congratulation and collegial disdain, Esparragosa declared in his article that "there remains to be dissipated [by] the brilliant light of my experience the darkness of whim and the ignorance with which it has been concluded [that Aguilar was a hermaphrodite]."[20] It is interesting that in condemning the "ignorant superstition" and "false philosophy" of the female midwives and other surgeons who had examined Aguilar, he was also criticizing the "ancient philosophers whose scholarship had underpinned conceptions of illness, healing, and the body into the medieval and early modern periods."[21] Interesting because, as we have seen in the case of Ramírez's death by rage, Esparragosa was in some ways still influenced by these strains of thought himself. It did not stop him from perceiving his own work as a repudiation of backward thinking.

In his testimony given as part of the original criminal case against Juana Aguilar, he offers ten handwritten pages of high-handed, erudite contempt. He begins as if standing at a lectern, scolding the masses for their collective ignorance— "From the earliest days in which Mythology placed among its fabulous creations [*fábulas*] the fair Hermaphrodite . . ."—and he goes on in the same vein, scoffing at the curiosity that common people feel for things peculiar and mysterious. This isn't typical writing for a criminal case, even for our overachieving, unpredictable Esparragosa. It is public invective disguised as testimony. He drops phrases in Latin, he references the Roman poet Martial, and he repeatedly refers to the Comte de Buffon, the aforementioned French naturalist whose theory of geographic determinism cast Americans in such a negative light.[22] As these mixed influences demonstrate, cutting edge was also classical, in a complex way.

Alongside Esparragosa, his colleague Doctor José María Guerra, who examined Aguilar as well, wrote three pages of precise anatomical scrutiny, insistent logical questioning (Did Aguilar menstruate? Was she able to have sex with men?), and uncomplicated common sense. He determined that the criminal charges against Aguilar for "concubinato"—having sex out of wedlock, in this case with women—could be explained by some women's desire to see what Aguilar was really about. Once they had succumbed to curiosity and discovered a manner of intercourse that was "less than appetizing" (*cohabitación nada deliciosa*), Guerra determined, they found themselves regretting it and took it out on her with legal complaints. This contrast neatly sums up the fine-grained difference between Esparragosa and his contemporaries. They relied on similar medical assumptions and came to similar conclusions, but while Guerra simply analyzed and explained, Esparragosa fixated on what being able to analyze and explain meant, socioculturally and intellectually. In offering his judgment, Esparragosa saw himself as part of a uniquely privileged, uniquely knowledgeable elite, and this, to him, was the conclusion worth emphasizing.

A rich irony, surely lost on her contemporaries, is that in this case Juana Aguilar happened to agree with her expert medical examiners. The provincial *india-mestiza*, who dressed in men's clothing and slept with women, indicated in her first defense that "without doubt some of these [women who have accused me] have been carried away by some passion and wanted to accuse me of complicity in this horrid crime." Clearly,

at least where a belief in the passions was concerned, Esparragosa did not succeed in distinguishing himself from the
masses.[23]

But in other ways, he was right: many of the methods
and mindsets of the enlightenment science Esparragosa was
devoted to were unfamiliar or even jarring to "the masses." Efforts to move cemeteries, with their dead bodies and possible
contagion, out of Spanish American cities often met with stiff
opposition and even revolts. Attempts to control the spread of
infectious disease with quarantines were likewise controver-
sial. Even the use of hospitals, those spaces that isolated patients from their families and lumped together people of diverse socioeconomic backgrounds, was opposed by many. As
Paul Ramírez has written in his study of colonial smallpox
epidemics in Mexico, these approaches all sprang from "a not
wholly consistent miasma theory that targeted noxious smells
and 'pestilential' airs and involved codifying distances, sepa-
rating hospitals and cemeteries from nucleated settlements,
imposing more rigid quarantines of people and communities,
and making professional caretakers available to the sick."[24]

Recall that Esparragosa was concerned with the "vapors"
that imperiled him, his assistants, and the neighborhood when
he examined Simona Villagrán's corpse. The threat of infection
was foremost in his mind, and only a matter of great importance could have persuaded him to exhume the corpse in the
first place. Esparragosa subscribed to the specific theory but
also to the broader agenda—the rational approach that Ramírez
describes as paramount for Bourbon enlightenment reformers
in the late eighteenth century. This approach had various manifestations, almost all of which claimed to benefit the "public,"
and many of which nonetheless managed to cast this public

as oppositional, or obstructionist, or merely ignorant. Where opposition could be avoided, it was thanks to a rather narrow definition of the "public." The Royal Economic Society of Guatemala, of which Esparragosa was a member, stated in 1811 that it published its results "to promote the enlightenment of the public in a period dedicated to such a sublime and worthy goal," yet as Martha Few points out, "the society's idea of the public . . . had explicit racial and class components; that is, they conceived of their 'public' as the educated elite population of Central America, called in the documents 'los españoles' (the Spanish)."[25]

Broadly speaking, enlightening Guatemala meant joining a global enlightenment by becoming a nation of people ordered by rational thought, ruled by liberal governance, and powered by modernizing ideas. Among elite Guatemalans, medicine was understood to be at the forefront of this enlightenment modernization. In 1803, Guatemala had a vibrant civil society with substantial intellectual output and professional development. The elites who participated in this development "looked to medicine as a way for Guatemala to join the other enlightened, modernizing nations of the world." In particular, the ambition manifested in "the emergence and development of Enlightenment-era humanitarianism among elites who considered it their moral responsibility to apply the new medical innovations of the era to cure and prevent disease among Guatemala's inhabitants."[26]

In other words, belonging to the enlightenment club wasn't just about having degrees and publications. It was also about making these accolades visible in social progress, and social progress required humanitarian efforts. This humanitarianism, along with its paternalistic language of "saving" and "rescuing" the unfortunate victims of illness—everything from Indians to fetuses—helps explain how a man like Esparragosa, so disdainful of common people and their common thoughts, could nonetheless devote himself to the care of commoners.

And devote himself he did. Esparragosa's diary from the surgery is a testament to the painstaking work he undertook, day by day, in the effort to treat injuries and save lives. It makes me wonder how on earth he had time to pester Josefa Paniagua. Most of the people he treated at the San Juan de Dios were poor people of mixed race. Most of the injuries he treated were inflicted violently, many in the kind of altercations that made their way before the criminal court judges. And most of the lives he saved would have been, from the vantage point of the scornful essayist who decried the ignorance of commoners, entirely unenlightened. Nevertheless, he was devoted.

"Petrona Morales," he wrote, on the first page of his diary for the years 1801–2:

> *India* from Petapa arrived at [bed] number 20 on the third of January with an injury made with a blunt instrument over her left eyebrow, three to four lines long, which did not damage the skin but did cause a significant inflammation in the eye, which clearly also caused internal inflammation since she is unable to see.
>
> The injured woman was left blind in her eye and remained working at the Hospital.
> March 17.[27]

Entry after entry details difficult injuries, and in each case new ink in the same handwriting offers amendments, indicating developing conditions or improvements, conjecturing about complications, and delivering a verdict on the patient's release.[28] The most striking quality of the journal as a whole is method. That is, the nature of the method and the consistency of the method. Esparragosa relies on a sophisticated medical vocabulary to describe injuries and treatments. He has a formula: he names the patient, he describes the injury, he details symptoms, and he recounts results. There is no description of the altercations or objects that caused the injuries; there are only bites, and bruises, and trauma from blunt and sharp instruments. Esparragosa has a keen sense of genre, and this is a surgeon's log par excellence.

But despite first appearances, the journal does not, I think, reveal an impersonal or unfeeling surgeon. As Esparragosa's entry on Petrona Morales demonstrates, he sometimes went beyond the humanitarian principle of healing. There is no indication that Esparragosa failed in his treatment of Morales, for she arrived having already lost vision in her eye, but a sense either of failure or of charity must have moved him to keep her on as an employee at the hospital. This is unusual; most often, the entry ends with a note that "the patient left the hospital in good health" on a given date. Sometimes, the patient leaves "almost in good health" and sometimes the patient leaves "without being healed." Most infrequently of all, a note in the margin goes something like this: "Deep injuries to the chest and abdomen; death of the patient and dissection of the cadaver." To get a sense of how Esparragosa approached these more extreme cases, consider the full entry:

> Anselmo Flores, mulato from Las Bacas, arrived at [bed] number 86 on the first of February with two injuries, seemingly inflicted with a sharp instru-

ment: the first at the top and a little to the left side of his abdomen near the area of his stomach, about half an inch long, having pierced the skin and the tissue and seemingly entered the stomach cavity, as the symptoms indicate some injury to the stomach or the intestines because he has a high fever, has lost his strength, has difficulty breathing, nausea, vomiting, and a great deal of pain in his entire abdomen that impedes movement of any kind; these internal injuries became greater than the original puncture wound and became the greatest obstacle to his recovery. The second injury lies between the fifth and sixth rib on the left side and near the back, half an inch long, having pierced the skin and the tissue and the chest cavity and having injured the left lung; he also had a small nick on his right arm over the bicep that was less than half an inch long and was only a flesh wound.

These symptoms were aggravated until February 3 at six in the morning, at which point the patient died. The cadaver was dissected at five in the afternoon. The first section opened was the chest and it was observed that the injury penetrating this region had only injured the lung; the abdomen was opened and copious hemorrhaging of blood was observed—the entrails were swimming in it and they were extraordinarily inflamed; the omentum had been stretched toward the site of the injury and the cutting instrument had made a small puncture in the stomach—about two lines long. . . . In addition to this in some inflamed parts of the stomach there were some gangrenous spots.[29]

Missing from Esparragosa's description of the dissection is some essential context that doesn't change his work with Anselmo's corpse but does change its significance.

In Guatemala in 1800, dissection was contentious.

Like quarantines and remote cemeteries, the anatomical study of cadavers was one of those aspects of enlightenment medicine that seemed essential to its practitioners and offensive to many others—not just "the masses," as Esparragosa might have said, but also the ecclesiastical elite. When the hospital was under construction, Esparragosa petitioned for an expanded and improved space to conduct dissections, and his reasons were explicit. Indeed, they were almost identical to the concerns that arose as he was examining the corpse of Simona Villagrán. After expounding on the importance of anatomical work, both for the teaching of medicine and for the comprehension of criminal cases and thereby the "public," Esparragosa complained that he was currently working in what amounted to a straw hut: it was tiny, it was uncomfortable, and it stank. "I am concerned," he wrote, "that myself or another who conducts this work will be contaminated and suffer from fever or some other illness."[30] Esparragosa eventually got a bit of designated space, despite the opposition. But because the corridor assigned to him was considered part of the hospital cemetery, the ecclesiastical authorities complained that the dissections were now violating canon law—the cemetery was consecrated ground.[31] Tate Lanning wryly observes that "since . . . the work on cadavers had to be done in the open, it was probably the olfactory senses as well as the canon law which were offended."[32]

So Esparragosa's pursuit of dissection ruffled some feathers.

Can it be any coincidence that this dispute occurred in 1800? In fact, there was a lot happening in connection with dissection and cadavers right around 1800. Only two years earlier, the first students passed their examinations in surgery, under the tutelage of Esparragosa. It was a major victory, given how hard both he and Doctor José Felipe Flores had fought for a proper program—a program worthy of modern, enlightened medicine. One of the principal obstacles was getting bodies. In 1793, Flores made an impassioned petition to the criminal court, asking for the body of Bernavela Blanco, the "beautiful husband-poisoner." It was one of many requests, and in this case it was granted.[33] But not always.

Flores wanted the bodies for two purposes: to teach anatomy and, vitally, to make wax figures. The wax figures were a second-best alternative, to be sure. He had undertaken the crafting of wax models in the first place because cadavers were so hard to get. But a labor begun out of necessity had resulted in something more; he had succeeded in making an extraordinary wax model in which all of the major organs could be removed and replaced. "He maintained later in life," writes Lanning, "that not even the wax figures of the famous Fontana could be taken apart and reassembled."[34]

The famous Fontana. That name may not ring a bell, but it's a reference to Felice Fontana, who in the 1770s began assembling a collection of wax models for the teaching of anatomy in Italy. Under his guidance, artists like Clemente Michelangelo Susini created lifelike, striking, and beautiful models.

Hidden below Flores's boast is a possibility: a speculative but suggestive connection between enlightenment science and the crime of the severed body parts. It has to do with how these wax models were created. Today, some of them are known as "anatomical Venuses" (Figure 19). Venuses because they are beautiful, to be sure—both aesthetically and scientifically.

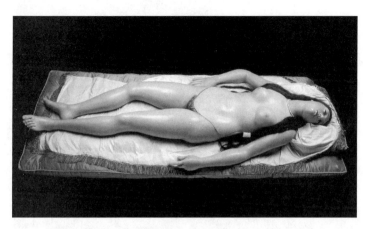

19. "Anatomical Venus" at the Sistema Museale dell'Università degli
Studi di Firenze Sez. di Zoologia "La Specola," Italy

But the Venuses are also notable for how their postures—
limbs relaxed, neck slightly arched, eyes half-closed—are erot-
ically charged (Figure 20). One holds her braid of long hair
between limp fingers. The so-called Medici Venus wears a pearl
necklace and tilts her head to the side in a posture of pleasure.
And yet beauty is no impediment to anatomical precision.
Below the necklace, the Venus's torso comes apart in layers.[35]

Alongside these full-length models, other wax repro-
ductions show individual pieces of the human form at different stages of imagined dissection. Organs, bones, nerves and
tissue—seemingly no portion of the body was too delicate for
Susini's artistry. Breasts, hands, reproductive organs, eyeballs:
each had its set of modeled perspectives (Figures 21–23).

To a viewer in the present day, the juxtaposition of erotic
pleasure and splayed organs is disturbing, even shocking. But
from the point of view of Fontana and others, showcasing anatomy through the display of a beautiful woman was a means of

20. Torso of a woman; wax figure at the Sistema Museale
dell'Università degli Studi di Firenze Sez.
di Zoologia "La Specola," Italy

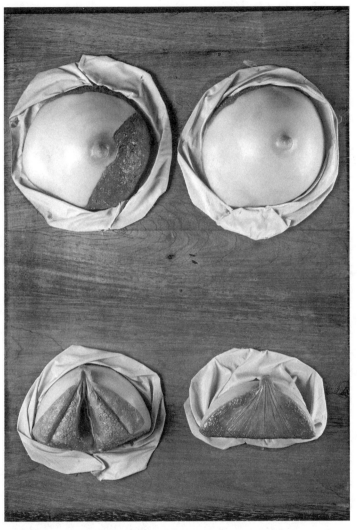

21. Wax model of female breast, Sistema Museale dell'Università degli Studi di Firenze Sez. di Zoologia "La Specola," Italy

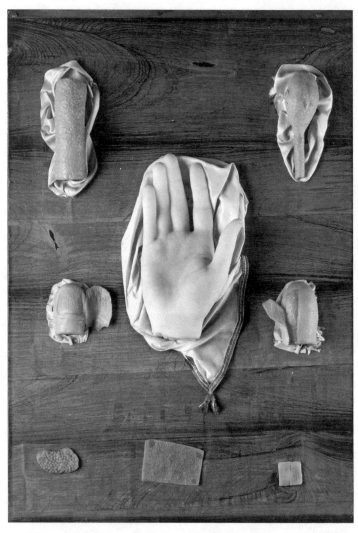

22. Wax model of hand and fingers, Sistema Museale dell'Università degli Studi di Firenze Sez. di Zoologia "La Specola," Italy

23. "Anatomical Venus" at the Sistema Museale dell'Università degli Studi di Firenze Sez. di Zoologia "La Specola," Italy

attracting people to anatomy; it made the argument that dissection was not disgusting—it was gorgeous. In her comparison of Italian and English models, Roberta Ballestriero writes that "Fontana's dream was ... to create anatomical models of scientific value for teaching purposes whilst removing the sense of repulsion produced by cadavers." And even to the modern eye, he succeeded. As Ballestriero observes, the Italian models are "graceful"; they seem like works of art, and there is something incongruous about their presence in the dissecting room. It is in the service of this objective, perhaps, that some of the more erotic qualities emerge. While English wax models from the same period embrace the marks of illness and death, showing "pallor, the livid flesh, glazed eyes," the Italian models seem "alive, pulsating; statues had a gentle look, a languid gaze;

the 'Venuses' had long hair left loose or gathered into seductive plaits and were often adorned by pearl necklaces." Ballestriero suggests that the placement of the Italian models on soft, silk surfaces (while the English waxes are on wooden blocks) encouraged viewers to "worry about their 'comfort'"—and, I would add, imagine them among the tossed sheets of a bed.[36]

Beyond attracting viewers to the practice of anatomy, the Italian models also make an argument about death and beauty. With the Florentine Venuses, "one feels in the presence of a beauty in agony." The facial expressions are "somewhere between agony and ecstasy," expressing "an idealization of the death agony of a young, beautiful woman, thereby capturing the essence of *Eros* and *Thanatos*."[37] To the present-day viewer, there may be something additionally disturbing in the observation that sexual ecstasy so closely resembles death agony—in the Medici Venus in particular, I think, one would be hard pressed to say definitively whether it is one or the other.[38]

With these examples before us, some possible connections to the crime become evident.

I haven't been able to locate José Felipe Flores's wax model, which probably no longer exists, but if the descriptions are anything to go by, it came apart in pieces. Perhaps even the breasts and hands could be removed, then peeled like onions. Lanning speculates that Flores was directly inspired by Fontana, and his reference to the collector makes it likely that if he were to follow any model, it would be this one.

So then imagine, if you will, what it would be like for students of surgery, well accustomed to Doctor Flores's wax model—possibly a woman, possibly a Venus—suddenly to find themselves confronted by an actual woman's body on the dissecting table. The wax model has prepared them—primed them—to see agony and ecstasy in a single form. But now that form, once inert wax, is real flesh. I can imagine that for some this would provoke unease, even disgust. Perhaps in others, it would provoke a spiritual reflection on the ephemerality of human life and the endurance of the soul. But for some the sight would prove titillating. We must at least consider that along with being scientifically stunning and aesthetically pleasing, the Venuses are also pornographically effective. That is, they could, for some viewers, stimulate erotic impulses rather than emotional, aesthetic, or intellectual impulses. They are quintessentially passive, submissive. They offer everything to the viewer—every piece of themselves.

So two more possibilities emerge. I cannot bring myself to suspect Esparragosa himself: arrogant and dismissive, without doubt; disrespectful of women, clearly; and also devoted to his work, unquestionably. The passions that moved him to dishonor Doña Paniagua do not strike me as the passions that would be stirred by a still corpse on a table. Besides, there are logical objections: he had constant access, so why *these* bodies, *this* month? The only plausible explanation I can come to— convoluted and too potboiler-ish—is that he might have used the body parts as an elaborate bit of evidence: proof to the authorities that his dissection room needed to be more formal, more secure. But this seems an extravagant and unlikely gesture, even for Esparragosa.

However, there were many other people with knowledge of how Esparragosa taught anatomy through dissection. Perhaps one of his students—or even one of the necessary staff who moved bodies from one place to another—found the shift from wax models to bodies provocative in an unexpected way. Or perhaps someone—and here the scope is larger—*objected* to Esparragosa's teaching of anatomy through dissection, and saw in these actions a means of protesting the practice. *Look at how you cut up woman's bodies,* we could imagine such a pro-testor saying. *You claim to do this in the name of science, but you are no better than the city butchers.*

These possibilities suggest a connection to either the hos-pital, where Esparragosa taught anatomy, or the cemeteries, where dissected bodies went to rest. Could these be the ac-tions of a vengeful priest? A disgruntled nurse? A grave dig-ger? A perverse student of surgery? Both the hospital and the cemetery seem possible places to find a perpetrator, but with the material we have so far it is hard to determine which is more likely.

The crucial question is when: when was the body taken to pieces? Where was it when the mutilation occurred?

5

In Hospital, at Home
In Which Simona Villagrán Is Buried Twice

A historian must painstakingly free herself from an innate "sympathy" with the archives, and instead see the documents as adversaries she must do battle with, scraps of knowledge that are unsettling and cannot be neatly squared away.

—ARLETTE FARGE, *THE ALLURE OF THE ARCHIVES*

When Dr. Narciso Esparragosa examined Simona Villagrán's corpse, he found evidence of how she had been buried. She wore slippers, a petticoat, and a garment from the Padres Recoletos—the friars of a local Franciscan order. She'd been laid to rest on a *petate*—a woven mat—and her head had been placed on a pillow. All these materials spoke of Simona's poverty—the petticoats and the petate were old and worn—but they also spoke of affection. Someone had buried her with care.

Simona's family was questioned by the authorities, and each relative offered a similar version of her final days. Her two sisters, Isabel Trejo and Thomasa Villagrán, gave the most extensive evidence. They identified the body and affirmed that their sister had been staying at Isabel's house, where she had gone to recover after a stay at the San Juan de Dios hospital.[1] Despite their ministrations, Simona had died of a fever on the evening of July 20, a Sunday. All through the night of the twentieth, relatives had kept vigil with the body, and she had been buried the next day, July 21. Both sisters insisted that Simona had been buried whole. They could not imagine who had mutilated Simona's corpse, or when the desecration had occurred.

Seeking more information about Simona's stay at the hospital, the court escribano visited the San Juan de Dios and asked to see their records. He reported that the name Simona Villagrán did not appear in the whole logbook; nor did any similar name appear. Inquiring further with the hospital staff, the escribano found two nurses who remembered a female patient—name unknown—treated for a fever and chills. As they recalled, the woman had been pregnant, and she had died of complications after leaving the hospital. The court brought Isabel Trejo back to clarify these circumstances, and she declared that the nurses were wrong: Simona had not been pregnant. "She had a baby who was one year and eleven months old," Isabel explained, "and the baby died on the thirteenth of July, seven days before its mother, who was sick and very downcast." Simona also had an older child, a girl of some nine or ten years named María Gil Villagrán, who gave evidence in court and echoed the observations of her family members. Other than to illuminate the particulars of the loss they had suffered—no less heartbreaking for being commonplace—María

Gil and her relatives could shed no new light on what had happened to Simona.

The clearest evidence comes at the end of the court's depositions with Simona's family, when an escribano was sent to examine the parish records at the church, Nuestra Señora de los Remedios. The record book stated clearly that "on July 21, 1800, Simona Villagrán, single woman of about fifty years of age, was buried with the Holy Sacraments she received at the Hospital, from which she emerged directly to her death." It was signed by the parish priest, Don Mariano García. Paired with this record, we have the testimony of Patricio Artiaga, who helped move the body from Isabel Trejo's home to the church, and then from there to the cemetery. Crucially, he also helped to bury the body. Patricio declared that "since he carried the body and buried it, as stated, he observed with great clarity that the body, until it was sepulchered and covered with earth, was entirely whole and was not missing any pieces."

Despite the sense of clarity, there were still doubts. At least three people insisted that the disinterred body was not Simona's. They claimed that Simona was smaller and slighter, had more hair and different feet. Even the relatives who identified the corpse as Simona had their doubts. They recognized the petate and the pillow, the slippers and the tunic, but they admitted that the body was swollen beyond easy identification, and there was more than a little conjecture in their determination that the mutilated corpse was, indeed, that of Simona Villagrán. The possibility remains, then, that the dismembered body was not hers. But if we work with the positive identifications of more than half a dozen family members, we can conclude the following: Simona and her baby fell ill in July. On the thirteenth, Simona's infant died. Simona went to the hospital, where she was not healed but also was not properly recorded as a patient. Released from the hospital, Simona went to her sister Isabel's house, where she died on July 20. She was buried the next day, her body whole. At some point after her burial on the twenty-first, someone dug up the body and cut it to pieces.

It is troubling to think of how the sacred ground was violated. It is troubling to think of all the painstaking marks of affection—the slippers and petate, the carefully placed body—thrown aside when the corpse was taken apart. But it is also troubling to think of Simona, still alive, suffering namelessly near the end of her days. Like the escribano who interrogated the nurses at the hospital, I wondered how Simona's visit to the San Juan de Dios had not been properly remembered or recorded. And like the officials pursuing the perpetrator of her corpse's mutilation, I sensed a connection between the cemetery where Simona was found and the hospital. Why this body, so recently tended at the San Juan de Dios? Was it merely coincidental, or were the associations of dismemberment something more than analogies?

Only in fantasy are hospitals exclusively for healing. In the colonial world, as in ours, hospitals and cemeteries are bonded by that powerful ligature, that unavoidable conclusion, death. But in contrast with our own time, in which medical institutions have a near monopoly on the experience of grave illness, death was also a frequent presence in a third place during the colonial period: at home.[2]

It's significant that Simona had living relatives who cared about her. Absent her family, she would have passed away without mention, unrecorded in the hospital logbook, probably buried in the San Juan de Dios's *campo santo,* the hospital cemetery. Instead, Simona's sisters brought her home to die. They did not describe the care they gave her, but the role they assumed was so common as to go without mentioning. Female relatives often cared for relatives who were ill or close to death, as Brianna Leavitt-Alcántara finds documented in Guatemalan wills. One doña in 1777 bequeathed her shawls to "the girls who have helped me in my sickness," making note that the best shawl should go to the one who had stayed with her to the end. A year later, another man of high social standing left ten cattle to a young relative who had taken care of him during his illness.[3]

The testators tacitly acknowledge that the illnesses their nurses tend will end in death, and the death will be met at home. And though there is less direct evidence to underscore the observation for Guatemala, it is also clear that medical professionals sometimes treated patients in the home. Consider the following remarkable case from late-eighteenth-century Mexico, familiar to us because of an ex-voto, a painting created to commemorate and express gratitude for divine intervention (Figure 24).

Doña Josefa Peres Maldonado underwent a mastectomy on April 25, 1777, in Aguascalientes, Mexico.[4] The operating surgeon, Pedro Maillé, of French origin and training, removed six cancerous tumors in her breast. Forty-one at the time of the operation, Peres Maldonado lived only a few months more before passing away—reputedly of other causes, since the operation was deemed successful—on September 5, 1777. She was much wealthier than Simona, and lived in a different region, but Peres Maldonado's ex-voto nonetheless tells us a great deal that is of interest for our case.

Most salient, the image documents the severing of a woman's breast. The surgery diary I read through does not mention a mastectomy, but it's certainly possible, given his ambition and self-confidence, that Dr. Esparragosa undertook

24. Unknown artist, the Peres Maldonado ex-voto, 1777

mastectomies at the San Juan de Dios. More than possible, it's likely that he discussed the process in the course of his teaching. And he may not have been the only one with knowledge of mastectomies and the will to perform them.

It was while contemplating this painting that I finally saw some sense in what had seemed the inane questions of the Guatemalan court officials, belaboring whether Simona had been mutilated at home before being taken to the cemetery. Their questions spring from the necessity of establishing that the corpse mutilator did not have access to Simona in her home, but they could also emerge from the speculation— far-fetched but conceivable—that Simona's body was somehow disfigured before death. Even with the seemingly straightforward evidence of the exhumation, officials were not quite sure what they were dealing with, and the prospect of other narratives—medical experiment gone wrong, depraved torture of a living person, witchcraft, or pact with the devil—hides between the lines of their questions and conclusions.

Only a few years later, in 1804, a man named José María Liverato Martínez was arrested for the death of Juana de Dios Callejas, a seventy-year-old widow who had suffered from a four-pound tumor in her left breast. Martínez, a forty-year-old Spaniard who called himself a gilder and a medical practitioner, did not have a license to practice medicine, but he had nonetheless operated on Callejas to remove the tumor, which was reportedly the size of a baby's head. Callejas died of gangrene, and Martínez argued in his defense that it was the transfer to the city center that had killed her.[5] The court took a dimmer view of this "curandero" and sentenced him to two years' labor. We know about this treatment because it went so badly awry, but there must have been other such high-risk experiments conducted outside the confines of the hospital.

This painting also gives us a sense of what an operation at home might have looked like. Pedro Maillé was assisted in the surgery by the depicted friars of the convent-hospital San Juan de Dios (not the hospital at which Esparragosa practiced, the identical name a coincidence), and the women are probably some of Peres Maldonado's daughters or relatives.[6] An ornate headboard, beautifully embroidered bedding, and a lavish folding screen all signal that this is the bedroom of a wealthy woman.

Even more important than the luxury goods are the devotional items. The painting makes a clear argument about their importance, both in the home and in the course of the surgery. Not only is the image itself an ex-voto, but the objects of devotion are prominently pictured. As Lisa Pon and James

Amatruda aptly point out, the gathering of earthly attendants on the left are divided from the cluster of devotional objects on the right, and they are divided by an open door, a "symbol of passage from here to the beyond."[7] The painting is doubly dedicated to El Señor del Encino (the Lord Christ of the Oak) and the Virgin Mary of el Pueblo, both of whom figure at the home altar: the Christ at the center and the Virgin Mary of el Pueblo at its left. At the foot of the Christ figure is a sculpted Virgin of San Juan de los Lagos, "recognizable by her conical blue mantle, lacy white collar and crown." She appears two more times in this room: in the framed picture at the upper right and in an oval frame above the door. Saint Joseph (Doña Josefa's name saint) is displayed to the right of the Christ figure. And these prominent figures are buttressed by others: nine images of sacred beings attend the crucified Christ of the Oak just as nine "members of her earthly community" attend Peres Maldonado in her trial, and the two realms are reflected in the painting's unusual two-part design.[8]

Though we do not know what tokens of devotion Simona encountered in her sister's home, it is almost certain that she relied upon images of some kind.[9] The Franciscan burial habit—a common practice in New Spain at the time—suggests that Simona's family was typical in its Catholic devotions. It is also likely that her sister's house featured a home altar like Peres Maldonado's: a collection of images, novenas, and perhaps prayer books or prayer cards. Such private devotional spaces could be found in even very humble homes, and over the course of the eighteenth and nineteenth centuries they only grew in prominence. William B. Taylor writes that the number of religious texts, notably devotional books, pamphlets, novena booklets, and broadsides, rose steadily after the late seventeenth century in New Spain, and hundreds of thousands of printed images circulated in the region.[10] Explaining why sacred images played such a vital role, even at the dawn of the nineteenth century and knee deep in the enlightenment, Taylor writes that the "mystique of sacred images and supernatural presence in the world" endured over the centuries for people of diverse class and ethnic backgrounds. "This enchantment of sacred images did not wane even as the Enlightenment impulse to dominate nature and apply scientific principles gained traction in political discourse, public works, and medical practice toward the end of the colonial period." We see proof of this in the prevalence of home altars and in everyday occurrences that melded devotional gestures with more modern practices. By way of example, Taylor describes a "late-eighteenth-century pharmacist who carried a statue of the baby Jesus in his medical kit for house calls to women in labor. It was what his clients expected."[11]

It's true that sometimes medicine and religion—especially as institutions—were at loggerheads. But it's also true that, as practices, they sometimes dovetailed effortlessly. The accommodations made by the pharmacist were typical of a mindset that understood medical acts to be enhanced by religious devotion. Perhaps, for some patients, this delicate balance could be better controlled at home. Staying at home during a grave illness had many advantages: the comfort of family members and friends as well as the spiritual aids and familiar devotional images that the sick person relied upon for support.

But many women did not have this choice. Many women went to the hospital not only because their conditions could not be treated at home but because they had no family to nurse them.

Following the lead of the escribano who went looking for Simona, I tracked down the hospital records for the year 1800.

I was fortunate to find two logbooks of women patients at the San Juan de Dios—logbooks for the years 1800 to 1802, the very same logbooks consulted by the escribano.

They felt like a discovery. Bound in leather, with no missing pages and remarkably legible handwriting, they are truly alluring, in Farge's sense: the promise of factuality, of completeness hangs about them (Figure 25). Reading these pages, I am tempted to imagine that I actually understand the comings and goings of people in the hospital, the types of patients who arrive, and the nature of their lives. Every entry records a name, an age, a race, the names of parents, an illness and a date of arrival. Notes in the right-hand column record the bed number, notes in the left-hand column specify the date of departure. In some cases, there is a cross in the left-hand margin; such a mark represents not a routine departure but a death. One can readily imagine the punctilious record keeper, perhaps a nurse or a doctor's assistant, standing by the patient's bedside and earnestly asking the questions that will result in neatly written answers, which will in turn result in accurate portraits of the hospital's new inhabitants.[12]

Yet as Simona's absence from these pages demonstrates, the impression is illusory. There are absences. And as I know from poring over the entries, there are mistakes. Some patients arrive multiple times within a single year (itself interesting), and there can be wild discrepancies in how such repeat patients are registered. A woman who was thirty-five years old in April might be forty-five in August. There are also assumptions recorded in lieu of fact, a tendency that is not discernible until one has read all these pages many times and found some of the corners too neat, some of the categories too pat.

Nevertheless, while the precision is illusory, the stories are real. The challenge lies in looking beyond the illusion of

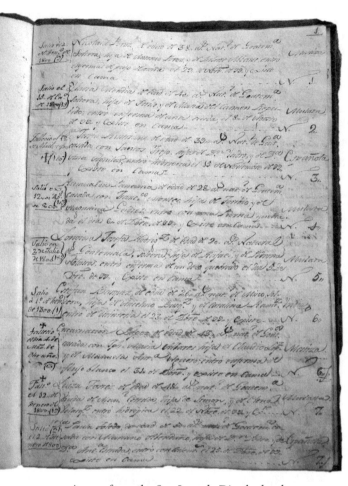

25. A page from the San Juan de Dios logbook
of women patients, 1800

completeness to the messier story beneath. Some of these stories emerge in the trends, and some of them emerge in the
details.

First the trends.

The San Juan de Dios Hospital opened its doors to everyone, but it catered primarily to Guatemala City's lower classes.[13]
This is evident in the overrepresentation of "Indias" and "mu-
latas," two races that track closely with low class in colonial
Spanish America. There are some 720 entries for the year 1800,
and more than 500 of these are identified as either "India" or
"mulata." Another 109 are "mestiza."

To get a sense of how this overrepresentation matters,
let's consider Guatemalan demography more closely. For the
entire colonial period, the province of Guatemala had the
lion's share of the inhabitants in the Kingdom of Guatemala
(spanning Chiapas to Costa Rica). Residents of the province of
Guatemala, some 519,000, comprised 62.9 percent of the kingdom's population in 1796. Because all data describing race is
to some degree flawed—consider the many good reasons for
"passing" and the subjectivity of the categories, to name only
two obstacles—pinning the racial distribution of the population is a challenge. At the end of the colonial period, in the
Kingdom as a whole, "65 percent of the total population were
Indian, 31 percent were ladino, and 4 percent were Spaniards
and Creoles, although in the province of Guatemala, Indians
were still about 70 percent of the population."[14]

This would seem to leave blacks and mulatos out of the
picture. But the explanation lies in the expanding uses of the
term *ladino:* "After about 1670 mestizaje appears to have so
blurred the lines of phenotypical distinction between free mu-
lattoes and mestizos that members of both groups came to be
lumped together as ladinos." Parish priests still asked about

race as if these were distinct categories, but their designation in parish registers began to blur or disappear altogether.[15] Changing attitudes about ethnicity resulted in lumpy categories. Long before the move to the new capital, a rough distinction had emerged between *gente ordinaria* (ordinary people) and *gente decente* (people of high social standing). These tracked along racial lines, but imprecisely: mestizos, mulatos, people of mixed race, and even some Indians were all part of Hispanic society as gente ordinaria.[16] They were all coming to be identified as "ladinos." Despite these attitudinal shifts that made distinctions murky, colonial treasury and judicial officials were compelled to continue using distinct racial designators for the purposes of determining tribute payments.[17]

This helps explain why some data is especially bad at identifying people of African descent and why, at the same time, the ineffectual categories remained in use. In case we needed reminding that racial categories are constructed, the demographics of Guatemala do the job: the casta paintings examined in Chapter 3 offer an illusion of genealogical precision, but the reality was anything but. The clearest view of this blurry picture requires "lumping" people of mixed race much as parish priests did.

Consider the figures for Guatemala City. In 1776, shortly after the city was moved to the new location, there were 5,917 people in Nueva Guatemala. (Recall that this grew to nearly 25,000 by the end of the century.) Spaniards made up 1,876 of these; 1,668 were Indians, and 2,373 were "mestizos, pardos, or another casta."[18] This fails to differentiate between people of mixed Indian descent and people of mixed African descent, but it still helps us see the imbalance in the hospital's admissions. If we follow the census's lead and consider only these three categories, it becomes clear that Indians and women of mixed race were overrepresented at the hospital. Spanish women made up 7 percent of the admitted patients; Indians made up 36 percent; and people of mixed race made up 57 percent.

These conclusions, which I draw from a single year of admissions at the hospital, fit with Lynda Craig's conclusions in her broader study of the San Juan de Dios. "The poorer and more transient elements of the population," she finds, "were more likely to come to hospital than the white and the rich."[19] Craig sampled logbooks like the ones I looked at, covering the period from 1788 to 1808. While her study offers less detail for 1800, it offers an excellent sense of the broader landscape. In 1782, 20 percent of the city's population was "Spanish," but only 10 percent of admitted patients (both men and women) were Spanish for the 1788–1808 period. Thirteen percent of Guatemala City residents were Indian in 1782, but 33 percent of hospital admits were registered as "Indian." Craig's work does indicate that the hospital tended to better reflect the city's demographics over time: in 1820, 15 percent of city residents were "Spanish" and 25 percent were "Indian," bringing both figures closer to the hospital admission rates.[20] This suggests that the hospital became less associated with the poor and transient as time passed. Craig notes that "after 1800, eighteen men who referred to themselves as 'Don' were admitted to the hospital" while five women titled Doña were admitted beginning in 1795.[21]

Zooming back a bit to understand the significance of this demographic data, there are two trends that matter. First, Guatemala was increasingly becoming a city with a dichotomous social structure: whites of high standing and ladinos of lower standing. While there had been finer distinctions earlier in the colonial period—tributary Indian, Hispanized Indian, mestizo, mulato, African slave, and so on—these had increasingly blended into "nonwhite," understood by Guatemalans to mean low-class. This may have placed even greater stress on the dividing line between high and low. Recall Don Narciso Esparragosa and his preoccupation with his title; markers of status were an entanglement—or, if you prefer, a matrix—of phenotype, reputational "race," economic position, and community standing.

Second, the hospital was originally a place exclusively for gente ordinaria, but as time passed it inched its way upward, becoming a place where people of high class might also seek services.

Consequently, the hospital was a place where high and low might mingle. Thanks to the hospital's detailed financial records, we also know what the staff looked like: seven salaried clerics, an administrator, a medical assistant, six nurses, a pharmacist, a female administrator for the women's wing, a barber, two laundresses, a bed maker, and three cooks. (Some monthly salary schedules have an entry for the designated *chocolatero*, chocolate maker, so the hospital couldn't have been *that* bad.)[22] This paperwork suggests that the staff was diverse as well. Alongside Esparragosa, with his titles and degrees and mostly untarnished reputation (cases of harassment aside), we have others of lesser standing. "On May 13, 1794," writes Craig, "Sebastina Ropel, a thirty year old single woman, [was] registered at the hospital to serve a sentence of seventeen months for an unspecified crime."[23]

She was not the only criminal in residence at the hospital. The proceedings from an unusual 1802 case reveal a surprising fact about the San Juan de Dios: it contained a "jaula," a cage, for sick prisoners.[24] And it seems, from the details of the case, that it was a clearly demarcated section of the hospital with regular inmates and established protocols. Authorities were first alerted to a problem with the so-called "cage" on February 15, 1802, when the hospital staff notified the alcalde that a prisoner had made his escape the night before. His name was Cesario Gramajo, and though I can find no documentation of the reason for his imprisonment, I do know that he was eventually tried for domestic abuse in 1819. It is possible, then, that the crime for which he was serving a sentence in 1802 was also a crime of violence.

The court's examination into Gramajo's escape illuminates the particulars of how inmates were detained at the hospital. Three men had gone in at 6 P.M. on the night of February 14 to give the prisoners (plural) their dinners: the *cabo de sala,* or chief of staff, Don Pedro Gonzales; the steward, Don Miguel Albarado; and a server, Mariano Rosales. A soldier tasked with guarding the cage, José Antonio Carrillo, had let them in and out. While all four men agreed that Gramajo had been there at the start of dinner and had been declared missing at 10 P.M. that evening, their versions of how the escape occurred differed greatly. The three hospital staffers, Gonzales, Albarado, and Rosales, all claimed that Gramajo had been safely locked away when they left the cage at the end of the dinner. Soldiers were known to drink too much or sleep on the job, they testified. In fact, one of them declared, it was not unusual for the guard to take a nap or sleep off the booze inside the cage, in one of the beds beside the prisoners. Carrillo, for his part, insisted that only two hospital staffers had gone into the cage and three had come out; he explained that the third had turned his face away as he walked out, and for this reason he had not noticed Gramajo sneaking out in the company of the (presumably complicit) hospital staff.

It is interesting that while all three hospital staff members described themselves as españoles, Carrillo was Indian. Perhaps this influenced the court in its decision to side against the soldier, imprisoning him for his role in letting Gramajo go free; surely the weight of three testimonies against his one also worked against him. But from this case we learn several remarkable details about the presence of prisoners in the hospital: they were a common presence, if the well-established routines are any indication; several prisoners might be there at one time, since it is hard to imagine losing track of a prisoner if there is only one or two; and security was lax. The prisoners were manacled to their beds, as the authorities' questions about *grillos* (handcuffs) made clear, but these were not foolproof. When they searched Gramajo's bed, they found a long, pointed tool like an awl beside the handcuffs. What's more, the case makes reference to the flight of two other prisoners from an unspecified earlier time, indicating that such jailbreaks were uncommon but not unheard of.

So we must conclude that criminals were a regular—perhaps constant—presence at the hospital, and they could have access to patients (and cadavers), either in the act of flight or in the course of serving out a sentence. This fact also puts into sharper relief the kind of mingling that occurred at the hospital. For in addition to the occasional perpetrator, there were living victims at the San Juan de Dios. Craig draws attention to the number of men who arrived at the hospital with injuries—many of them no doubt involved in the feuds and bar fights that kept the police busy—but the injuries of women go unmentioned. This must be because, taken as a whole, women do not seem to have suffered disproportionately from injuries. It is only when we separate married women from unmarried women that particular trends come into focus. If we look at all the ailments that had ten or more occurrences throughout the

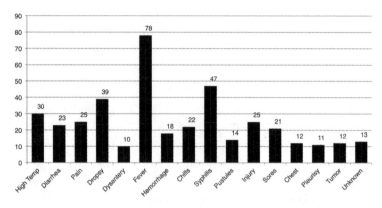

26. Reason for admission in the year 1800 to the San Juan de Dios
Hospital among women who are not married

year among unmarried women, fever (78 cases), syphilis (47),
and dropsy (39) are the standouts (Figure 26). There are only
25 unmarried women with injuries, roughly as many as complained of "pain" and "sores." But if we look only at married
women (Figure 27), the trend is startlingly different. Injuries
are the most numerous: 57 patients, almost a quarter of all
married women, are admitted for this reason in the year 1800.[25]

So married women were much more likely to suffer injuries. Why? For the most part, married and unmarried women
engaged in the same occupations. More unmarried women and
girls worked as household servants, an occupation more prone
to beatings than not, so this cannot explain the disparity.[26]
Since "unmarried" includes widows, we cannot infer that
married women necessarily had more accident-prone children.
And from Esparragosa's surgery log, we know that the vast
majority of injuries treated at the hospital were inflicted by
other people. There's the occasional dog bite or accident at the
sugar mill, but men and women alike are almost always hit with

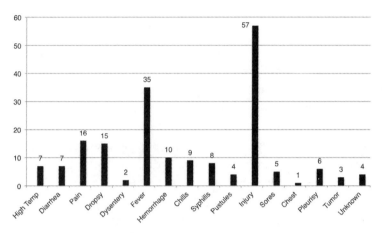

27. Reason for admission in the year 1800 to the San Juan de Dios
Hospital among married women

rocks, flogged with sticks, stabbed with knives, and pierced with swords. The unavoidable conclusion is that married women were being injured by their husbands.

It is interesting to compare these figures with the number of domestic abuse cases that appear in court; we might even infer from the hospital records a more accurate figure for the number of women who withstood abuse. Only eight cases of domestic abuse were heard in the year 1800, and of these, four took place beyond Guatemala City. While we cannot assume that all fifty-seven of the injuries logged at the hospital were the result of abuse, we can use the rate of injury among unmarried women to estimate how many injuries belong to each category. (This is a little fuzzy, of course, since unmarried women could also suffer abuse from domestic partners, parents, or others.) About 4 percent of unmarried women arrived at the hospital with injuries. At this rate, only nine married women would have been admitted with injuries, suggesting that more than forty of these cases were likely due to abuse. We should also keep in mind that women showed up at the hospital only with injuries that were too serious to treat at home.

Apart from the fact that marriage was bad for a woman's health, what can we learn from this data about women and illness? Widows died at a much higher rate than married women and single women, 50 percent as opposed to 17 percent, no doubt because they tended as a group to be older. Apart from injuries, the patients' reasons for admission are distributed pretty evenly across marital status and race. There are eight cases of "insulto," occurring to women of varied ages (as young as sixteen, as old as fifty-eight) and races. It's unclear exactly what this means. Rape? Verbal insult? They stand out because no one today would go to the emergency room complaining of insults, but they obscure the more general distortions in every category. "Fever" is recognizable to us, but the category "fever" doubtless groups together many illnesses, everything from flu to meningitis. We don't make quite the same distinction between "chills," "high temperature," and "fever." So we both split and lump differently. It's safe to say that almost all of these categories would be parsed differently by current medical practitioners. As a result, the illnesses tell us more about how the hospital framed and grouped conditions than they do about what patients actually had.

Considered together, these trends tell a few stories. They corroborate—somewhat obliquely—the incidence of violence against women. They also offer a fuller racial portrait of the city. This portrait is necessarily skewed, since the very terms used by patients and hospital staff required a measure of invention and interpretation. But we can observe that in the eyes of a contemporary, the hospital was a place where high and low met: a place where people of high social standing could seek treatment without entirely sacrificing their reputations; but a place dominated nonetheless by gente ordinaria—women who were poor, who had compromised their virtue, who were of mixed race. It was even a place where one might come into contact with a prisoner, a person serving a sentence for a violent crime.

Now the stories that emerge in the details.

Lynda Craig's dissertation on the San Juan de Dios Hospital counted 40,065 civilian patients in the admissions books and sampled 3,121 cases—nearly 8 percent of the patients admitted between 1788 and 1808.[27] The roughly 600 cases from the year 1800 that I pored over were certainly included in her sample, but they take on a different aspect when they are scrutinized as a narrative—slow, piecemeal, and laconic, it's true—about the admission of women into the hospital. Individuals emerge. Fragments of personal stories appear.

Some entries in the hospital logbook tell their stories by connecting with documentation in the contemporaneous criminal cases. Consider the entry for a forty-year-old mulata named Josefa Anastasia Tortola, who was admitted on January 28, 1800, with injuries. The circumstances of her injuries are detailed in a criminal case against her husband, Josef Gregorio Barrientos, a shoemaker with a tendency to drink. Tortola had gone to find him at the house of a friend where he had been drinking for several days. She persuaded him to leave, though they argued bitterly all the way home. The moment they returned, her husband stabbed her in the chest, back, arm, and hand. She was still conscious when the escribano arrived at the hospital to take her testimony, and she named several witnesses to the altercation, including one of her three children. The boy, a twelve-year-old, had tried to defend his mother from his stepfather, but neither was any match for a grown man, described as "thickset" and "round-faced." Dr. Narciso Esparragosa judged the injuries to be grave, a judgment underscored by the fact that Tortola arrived with her intestines bulging from the wound, and he made note of the fact that she was four months pregnant.

In some cases, like this one, we are fortunate to find an inventory of the victim's belongings, and the material objects give us an immediate and incontestable snapshot of how Tortola, her three children, and her drunken husband lived. The escribano listed, as follows, all of the items to be found in the victim's house:

> An image of Saint Barbara in a frame, two very old shelves, three little tables, two old chairs, one box for measuring maize, two crates and store counter, all very old; two other counters of little value; a case with various dishes; six old pieces of pine wood; a store stepstool; a basket with earthen jars and bowls.[28]

We could not ask for a clearer depiction of Tortola's home. The vision that comes to mind is one of painful scarcity, spiritual devotion in the midst of material poverty, and hard work wrung from the use of worn objects. Recall, by point of contrast, the extravagant interior of Doña Peres Maldonado's room in Aguascalientes: the rich textiles and furniture, the effusive display of devotional images. In Tortola's home, most of the items inventoried—the measuring box, the counters, the jars and bowls, the shelves and pinewood planks—relate to her work as a food vendor in the city plaza. It is notable that there are no personal items apart from the image of the saint; the absence of extra clothing or luxury items of any kind testifies starkly to the family's diminished means. And to the vital necessity, even for such a family, of the sacred image.

After Josefa Tortola gave her testimony in the San Juan de Dios Hospital, many witnesses supported her account with their own versions: the attack had been loud and prolonged, and it had drawn out most of the neighborhood. Though the court seemed inclined to pursue the matter, it did not get far. Tortola died of her injuries on the second of February, and her husband fled the city. Though a notice was sent to officials throughout the *audiencia,* Barrientos was not found. Not until eleven years later, weighed down by a guilty conscience, did he turn himself in. Barrientos was sentenced, only to be exonerated soon afterward; the officials judged that his quiet life after the crime counted for much, and they noted, with unintentional irony, that he had shown himself to be penitent.[29]

Rarely can we unfold such a rich story around the scant twenty words of a hospital entry, but we must imagine that for each entry such a story exists: remembered in the moment, complex in its causes, confused and perhaps contradictory in how it was interpreted, and lost now to us. With some entries, fragments of stories emerge in repeat appearances: a castiza widow named Barbara Rodríguez arrived on March 23 with unspecified pains and stayed for a week; she returned only a few weeks later on April 27, still with unspecified pains, and died after two months in hospital. A married mulata named Crestina Cutiño, in her seventies, went to the San Juan de Dios four times in the early months of 1800. She was diagnosed with and treated for dropsy each time, and she died in early May. There are also poignant stories that can be inferred from a single line: the story of a woman judged to be Indian who could not give her name, ailments, or parentage because she was mute. The story of a three-year-old mestizo boy admitted on July 11 with worms (which I take to mean parasites), who died on July 14. The story of an Indian widow named Sebastiana from the town of San Lorenzo del Tejar, of whom the logbook says, "No account could be made because she arrived already dying and was brought here by a young man."

These partial narratives signal misfortunes of circumstance. They signal the impotence of medical practitioners in dealing with common ailments that they saw all too often and frequently could not defeat. They also signal the practical obstacles that made medical work challenging: illiteracy, the difficulty of transporting gravely ill patients to a central care facility, the absence of specialized practices for children and patients with disabilities. As Sebastiana's entry makes clear, patients often arrived already at death's door, and even better doctors with better facilities could have done very little.

This is exactly what occurred to a patient who arrived on July 1, 1800, in the very early hours.

Though I had read through the hospital logbook more than once, it was not until the third or fourth perusal that I spotted her: at the very top of the page, the very first entry for July: Manuela Trujillo, "a poor woman who gave no account apart from her name, *natural* of Guatemala, died the same day" (Figure 28).[30]

The significance of the entry sank in. Manuela was the only woman who had died in the several days before July 1. She was a mestiza, meaning that her skin tone would have been judged a match to the severed breasts. They had to be hers.

Why had I not seen her before? Perhaps because at first I'd been looking for the victim of a violent crime, not a woman dead of illness. (Though it should be made clear that the entry leaves open the possibility that Manuela did die of injuries.)

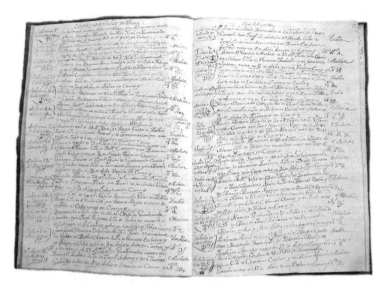

28. The first pages for July 1800 in the logbook for
the San Juan de Dios Hospital

Or perhaps because I'd been looking for a crime that took
place at night, and I was overlooking that for the hospital staff,
July 1 would begin at the stroke of midnight. Before the hours
of dawn, Manuela Trujillo would have had plenty of time to
arrive, meet her death, and be set aside in the morgue.

However the oversight occurred, it gave me a strange
sense of sudden affinity with the escribano who had gone in
July of 1800 to consult this very logbook. He had overlooked
this too, perhaps for the same reasons. It's true that he was
looking for Simona Villagrán, but it would have taken little
imagination to consider the importance of July 1 and the death
of a woman around that date. I am certain that if the escribano
had realized the significance of the hospital entry for Manuela
Trujillo, the circumstances of her illness and death would have

been the next lead in the investigation. The officials would have interrogated the hospital staff about who she was, how she arrived, where her body was placed after death, and where it was buried. Some answers, however partial, would have emerged.

Absent this line of investigation, I set off on my own mad scramble to learn something—anything—about Manuela Trujillo. But when you are looking for one person, and an obscure mestiza with a common name at that, sometimes the archive will not yield. The colonial archive is not designed to find individual people. It is immeasurably easier to find circumstances, trends, experiences, and realities based on the individuals closest to hand. So historians write about the people offered to them by the archive, and the pursuit of a single person becomes a quixotic affair. There is something deceptively satisfying, I realized as I tried to find Manuela, about the kind of history we've done in the past several decades—that is, the history of marginal people, the history of the obscure. It's satisfying because there's a sense of (self-congratulatory) recovery: "Those people may have been obscure then," you say to yourself, "but I am bringing them into the light. I am making them *un*-obscure, by attaching significance and historical meaning to their stories. Their lives *do* matter; their lives *do* tell us truths about the past." But it's deceptive because we did not really choose these particular representatives of obscurity. Sure, we decided to write about them because their stories were interesting, or their circumstances were especially compelling, but we did not go looking for *them,* specifically. They are still tokens.

Trying to actually find a particular obscure someone is soberingly difficult. It is a manner of doing battle, as Arlette Farge writes, with scraps of knowledge, and the battle to find Manuela Trujillo was getting me nowhere. I searched in Pardo's vast *indice onomástico,* the AGCA card catalogue that lists people by name, and there was no mention of her, which meant that she had never generated a legal document—a land claim, a legal agreement, a criminal case—that passed through Pardo's hands. The possibility existed that she might be mentioned in the *protocolos,* the bound books kept by notary scribes, but there are hundreds of these, and they have no internal organization other than chronology; finding Trujillo in such notebooks would mean hundreds of hours of reading or extraordinary luck. I asked my colleague Brianna Leavitt-Alcántara, who has worked closely with women's wills in Guatemala from this period, but unfortunately she had never come across Manuela's name. Brianna did recommend looking through the censuses of 1796–97, which she kindly shared with me as images, and I began the slow search through hundreds of folios, hoping to catch a glimpse of Trujillo there. I learned the names of tailors and musicians, bricklayers and bakers, their wives and their children, and the many cohabitants whose relationships to each head of the family remained obscure. But even as I read through the censuses, scanning thousands of names over many hours, I knew it was likely that Manuela would not be there. I did not even know whether she was a resident of Guatemala (though the entry told me she was native to the city). It was possible that she had traveled to the hospital from far away, arriving in the dead of night with the last of her strength.

I was forced to accept that this might be as much as I would ever know about Manuela Trujillo. Her name. Her supposed race. An escribano's inference that she had been pregnant. The consequent likelihood that she had been young. And the fact of her abrupt death at the San Juan de Dios Hospital on July 1, 1800.

6

An Urban Space
In Which the Perpetrator Communicates
a Third Time

*How to explain—without seeming to brag and without disdain
for historical fiction—that if we are to do right by these many
forgotten lives, lives ground down by the political and judicial
systems, we can only do so through the writing of history?*

—ARLETTE FARGE, *THE ALLURE OF THE ARCHIVES*

The Guatemala City officials were also frustrated, as
the days wore on and no suspect emerged. Toward the
end of the month, the Guatemalan *fiscal,* the attorney
for the crown, Don Juan de Collado, decided to take
action. On July 28 he summarized the actions taken by the
perpetrator to date, and he commented on the "horrific and
atrocious nature of this crime." The supervising judge had
taken considerable trouble with the case, he noted, ordering

the exhaustive work of identifying recent graves and undertaking exhumations. Collado's next observation and the related orders are worth citing in full:

> Consider for a moment the actions before us: ex-
> posing those tragic and horrific fragments in such
> public places, and in the most recent case, at such
> an hour [in the middle of the day]; it demonstrates
> an incredible audacity, a direct insult, a flagrant con-
> tempt for Justice, and a shocking absence of fear; all
> of which suggests to me the following course. There
> are so many Judges in the Capital, twelve Alcaldes
> de Barrio, comisarios Bances and Lorenzana [offi-
> cers of the Holy Inquisition], and officials of the
> audiencia chamber; we could arrange a certain dis-
> tribution of patrols so that every day three or four
> men head out in different directions, expanding
> the reach of the Alcaldes de Barrio to the whole city
> and its suburbs; meeting beforehand at each patrol
> leader's home, a plan would be made regarding ap-
> proach and area covered.[1]

Collado detailed a few more particulars of how the patrols
would be organized to the greatest advantage, and then the
orders were put into effect.

Only two days later, as if to underscore the audacity, contempt, and absence of fear noted by the fiscal, the perpetrator
acted once more. On July 30, the escribano for the case wrote
that one of the alcaldes, Don Ambrosio Rodríguez Taboada,
had reported the appearance of a pair of ears on the windowsill of his brother, Don Cayetano Díaz. The ears were duly
handed over to the escribano, who described them as "dry,

looking as if they had been in smoke," and who immediately gave them to a priest so that they could be buried in the sacred ground of the cathedral.

The ears. No doubt the very ears that had been missing from Simona Villagrán's body, given their advanced desiccation. The ears that fit so neatly, I must point out, with a potential message about the efficacy or inefficacy of prayer. *Your gods are not listening. You place all your faith in them. But they do not hear you.*

We have no record of the fiscal's response to this event, but we can easily imagine his frustration. Don Cayetano Díaz was persuaded to conceal himself in his home to maintain a lookout, in the hope that the person who had left the ears might return. Nobody did.

The perpetrator's choice to leave the ears once more at the same house is interesting, and it raises several possibilities. The first, of course, is that Don Cayetano was an intended target; the messages might have been meant for him or for someone in his household (perhaps even his brother, the alcalde), or they might have been a message directed at the greater community *about* him. A second possibility is that the perpetrator took advantage of the ambitious new patrols and committed the next crime where officials would least expect it: at the site of a previous crime. A third possibility is that the area had some other kind of meaning to the perpetrator. Consider that the hands had been left across the street, at a different home but on the same block as Cayetano Díaz's house. *Something* about that block was significant, strategic, or convenient.

So what was important about this place? *Where* was it?

In court documents, individuals gave their addresses only as general locations, sometimes in relation to other well-known homes or landmarks. So locating Don Cayetano Díaz in Guatemala City was surprisingly hard. With the assistance of documents created during the postearthquake transition, I was able to identify the *manzana* or city block allotted to him—manzana 31.[2] It was located just north of the Plaza de San Francisco, which itself sat diagonally southwest of the Convent of San Francisco. In the contemporary map of Guatemala City (Figure 29, oriented with north to the left, east at the top), this block is in the lower right-hand quadrant, just to the left of the plaza. By itself, this location tells us very little. We know it was a place of relative prominence—close to San Francisco—and it adjoined a public space. But what other significance does the location have?

William B. Taylor writes of place as something fluid in colonial Spanish America, something that "has as much to do with what was understood to have happened there, the circulation of people and images, and news and memory of divine presence."[3] Taylor's conception draws upon and complements that of geographers like Yi-Fu Tuan, an eminent scholar whose book *Space and Place* has proved influential in many fields. As Tuan explains with characteristic simplicity, we can understand immediately the way place matters by contrasting the experiences of children and adults. "The child not only has a short past," he writes, but a tendency to focus on the present and immediate future. A child's "vitality for doing things and exploring space is not suited to the reflective pause and backward glance that makes places seem saturated with significance." So a child might be able to quickly conjure up a fantasy world around an object close at hand, turning a block of wood imaginatively into an airplane, but the object isn't heavy with emotional associations: "A broken mirror or an abandoned tricycle has no message of sadness." For this reason, "children

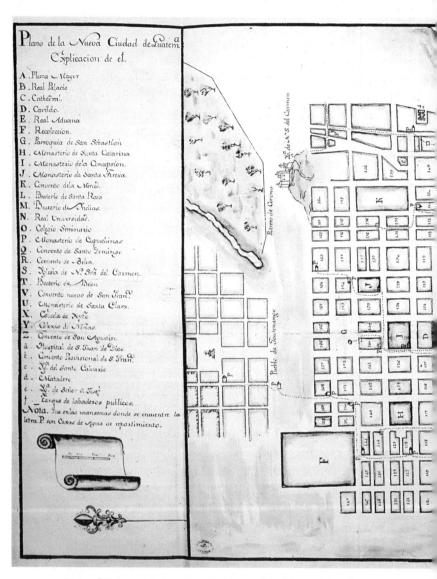

29. Map of Guatemala City in 1787. A translated legend for the map:

A.	Main Plaza	I.	Monastery of La Concepción
B.	Royal Palace	J.	Monastery of Santa Teresa
C.	Cathedral	K.	Convent of La Merced
D.	Cabildo (city council)	L.	Beaterio of Santa Rosa
E.	Customs House	M.	Beaterio of Indias
F.	Recoletos Convent	N.	Royal University
G.	Parish of San Sebastián	O.	Seminary College
H.	Monastery of Santa Catarina	P.	Monastery of Capuchinas

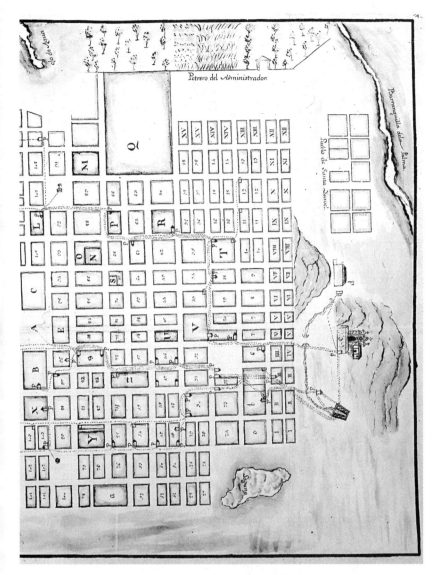

Q.	Convent of Santo Domingo	a.	Hospital San Juan de Dios
R.	Convent of Belén	b.	Provisional convent of San Francisco
S.	Church of Our Lady del Carmen	c.	Church of the Calvary
T.	Beaterio of Belén	d.	Slaughterhouse
V.	New Convent of San Francisco	e.	Church of San José
U.	Monastery of Santa Clara	f.	Public fountain (for laundry)
X.	Escuela de Cristo		
Y.	School for girls	*Note: Smaller P indicates public water supply.*	
Z.	Convent of San Agustín		

are baffled when they are asked to interpret the mood of a landscape." In contrast, adults associate objects and scenes with
moods. That is because "place can acquire deep meaning for
the adult through the steady accretion of sentiment over the
years. Every piece of heirloom furniture, or even a stain on the
wall, tells a story." The places a child sees matter-of-factly, Tuan
says, are for adults "haunted by memories."⁴ Adults associate a
memory with a place—at this turn in the road I hit a deer last
winter, on that hill I fell asleep waiting for sunrise, on this block
I met the love of my life—and the memory becomes inseparable from the meaning of the place. Sometimes it is even enough
to have other people's memories—secondhand stories, family
lore, significant current or historical events. Visit Gettysburg,
or Teotihuacán, or Auschwitz, and you will have difficulty *not*
seeing meaning in the place.

This may well prove irrecoverable for the thousands of
people who walked by and around manzana 31. We cannot look
into their memories to uncover the joy, embarrassment, anger,
grief, boredom, and lust that Guatemalans may have felt and
associated with that corner of their city. But we can, to a certain
extent, suggest possible meanings of this manzana by contex-
tualizing it in the broader experience of Guatemala City. That
is to say, we can create a textual (and perhaps visual) sketch
that is animated: a description of how the place was lived and
felt, and how manzana 31 fit into it.

Recall that the city was established as the capital only in
1775, twenty-five years before the events of our case. In laying
the groundwork, officials and planners followed the guidelines set two centuries earlier by the Spanish king Philip II: a
grid with a large plaza at the center; streets dividing *manzanas*
(blocks) and *solares* (land plots); single-story construction with
interior patios; and a deliberately peripheral distribution of the

population, with wealthier residents at the center and poorer residents at the edges.[5] This follows Tuan's general observation about the well-established "prestige of the center."[6] In fact, the new city allocated plots of land based on the locational prestige of each person's prior residence in Santiago. Tanners, butchers, and others with professions deemed unpalatable were effectively kept at the periphery.[7] Planning a new city from scratch allowed for some beneficial changes, as well. The plaza was twice as large as that of the abandoned city of Santiago, and the roads were significantly broader. Overall, the planners favored spaciousness and anticipated outward growth. Its landmarks included the cathedral, the archbishop's residence, more than a dozen convents and monasteries, the customs house, the national palace, the central market, numerous plazas, and several *garitas*—entrance gates at the edges.

In 1791, the city was divided into six *cuarteles*—roughly, districts—and each cuartel was divided into two *barrios*—neighborhoods. The southwest corner of the city, where our events took place, was the cuartel de San Agustín; its two neighborhoods were the San Juan de Dios, after hospital, and the barrio del Perú. These designations mattered not only in how they formed communities but in how they functioned legally: each barrio was assigned an alcalde who answered to a superior in the cuartel. Each district also had its own assigned escribano—thus the census books I consulted in search of Manuela Trujillo. From early on, "the new city organized the administrative structure of authority and control parallel to the spatial structure of the neighborhood and district."[8] In other words, state power can be articulated spatially (locationally) in any number of ways: it can be held in a central place and demand that people travel to it; it can be distributed hierarchically, so that a central power exists but delegates represent power in a more expansive way; it can be distributed, with no centralization at all. In Guatemala City, residents would have been sharply aware of the presence of the alcalde and his delegates as enforcers and representatives of the king's power— at the neighborhood level.

These elements give us an aerial view of the city, a sense of its principal features, and a rough sense of how administrative authority was articulated through place; but they don't tell us much about how the city felt. Perhaps we can learn a little more about how it was experienced by peering into it through the eyes of a visiting contemporary.

"In walking through it," wrote an English traveler named Henry Dunn, who resided in Guatemala for a year during the 1820s, "the first thought that strikes a stranger is, that Guatimala is one of the dullest places he has ever entered."[9] Well! Perhaps if he had visited a little earlier, in 1800, Dunn would have found enough excitement to keep him occupied. Or perhaps not, since his objections had primarily to do with architecture. "This melancholy appearance is chiefly occasioned by the way in which houses are built," he laments. He observes that they are all single-story and spacious, and "they present to the street only a series of white-washed walls and red-tiled roofs, with here and there a window, carefully guarded by large bars of iron, and a pair of massive folding doors, studded on the outside with heavy nails; thus giving to it, at the best of times, more the appearance of a deserted than an inhabited city."[10]

What struck Dunn as dull strikes others differently, but his description is apt. There *is* a kind of fortress feel to Guatemalan houses—iron bars, heavy nails, massive doors—that can be both imposing and silencing. From the sidewalk, one can guess at what lies within each manzana only by the height of the patio trees and the voices that drift out from the open cor-

ridors. Despite Dunn's avowal not to impose upon the reader
any rhetorical "painting," he nonetheless offers a lovely description of the typical Guatemala City home. Consider Dunn's
extended portrayal here as a kind of initial immersion in Guatemala place:

> Let us enter, then, at that great folding-door, look-
> ing like an inn gate, with blank walls on each side.
> We open it, and immediately find ourselves in a
> large square court-yard, in the middle of which
> is an orange-tree in full bloom. All around it is a
> covered walk, or piazza, raised about a foot from
> the ground, the roof supported by wooden pillars.
> Under this piazza are seven or eight doors, leading
> into different apartments; each one having an inte-
> rior communication with the rest, and all, of course,
> on the ground floor—stairs being almost unknown
> in Guatimala. The first room will probably be a
> common chamber. The next, a *sala,* or drawing-
> room, furnished with ten or a dozen antique chairs;
> an old-fashioned settee, with a slip of mat before it
> for a carpet; and two small dressing-tables, placed
> at an immense distance from one another, each
> bearing the image of a saint carefully enclosed in
> glass. Three or four pictures adorn the clean white-
> washed walls; and two lamps, cased in silver, hang
> from a roof in which all the naked beams are to be
> seen, with here and there a straggling cobweb. The
> floor, like that of all the rest of the rooms, will be
> paved with red tiles; its cleanliness depending upon
> the civilization of its owner. From hence we pass
> into a third apartment; probably the chief bed-

chamber; serving also for a daily sitting-room, in which to receive visitors. It contains a handsome bed, a large mahogany wardrobe, a few chairs, and a cupboard with glass doors, in which may be seen carefully arranged all the stock of china, from the blue wash-hand basin down to the diminutive coffee-cup, till lately a more valuable property than a similar service of silver. By the side of the bed hangs an image of the Saviour on the cross, under a little scarlet canopy; and on a small table, in another corner, is placed St. Joseph, or the Virgin. The next two rooms will have little furniture besides a bed, a chair, and an image: we shall therefore pass on to the *comedor,* or dining-room, which contains only one large oak table (a fixture), and seven or eight common wooden chairs. Next to this will be the kitchen: in one corner a large baking oven, of an oval shape; and in the middle of the room a mass of solid brickwork, three or four feet high, containing six or seven cavities for small charcoal fires, and conveniences for preparing the thousand different stews which are compounded in a Spanish *cocina.* To the right of this will be an inner yard, with its *pila,* or cistern of water; and further on the stables, with a second *pila* for the use of cattle. . . . And this is a fair description of a respectable house.

Dunn's detailed portrait concludes with a practical matter: such a house may be rented for eighty pounds sterling. Perhaps Don Cayetano Díaz or Doña Josefa Paniagua would have lived in houses of these dimensions, while we know that poorer residents like Liberata Bejarano stayed at the city edges in two to three rooms, with packed dirt floors and outdoor kitchens.

But Guatemalans lived as much outdoors as in, and they shared places—streets, plazas, watering holes, the open market, the churches and cathedral—with one another. Combining the observations of Dunn and other travelers with comments by Guatemalans, we get some sense of how these places mattered in everyday ways. And since we could view these places from any number of perspectives, let us consider them more specifically in three related ways: according to the time of day; along the spectrum of light and dark; and in terms of how they contained stillness or movement. Dunn's painting of the house interior conveys stillness, and there could be stillness outside of the home, too—the stillness of an empty street at dawn, the stillness of a chapel after mass, the stillness of a bricklayer's or a bakery or a laundry during the midday rest. But more often than not, there was movement, beginning with the most ordinary and necessary movement of walking down the street.

What was it like? Dunn concedes that the streets were broad "but wretchedly paved, with a considerable declivity from each side," so that heavy rain made the roads impassable. "At other times," Dunn complains, "the sharp-pointed and ill-arranged pebbles extort groans from the un-happy sufferer who in light shoes is doomed to undergo the miserable penance of passing over them."[11] We should take his complaints with a grain of salt, since Guatemalans didn't find the roads as onerous, but we can still imagine that travel across these streets wasn't easy. Walking could be slow, and riding on horseback might be only slightly faster.

The city is crisscrossed with paths taken each day by its residents. Some journeys are exceptional, taken only once and remembered forever, like the route taken by Manuela Trujillo to the door of the San Juan de Dios Hospital. But others are taken often, even every day, and have the comfort of routine. A young man goes to work at the blacksmith shop, walks home to have lunch with his mother at one in the afternoon; then he walks back to work for the afternoon and returns home at five.[12] A maid goes out every day at the same time to buy tortillas. A woman hurries home after mass because she has gone too long without the drinking chocolate that Guatemalans use to punctuate the day, to warm themselves in the cold air, to sweeten their tongues as they gossip.

We might go farther and imagine particular walks at particular times of day. At nine o'clock in the evening, the city is in darkness, for there is no illumination on the city streets.[13] Walking even a few blocks to the home of a sick friend feels like a perilous business. Your senses are sharpened; you hear the strumming of a guitar in a patio, an argument between a man and woman across the way, and the disconsolate barking of a dog. The smell of tobacco smoke alerts you to the fact that someone else is walking nearby, for Guatemalans smoke like chimneys, and you lift your nose to determine whether it is a man's cigar or a woman's *cigarillo.* Cigar—decidedly. A door opens near you and you stop; out of the block of yellow light two men stumble out, drunk, half pushing one another and still disgruntled at the money they lost over cards. They do not see you as they pass, and you walk on, a little more quickly. The strident voices at the corner up ahead could only belong to the alcalde and his *alguacil,* and they are best avoided, too. You walk quietly, listening to snatches of their assured conversation, and moments later you finally reach your friend's house. You knock on the great wooden door, relieved to have arrived safely.

A walk at midday is a different matter. Whether you are out for a rushed errand or a leisurely *paseo*—a term Guatemalans used and still use to describe a short excursion, a jaunt—something is bound to happen. As you walk to the market to buy chocolate and bread, you see a couple whispering furtively across a wide windowsill, the woman inside holding the shutter mostly closed, the man in the street reaching in to clasp her hand. On the next block, at one of the public pilas, half a dozen women are washing clothes, scrubbing against the stone and slapping the wet fabric down to dry. Farther on, you see two women standing in a doorway, mending in the bright sunlight, shooting the breeze. Beside them, in the scant shade of the window balcony, an older woman rolls cigarettes and stacks them neatly on a tray. Then a few blocks later, as you near the plaza, two men on horseback ride by, laughing and whistling, setting all the young women within striking distance on edge. You can tell by their finely made hats and boots that they are men of some means; one of them might even be an Aycinena, the most renowned family in Guatemala. He doesn't seem to notice anyone, until his eye snags on the demure figure of a woman wearing a veil, and she ducks her head, willing him to look away. You reach the market and your favorite vendor is there, pouring chocolate with quick hands into bowls. The chocolate is perfect: rich, hot, heavy with the scent of cinnamon. The bread vendor gives you an extra-large piece, so the outing has been a success. Even if it is a very uneventful walk home, you will probably run into someone you know; you might have to avoid someone you'd rather not see; or you might take a brief detour for a drink stronger than chocolate and find yourself in unexpected circumstances, as so many city people did.

So it was for María Inés Barrios and her mother, who

were out walking when they ran into some friends, Manuel *el Dulcero* and Nicolás Alvarado. Nicolás complained of thirst, so they decided to stop by the house of a woman named María Gregoria. She sold them a few drinks, and they all sat out in the street to enjoy them. One of the company started to play the guitar, and the gathering got very merry. Until María Gregoria, who apparently did not have a license to dispense alcohol, came out of the house and told them to scram. Barrios and her mother protested, declaring that "the street belongs to the king," and to no one else, meaning that it was a public place in which they were free to drink, sing, and more. They also added, for good measure, that María Gregoria was a stupid drunk. Not surprisingly, the moonshine vendor took offense and got rid of the unwelcome guests outside her door with the assistance of a heavy stick.[14]

Altercations over public places were not uncommon, and they bring to the foreground the conceptions people held of shared space. The street may have belonged to the king of Spain, but people swept their thresholds and the space outside their doorways, and they occupied corners of the plaza as vendors, and in other similar ways they understood shared space to be also possessable and particular.[15] María Candelaria de Herrera, an Indian woman from San Cristobal who sold tortillas in the central market, clashed in public with a Spanish vendor of higher standing, Don Joseph, over such a matter. He objected to Herrera's placing trash next to his stall, and Herrera replied that he shouldn't worry about the trash because there were Indians who swept the plaza clean every day. Besides, she replied, "the plaza belongs to the king." Don Joseph, apparently incensed by this reply (leveled by a social inferior, to his eyes), threw an orange at Herrera and then set upon her with a bowl, finally seizing her by the braids and dragging her over the ground. Herrera was upset about the injuries, but she was even more upset about the embarrassment to her honor, since this had all occurred in the public plaza: her braids had been pulled—a particularly offensive defamation—and her clothes had been torn off her body.[16]

The market in the plaza beside the cathedral was the most public of public places, but to the residents of the city there must have been several such nodes of dense activity in their mental maps and, conversely, quiet spots that remained quiet even in the bustle of midday. Recall the case of Josefa Gonzales, whose husband, Marcelo Contreras, pulled her off the road and whipped her.[17] They had been walking along the calle del Calvario, at the very edge of the city and near the cemetery where Simona Villagrán was buried. Contreras evidently knew the quiet spots along this route; otherwise he would not have chosen such a place for the mistreatment of his wife. So it must have been for the perpetrator of our crime.

Let's look again at a map of the city, holding in mind this more elaborated sense of place—as something active, something with events in it, something unfolding along a route (see Figure 29). First, let's find some other places on this map that matter to the story. We see the Hospital San Juan de Dios, at the far west of the city (bottom of the map). The Calvario, where Simona was buried, is at the far south of the city (right edge of the map), distinctly apart from it and up on a hill—thus the "Calvary" in the climb. Right away, their locations are interesting. We already knew that the hospital was at the edge of a ravine, but without city maps we wouldn't have known that the Calvario was quite so close to the city slaughterhouse. On the other side of the Calvario, farther west, is the Guatemala City aqueduct, which carried water to public pilas—reservoirs and

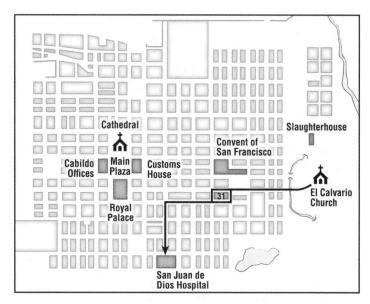

30. Guatemala City, showing the perpetrator's likely route

fountains—by means of underground pipes.[18] These waterways flow past manzana 31 as part of their northward current.

But the most significant route here is not a waterway. It is a pedestrian route (Figure 30).

To see this route, we have to imagine El Calvario and the San Juan de Dios as pieces of a story. It might be a story about someone who goes every morning to El Calvario for morning services and then walks several blocks to his job at the hospital. It might be a story about someone who works at the slaughterhouse and stops by El Calvario for a second, more gruesome kind of butchery before continuing on to visit a sick relative at the San Juan de Dios. It might be a story about a student of surgery who spends long hours at the hospital and whose uncle is a priest at El Calvario. We don't know exactly what the story is, but somehow the story unfolds along this route. If we consider this route in terms of stillness and movement, light and dark, a new aspect of the story emerges. The plaza is not just a public space; it is a place where one can be still. Imagine: whether it's nighttime or daytime, the perpetrator can sit in the plaza, watching manzana 31, waiting until everything is quiet and the streets are deserted. Then he can get up, walk at a normal pace by the barred windows, and drop something from his sack on the sill. If someone starts to come around the corner, he has only to go back to the plaza and wait again. Manzana 31 is perfect because it connects the two places that matter, and the plaza beside it offers a vantage point.

There is no record of it in the case documents, but it could be that the Guatemala City authorities realized that this was so. Even if they did not see manzana 31 as part of a route, they certainly saw it as a place of importance in the case. You'll recall that we began this chapter with the fiscal's determination to monitor more closely and deploy more effectively the resources of the alcaldes' offices. There can be no doubt that their zeal was in some way effective. Perhaps in the very same plaza where the perpetrator had waited and watched, the alcaldes now waited and watched. They did not get their man, but he felt their presence. We know this because more than a month passed before he struck again. And when he did, it was in a new place, with greater vehemence.

7

Death, Sex, and the City
In Which María Rosa Padilla Is Found in the Morgue

History is not a balanced narrative of the results of opposing moves. It is a way of taking in hand and grasping the true harshness of reality, which we can glimpse through the collision of conflicting logics.

—ARLETTE FARGE, *THE ALLURE OF THE ARCHIVES*

The perpetrator was quiet in August. And then on September 8, he made his mark once more.

A Friar Cerezo wrote to the court with the following disturbing message:

A woman passed away yesterday in this Royal Hospital and her daughter arrived today to prepare her for burial, at which point she saw that her mother's genitals [*partes pudendas*] had been cut; but the daughter notified her brother who gave me notice.

This cadaver is of a woman who was placed in the morgue under lock and key, which fact surprises me greatly. It being necessary to acknowledge these events, I bring them to your attention so that license may be given to move the cadaver to a protected place.[1]

The woman was one María Rosa Padilla, and the morgue in question was part of the campo santo, the cemetery and chapel, attached to the San Juan de Dios Hospital. Officials acted at once to investigate the crime. From the hospital staff they learned that María Rosa Padilla had arrived at the hospital on the first of the month suffering from dropsy. She died on the seventh in the hospital and was moved to the morgue. At that point, several members of the staff had seen her and verified that she was in one piece.

Padilla's daughter, Petrona, had also seen the body in the morgue on the seventh. It was only upon returning on the following morning that she found her mother's condition altered: "Opening the door of the chapel, which she found unlocked, she saw that her skirts were lifted and her shameful parts exposed," and the corpse being in this state, it was impossible to ignore that "the entire region had been cut up all the way to the buttocks." Then, "filled with horror and fright," Petrona went to tell her brother what she had seen.

Dr. Narciso Esparragosa examined the cadaver, giving a detailed account of what he described as a "disaster." The genitals had been entirely removed from the body with a sharp instrument. Parts of the internal organs and thighs had also been mutilated. The cuts extended all the way around from the hips to the buttocks, which had been completely removed. Esparragosa declared that "neither he nor his students could have executed such butchery," which bore no similarity to the kind of anatomical dissection practiced at the hospital.

The buttocks and genitals were not just cut; they were missing. There was a pool of blood near the body, and there was blood smeared by the doorway to the morgue. Clearly someone had mutilated the cadaver during the early hours of September 8 and carried away the spoils. No one could shed light on who.

Does this discovery seem different from the others? It struck me as different when I first came upon it—more violent, more transgressive, and less considered. Also more obvious, since the placement of twin body parts—breasts, hands, ears—has a runic quality that the hatcheting of female genitals does not.

But I think this sense of difference is an illusion. It certainly *feels* different, and that's because in this case it was the mutilated body that was found, not the purloined parts. Recall that Esparragosa, when he exhumed the body of Simona Villagrán, observed that the genitals and buttocks had been cut away. Then he discarded the observation, finding its implications unfathomable, and determined instead that the body had decomposed quickly, leaving the *partes pudendas* of the corpse more damaged.

While the treatment of María Rosa Padilla's corpse may feel like an escalation, from the perpetrator's point of view it wasn't. He had done this before.

Yet it matters that the corpse, not the parts, was found. It matters because this hatcheted corpse communicated something different to Guatemalans. However confounding the messages sent by the breasts, hands, and ears, they did express a few things very clearly. They expressed anonymity. They expressed deliberation, even restraint through that deliberation. And they expressed ambiguity regarding the perpetrator's stance in relation to the corpse.

In contrast, the mutilated corpse of María Rosa Padilla expressed something personal and specific. The perpetrator remained anonymous, but his target did not. Here was a mother—found by her daughter, no less—with a name and a story of recent illness, utterly savaged. She could be identified by face and feature and dress. She was still a *person,* in the way that we acknowledge corpses to be still people-ish. "Personhood persists where it manifestly no longer resides," as one historian succinctly observes.[2] This is tangibly different from what the perpetrator accomplished with the breasts, hands, and ears, which were, in a clear (if shocking) way, already *made into* objects before they were placed. They were objects that *implied* a corpse—a missing corpse. But no one would have considered the breasts, hands, ears "a corpse."

María Rosa Padilla *was* "a corpse." She was "a person," but with pieces of her taken away. Therefore the actions taken by the perpetrator in the morgue were no longer actions taken through objects (breasts, hands) but actions taken upon an individual. And they did something particular to that individual, to that person. As Laqueur writes in his recent cultural history *The Work of the Dead,* "To treat a dead body as if it were ordinary organic matter—to leave it lie as if it were the body of a beast—or willfully to desecrate and mutilate it is to erase it from culture and from the human community: to deny the existence of the community from which it came, to deny its humanity."[3] The angle on community is interesting, and we'll return to it, but at this point consider just the dehumanization effected by this treatment. Instead of using the body parts as a vocabulary to say something (what, we still wonder), here there is one very loud message about the body itself: *I have destroyed María.*

This is also a message without restraint, or at least without the appearance of restraint. There may still have been deliberation: September 8 is a Catholic feast day—the Nativity of Mary.[4] Can it be that this attack upon a mother's reproductive system—that is, violence to the organs that made her a mother—was pure coincidence? Is it also a coincidence that the woman's name was María? Or did the perpetrator intend once again, in an oblique way, to offer a Christian symbol, upended? Even if the decision was made carefully, the cuts were not. They could be read only as violent and even wild: the lifted skirts, which speak of haste and disregard; the splatters of blood, which speak of messiness and incaution; and the very breadth and number of the cuts, which suggest a loss of control or, at a minimum, an undisciplined approach to the body.

And last, and related, the state of the corpse seemed to eliminate the ambiguities and nuances accompanying the perpetrator's prior messages. Targeting the genitals could leave no doubt: this was a sexual assault. A confusing and unnatural sexuality perhaps, but undeniably sexual nonetheless.

In all these ways, the discovery of María Rosa Padilla's corpse can seem like an escalation. It violated the integrity of the morgue and the campo santo. And undeniably, it offended Guatemalans' sensibilities about death. There were good deaths and bad deaths, and this, this "disaster"—to use Esparragosa's word in a different way—was decidedly not a good death.

A good death? How is such a thing even possible?

To us, the phrase verges on oxymoron. We are somewhat past the mid-twentieth-century moment when social critics observed that death was the greatest taboo of the modern Western world, but we are still close enough to feel its ripples. The sense that "contemporary western society shuns and fears death" is yet visible in how we relegate the dying to separate spheres, erect unwieldy and costly institutions for their isolation, and struggle in personal interactions for comfortable ways of speaking about the dead and dying.[5] In its simplest expression, this aversion might be summed up as the conviction that death is bad because it is an end to life, and life is incontestably better. It is this love of life that blossoms into other, more complex and more poisonous, mindsets: the cult of youth and youthfulness; the lack of reverence for the elderly, bordering on neglect; the obsession with manipulating—even defacing—our bodies so that we appear younger than we are. Life is where we find meaning, and youthful life is the pinnacle of that meaning—the most desired state, the ideal around which we build our world.

This is not so for the early modern world, in which it was widely understood that being dead had many advantages over being alive. But it was important to not just die, but die well. "Dying well—holy dying, dying in peace and without fear, dying perhaps in the hope of another life, dying with acceptance of fate" was not only possible and constantly discussed, it was central to Christian practice.[6] For certain time periods in Spain and Spanish America, I can say without fear of overstatement that dying well was as important as or even more important than living well.

To understand how this can be so, we need to contend with colonial Guatemalans' conception of death, a conception very different from our own.[7]

We must grapple with death's prevalence, for one thing. And I don't mean "prevalence" in the sense that people were dying all the time, though it's true that mortality rates were high. In New Spain, there appears to have been no real population growth during the nineteenth century thanks to ongoing epidemics and wars.[8] Guatemalan women's wills point indirectly to the high mortality rates of spouses and children: 55 percent of women sampled in the late colonial period had lost spouses; 55 percent had lost at least one child; and 16–18 percent had lost all of their children by the time they made their wills.[9]

Mortality rates aside, what I mean by "prevalence" is the way in which the specter of death—the idea of it, the topic of it, contemplation and preparation for it—was entirely ordinary and necessary to living. Indeed, well into the early nineteenth century, "death permeated the very meaning of life."[10] To more fully understand the Spanish colonial mindset, we must imagine a culture entirely interpenetrated by death; we must accept that premodern people saw themselves living in a shared community with the dead. That's not to say that they saw ghosts everywhere, but rather, in an entirely un-supernatural way, that the dead were integral and significant to daily life. They had not been exiled. "Thano-politics—the control of dying, the rules according to which one dies, the rules over the possessions of the dead and the possession of the corpse, the exchanges tying the ancestors to the living, etc.—made up the fabric of everyday life."[11] Consider this rough analogy: the way in which we easily and naturally accommodate to the existence of people we love who live far away. Family and friends who reside in different states or in different countries don't become topics of lamentable whispers, strange silences. They are thought of and spoken of and corresponded with; we allow for reminders of them in everyday routines; we invite them to stay in our lives as much as possible.

In the memorable words of Carlos Eire, "Heaven, hell, and purgatory were as much a part of [Spanish] topography as Madrid, Gibraltar, and the Pyrenees."[12] Eire's classic study of death and dying in sixteenth-century Spain explores how the "fascination" with death in the early modern period, a fascination rooted in Catholic beliefs, influenced the practices of saints, kings, and common Spaniards. How could Spaniards find meaning and inspiration in detailed stories about the death of King Philip II, who "practically rotted away in his own excrement"?[13] How could they, almost simultaneously, insist that the body of Saint Teresa of Ávila exuded a "marvelous fragrance" after her death, an odor of sanctity that could not be washed away from anything she had touched?[14] The explanations for both, as well as the Spanish (and Spanish American) preoccupation with will writing, emerge from a cluster of ideas about dying well. The king might have died in terrible pain, but he suffered with magnificent humility and piousness, showering kindness on those who attended him. This was a "good" death that could lead by brilliant example. And Teresa's odor of sanctity offered proof—undeniable, physical proof—of her saintliness: another invaluable lesson.

Spaniards needed their lessons. Conceptions of the Catholic afterlife—the slim possibility of heaven, the much greater likelihood of purgatory—are more familiar to us; less familiar to us is the conception of death as a pitched battle for the immortal soul. During this "final death struggle," demons would swarm the deathbed like hornets while saints offered support to the resistance; friends and relatives would assist with prayers; and, vitally, the dying person would deploy all the techniques acquired through a lifetime of preparation. The *Ars Moriendi* texts, books devoted to the art of dying, constituted an essential part of this defense. In works like *Victoria de la muerte*

(1583) by Alonso de Orozco, Catholics learned detailed and extremely practical instructions for the final onslaught.[15]

Following these instructions could facilitate a good death, even if few could come close to the glorious suffering of Philip II or the gorgeous aroma of Teresa. And though ideas had changed to some degree in both Europe and the Americas by the eighteenth century, Spanish Americans continued to practice most of the elements of dying well that were practiced in the sixteenth: accepting the sacraments—confession, communion, and extreme unction; preparing a will; washing and preparing the body for burial; keeping vigil with the body; performing the burial procession and mass; and undertaking the burial in sacred ground.[16]

It is among these practices that we encounter a curious contradiction—or at the very least, a puzzle—about how the corpse should be treated after a good death. It's clear that colonial Guatemalans (and Catholics more broadly) share the general respect for the corpse described by Laqueur, who comes as close as I have seen to arguing that such respect is universal. Bodies in Guatemala are not left out for the dogs; such a fate is regarded with contained disgust, remember, at the opening of our case. No—bodies are treated as Simona Villagrán's body was treated: washed and dressed, carefully tended, watched over by family, carried to and buried in sacred ground. This is the reverence that we would expect. And yet . . . this insistence on keeping the body intact is *not* universal. Consider the treatment of saintly bodies and the creation of saintly relics. What happened to that aromatic body of Saint Teresa's? As Eire writes, "the relic hunters prevailed." A few years after her death, one witness testified that "there was a great deal of flesh missing from the back, and almost half the belly was gone." Another commented that only her legs and feet had not been scavenged.

Teresa's niece complained, "I have been told that the body is all cut up, and that they parcel out pieces of flesh to those who ask for them out of devotion."[17]

The taking of relics does not damage the soul of a saint. But if this is true, then cutting up a corpse shouldn't matter. Right?

The seeming contradiction underscores the ambivalence around dissection in the late colonial imagination. On the one hand, anatomical science grew in importance as both methodology and metaphor in colonial New Spain. People began to understand anatomy as one of the building blocks of empirical analysis. Political treatises talked about understanding the kingdom through dissection. It became more common to use corporal metaphors about members, organs, and limbs as a way of describing pieces of the political *body*.[18] An excellent example of this comes from a Guatemalan criminal case, in which one Manuel Silvestre Rodríguez was tried in 1800 for carrying a weapon. The arresting official described Rodríguez as a wastrel, a good-for-nothing who spent all his time vagabonding in the street, "perverting" women, gaming, and drinking. "He is one of those many individuals," the official wrote, "who like a rotten member must be separated from the public body."[19] Using this corporeal metaphor, the official was advocating a kind of community amputation.

But on the other hand, even as dissection gained credibility in these ways, dissection was still seen as an "extreme form of punishment beyond death," practiced primarily on criminals. This is so despite the continued importance of relics: "Yet, at the same time, the fragmentation and dismemberment of the body postmortem was associated, from early Christian times, with kings, saints, and martyrs, whose relics played a foundational role for the communities of believers in the Old and New Worlds."[20] So how did colonial Spanish Americans really feel about mutilated bodies? Did they abhor mutilation while turning a blind eye for a piece of possible salvation? Or did they not find mutilation as abhorrent as we might have thought?

In a phrase, neither and both. Method and manner made all the difference.[21] Taking a fragment of bone and placing it in a beautiful reliquary, cherishing it as treasure, was one thing. Taking a body apart like a carcass to study the shape of the uterus, or violently tearing a corpse apart to satisfy some perverse pleasure—those were something else altogether. Reverence, in the first case. Scientific (or morbid) curiosity, in the second. Unhealthy passion—or malice, or demonic impulse, or *something* just as awful—in the third. It may feel unsatisfying, as far as rules go, because it seems like a vague distinction too open to interpretation. Does it really just come down to intention? Mean-spirited mutilation is wrong but respectful mutilation is fine?

Yes. Or perhaps, more precisely, taking a corpse apart with ill intent is mutilation; taking a corpse apart with good intentions is not mutilation at all. Mutilation implies violence, and the partitioning of a saint's body for the purpose of devotion is more correctly understood as a nonviolent fragmentation and dispensation of material sanctity.

Two considerations help explain how something seemingly so crucial could boil down to a fuzzy distinction. First, think back to the idea of the dead as participants in daily life—still part of the familial unit, still part of the everyday imaginary. With living people, the intention of an action is what matters, too. The same act rendered with cruelty or kindness can be respectively illegal or tender. For example: among the Guatemalan criminal cases, there are a handful of disputes around hair cutting or braid cutting. Seizing a woman (mostly Indian women, in these cases) by the braids was offensive; cutting the braids off was a shocking act of violence, a stab at the woman's honor and an ultimate insult.[22] Yet cutting a lock of hair as a keepsake could also be a loving gesture, a promise to treasure the token of the beloved. So it was with a corpse. Similar actions, motivated by vitriol or devotion, had distinct meanings.

The second reason this is fuzzy has to do with another belief, a cornerstone of Catholic thought: resurrection. While there was broad and enduring agreement that a corpse deserved respectful treatment, there was debate and disagreement over how the buried body mattered to that most significant stage of the afterlife. Medieval thinkers in particular worried over how the self would appear during resurrection. There would be *some* kind of bodily resurrection, most believed, so what would the body look like? Old or young? Damaged or not? What about people who had undergone amputations? Would their limbs be restored?[23] In the early modern period, and verging on our moment in 1800, these questions about resurrection were not taken up with as much energy, leaving an array of answers and resolutions that can be best described as heterogenous.

One caricature of this period depicts corpse-hungry anatomists on one side and righteous, pious churchmen on the other, battling for science and religion respectively. This oversimplification is misleading for many reasons: among them, the practice of anatomy was centuries old by 1800, the categories "scientist" and "churchman" were not as rigid as we might imagine, and anatomists did not necessarily view what they were doing as violating God's laws.

But the debate over how bodies should be treated was real, and in Spanish America it was less about anatomists pilfering corpses than about the placement of cemeteries. As mentioned in Chapter 4, enlightened reformers pushed for the removal of church burial grounds, advocating their placement at the outskirts. The principal motive was hygiene. Recall that Esparragosa worried about the "miasmas" roiling through the neighborhood when he examined the corpse of Simona Villagrán. Miasmas were much more than a bad smell; it was believed that "a poisonous atmosphere resulted from the vapors of decomposing bodies."[24] Therefore burying a corpse—and especially a diseased corpse—in a church was, to reformers, tantamount to placing a powder keg of contagion where it would do the most damage.

A practice already seen as questionable by reformers was aggravated by the epidemics—mostly cholera—of the late eighteenth and early nineteenth centuries. In Guatemala, this resulted in "numerous bodies being crammed into small public spaces adjoining the local church buildings, and fetid conditions for the priest who daily inhabited these walls."[25] Ordinarily, the situation was not quite so dire. Buried corpses were placed beneath church floors, echoing European practices.

You might wonder how they all fit, even without the epidemics. Not very well. Buried corpses were "crushed beneath the blows of a pounder replacing nearly all the removed dirt so that the church floor would not sink."[26] John Lloyd Stephens, the explorer and author from the United States who traveled extensively through Central America in the nineteenth century, described with horror how the pounder was used in the burial of a child. The sexton rested the boy in the grave in the church floor, "folded his little hands across its breast, placing there a small rude cross, covered it over with eight or ten inches of earth, and then got into the grave and stomped it down with his feet." This was deemed insufficient, so more earth was shoveled in before the sexton returned with "a pounder, being a log of wood about four feet long and ten inches in diameter . . . and again taking his place in the grave, threw up the pounder to the full swing of his arm, and brought it down with all his strength over the head of the child." Stephens reports that his blood ran cold, and when he attempted to halt the process, his objections seemed "only to give him more strength and spirit." It was difficult work, and it required more hands. To Stephens's utter horror, the boy's father then proceeded to lay down his hat, get into the grave, and take the pounder to the dirt "with a dead, heavy noise."[27]

No doubt you're thinking right now about that distinction we discussed a page or two ago: taking a corpse to pieces with reverence or . . . not. It's true that this comes across as rather violent. And while we may sneer at Stephens's poor anthropological sensibility, we may, at the same time, know just what he means when he writes, "I never beheld a more brutal disgusting scene. The child's body must have been crushed to atoms."[28] Nevertheless, it's important to understand why Spanish American Catholics considered this preferable to moving burial grounds out of the city, or town, or village. If the dead are still part of everyday life, still active members of the family, pushing them to the physical edges of the community is a terrible sundering. Moreover, placing them in such a place—even if it is consecrated—removes them from the sacred sphere of the church. Much better to keep them close, where their presence can be felt and their memory honored every time one crosses the threshold to hear Mass, to confess, and to pray.

One of the arguments in favor of church burials (with the pounder), in fact, was that burials outside of town resulted in corpse desecration. "When burials were relocated to the new cemetery," a priest from Cahabón in Guatemala reported, "animals desecrated the bodies. In response, the people buried bodies in the grounds of their own houses." In Escuintla, a priest sympathetic to the reforms worried that the authorities making the rules just didn't understand conditions on the ground. "To bury outside a town, the priest wrote, residents had to rip trees out of the ground just to be able to bury a body. By the time the mourners returned to their homes, pigs had already dug up half-buried bodies and were dragging them through the town streets."[29] So people revolted, sometimes staging demonstrations that turned violent, sometimes taking quieter approaches like the people in Cahabón. In Guatemala, most of these revolts did not occur until the 1830s. Similar revolts occurred throughout Spanish and Portuguese America— in Brazil, Lima, and Mexico, as historians have examined.[30]

Even though the revolts in Guatemala occurred mostly in rural areas and a few decades later, there are intriguing antecedents directly relating to our case and touching on the same themes: sacred and profane ground, the proper treatment of a body, and the appropriate role of medicine and religion in relation to that body.

Curiously, the friar who reported the discovery of Padilla's body refused to give evidence in the investigation. When pressed, Friar Cerezo said that it was not fitting to his station, and that he did not see how he could be compelled by even his superior, let alone the secular court, to give testimony in a criminal matter. Or, to use his phrase, to be "mixed up" in a criminal matter.[31] As you might imagine, the court officials were miffed. And from our vantage point, it's a little mysterious. To readers trained by the twists and turns of paperback mysteries, it probably seems like he has something to hide.

Maybe, but I think something else is going on. The answer, to my eye, arrives in a seemingly unrelated complaint written a few weeks later by Esparragosa.

In mid-October, Dr. Esparragosa wrote to the court complaining about the conditions of his dissection laboratory. In typical Esparragosian manner, he protested that the work undertaken in this space was critical—for teaching, for forensics, for the development of medical treatments—and that the limitations of it were dire: too small, conducive to contagion, and dreadfully uncomfortable. "I prudently fear," he wrote, "that either myself or another one of us dedicated to this work will be stricken by a fever or disease, and knowing this it seems necessary to have the best possible conditions in order to avoid the risks inherent to work that is so cumbersome but so useful."[32]

When you consider that the space used for dissection was adjacent to where Padilla was found, this complaint looks a little different. A month had passed since Padilla's death, and the San Juan de Dios was in the midst of a multiyear renovation project. Esparragosa probably took stock of the situation after the Padilla "disaster" and then learned that the renovations were going to take longer than expected (don't they always), which prompted him to agitate for a faster timeline. Don Pedro Garci Aguirre, the project overseer, wrote back with disappointing news and a fascinating—for us—description of the current and previous facilities.

> These [dissections] were previously conducted in the open air, on a table made of wood, and with a thousand attendant inconveniences, and for this reason a tiled lean-to roof was constructed, adjacent to the little chapel that is used for the deposit

of cadavers, where it would be possible to work shielded from the sun and rain. But the stated lean-to roof does not offer more than a narrow corridor in which to work, since it is, for now, a temporary place in which there is hardly room for all the medical practitioners and ministers of Justice who attend to observe [the autopsies] of those who are assassinated or other deceased persons.[33]

It was true that a new dissection laboratory was part of the plan, Garci Aguirre acknowledged, and he was sympathetic to the needs expressed by Dr. Esparragosa. But he did not intend to deviate from his current course, which gave priority to the renovations of the women's wing.

The "little chapel" is not described in more detail, and it's almost certain that Padilla was there, not in the dissection corridor. (Remember that the room was locked, and there was blood on the door; there could be neither lock nor door on an open corridor.) But the fact that they were adjacent to each other and that both abutted the hospital cemetery is significant. Other people thought so, too. In December of the following year, one of Guatemala's elites weighed in on the issue. Antonio Larrazabal, a cleric with impeccable Spanish pedigree who was then at the parish of Los Remedios, had heard from an alcalde (Señor Marquez de Ayzinena, even more impeccable) that in the campo santo of the hospital there was a "tile covered gallery in which bodies are anatomized." Larrazabal had to see this with his own eyes. He went, he saw, and he protested vociferously.

Why? According to Larrazabal, the dissection gallery stood on sacred ground. Remember that the hospital stood at the very edges of the city, bordering a ravine that was viewed as little better than a dump, a no-man's land. A patch of hallowed ground defended the city from this ravine like a bulwark. But there was a flaw in these defenses, a chink in the wall. The hospital cemetery had been sanctified, along with the little chapel, and then this lean-to had been constructed right next to it, which meant that all those dissections and autopsies, whether for medical study or criminal inquiry, were conducted in violation of that sacred purpose.

Here, I think, is the cause of Friar Cerezo's indignation, and with it an interesting window onto some of the frictions and alignments among city elites. Friar Cerezo was surely horrified that a woman's body had been so defiled in a sacred space, but he was probably just as horrified that dissections were occurring day by day adjacent to that space on sacred ground. I'm not saying that he saw dissection and Padilla's mutilation as the same thing, but they were both atrocious abuses. And since Esparragosa conducted autopsies in the service of criminal investigations (remember that he complained about doing too many), Friar Cerezo saw the criminal court and the surgeon bound up in it together. He had probably been festering with frustration at the dissection lab for months, unable to do anything for lack of influence.[34]

Larrazabal's complaint did the trick. The sheaf of documents was passed on to Don Antonio González Mollinedo y Saravia, who held the highest office in the kingdom: the presidency of the Guatemalan *audiencia.* His reply is not part of the record, but he must have demanded some kind of reckoning, because Don Garci Aguirre, the project overseer, felt compelled to write a long justification. Sounding rather beleaguered, he explained that the lean-to had been built before the ground was consecrated, and that the archbishop of Guatemala (now deceased, unfortunately) had himself come to see the space and had tacitly approved of the gallery—by saying nothing—before consecrating the cemetery and chapel.

The response from the two clerics assigned to the chapel is a rhetorical masterwork of high-handed condemnation. They began by acknowledging their error about the sacred ground, and they praised—in muted terms—the necessary work performed by the anatomists. But they also gestured to the incongruity of anatomical work, signaling how "the blood spilled by these operations, which drains through a hole in the masonry bed designed for these bodies," had no consonance with preparations for Christian burial. In other words, the friars drew a line in the sand—or the soil, perhaps—stating with unequivocal if quiet conviction that anatomy belonged to one realm and Christian burial to another.

In reply, the fiscal wrote a few terse lines that left no doubt whose side he was on. The dissection work was "greatly needed" and of "great public utility." If the friars so desired it, he decided, ignoring the concession and counterargument made by these interlocutors, the area could be deconsecrated.

To my eye, this rather convoluted debate matters for the light it sheds on the tensions and alliances among the elites who were compelled to reckon with this sordid case. It's not as simple as the caricature would have it: enlightened scientists on one side and recalcitrant priests on the other. But clerics in Guatemala did seem to find some of Esparragosa's "enlightened" practices problematic, and they associated them with the workings of the criminal court. This may be a stretch, but I think it's also significant that an alcalde (of high social standing) sided with the clerics. You may remember from Chapter 2 that alcaldes and judges did not always see eye to eye. It seems to me no coincidence that Esparragosa and the fiscal saw it one way while the clerics and an alcalde saw it another. Esparragosa and the fiscal have in common the confidence (or arrogance) of believing they know better: they judged themselves enlightened, implying that those who saw differently were not.

Despite these tensions, illuminated and partly occasioned by the finding of María Rosa Padilla's corpse, there was probably more agreement on how the perpetrator's actions could be interpreted as a sexual crime. Or, perhaps more accurately, a crime motivated by a sexual impulse. We need to be clear about what this means, because for us, "sexual crime" carries some baggage that it would not have carried for anyone in Guatemala in 1800.

Let's unpack that baggage for a moment, in an effort to distinguish our own notion of "sexual crime" from theirs.

The first thing that weighs us down is Freud. Whether we realize it or not, Sigmund Freud and psychoanalysis, usually through the prism of popular psychology and pop culture, shape our understanding of sexual crimes: rape, assault, and so-called "sexual murder" (which can include sexual mutilation of the victim, pre- or postmortem). Most conspicuously, psychoanalysis primes us to think of sexual crimes as expressions of sexual deviance or perversion. If pushed to characterize these perversions, you might find yourself turning to something called "sadism," a term coined in the late nineteenth century by the German psychiatrist Richard von Krafft-Ebing, referring to the Marquis de Sade (1740–1814, and more on him later). Freud took up the term in the early nineteenth century, remarking in this manner on male sexuality:

> The sexuality of most male human beings contains
> an element of aggressiveness—a desire to subjugate;
> the biological significance of it seems to lie in the

need for overcoming the resistance of the sexual object by means other than ... wooing. Thus sadism would correspond to an aggressive component of the sexual instinct which has become independent and exaggerated and, by displacement, has usurped the leading position.[35]

As Deborah Cameron and Elizabeth Frazer discuss in their analysis of sexual murder, Freud does not really believe in any kind of "natural" sexuality. Reproductive heterosexuality is convenient for society, but there's nothing innate about it. "Perversions arise precisely because the path to socially valued 'normal' heterosexuality is a tricky one, offering many opportunities for deviation."[36] That path begins in childhood, according to Freud, and it requires boys to resolve their Oedipal desire for their mothers with the "castration complex" (overcoming the fear that their father-rivals will castrate them), and it requires girls to realize they are already castrated and transfer their desire from mother to father (and then, by extension, to other men). I love the dry understatement with which Cameron and Frazer observe that "given this complex developmental process, it is hardly surprising that things can go awry."[37] Quite. There are opportunities for trauma aplenty when fear of castration and a death wish against your parents are lurking in every interaction.

So where does this leave us with sadists? According to Freudians, their actions are a defense against the anxiety of castration, an assertion that they are the castrators, not the castrated. You may not have had this exact formulation in mind as you contemplated the attack on María Rosa Padilla, but you've nonetheless felt its effects through the diffuse influence of psychoanalysis. It's what shapes the popular conception of the angry, emotionally stunted serial killer. It's why this killer is always imagined as male. And it characterizes sexual crimes in relation to these early childhood developments. As fantasized acts of revenge, for example, and as gross hatred against the desired sexual object. These are all variations on a Freudian theme.[38]

Another kind of baggage for us emerges not around sex but around gender. Because it cannot go overlooked that all of the bodies targeted by this perpetrator belonged to women. How is this different from sex? It's different from sex because it suggests that the perpetrator is targeting these women because they are women. Sexual crimes can also target men (and in the colonial period, some do), but in this case they don't. That fact places this case squarely in the category of what we could consider a sexual crime motivated by misogyny—a hatred of women. Feminist critiques of male violence against women have allowed us to understand that these crimes are not "merely" about sex and not "merely" expressions of deviance. They are also political. Male violence targeting women "expresses not purely individual anger and frustration," Cameron and Frazer explain, "but a collective, culturally sanctioned misogyny which is important in maintaining the collective power of men." Indeed, they go on, framed this way it may be apt to consider these crimes acts of sexual terrorism.[39]

And what, exactly, is sexual terrorism? Well, unfortunately, it's an approach all too familiar to women in Guatemala today, where a new legal category—femicide[40]—was created in response to the rampant and often spectacularly gruesome murder of women. You might wonder why a special legal category is necessary for women, when it is already illegal to murder people. Therein lies the problem. However well intentioned, its creation speaks tragically to the apparent exclusion of women from the wider category. Criminalizing "femicide" reads like an act of desperation in a world where the bodies of women (and very young girls, even infants) turn up disemboweled, sexually mutilated, beheaded, or with insults carved into their flesh.

But it's also true that the term "femicide" is more than a legal category: it's a label that draws public attention to the singularity of the crime.[41] In her thoughtful treatment of these crimes, Ninna Nyberg Sørensen understands mutilations of the female body as a form of discourse. She agrees that bodily mutilations can be interpreted as "semantic operations permeated with enormous metaphorical force that dehumanises the victims and their bodies."[42] But why would men resort to this convoluted and extreme form of conversation? Why would the mutilation of women's bodies become a form of "governing"— a way of making claims to power? Now it gets interesting, and closely related to our case. Because, it turns out, corpses are an incredibly apt way to argue over the boundaries of sovereign power. How? "On the one hand the corpse is a material object, while on the other hand it is a signifier of wider political, economic, cultural, ideological, and theological endeavors." That is, the corpse is meaningful in all these spheres. Recall Laqueur's comment, earlier in this chapter, about community in relation to the corpse. Communities to some extent define themselves by how they treat corpses. Or, put another way, the state of a corpse is a measure of the community. And the disposal of a corpse says something about a community's politics, economics, culture, theology, and so on. As a result, it can be deeply threatening for the community when someone disrupts the usual way of things, hijacking the treatment of the corpse and its related meanings. Sørensen goes on: "Whereas sovereign practice establishes who is disposable and who is not, the power to dehumanise the disposable lies in the power to re-duce bodies to undignified trunks of flesh."[43]

So to dehumanize a body—to make it an un-person by chopping it up with malice—is to exercise a claim to power in all of the spheres in which a corpse is meaningful.[44] Here's where it's important to distinguish this line of thinking from the Freudian line of thinking. Because according to people who look at femicide, these acts of violence "are not the work of deviant individuals, the mentally ill or other social anomalies." Perpetrators work together, are quite sane by ordinary mea-sures, and operate with a shared "gender imaginary." The act of violence is "directed towards the annihilation of the victim's will with the purpose of denying her control over her body, and is as such an allegorical example of a sovereign practice."[45] Through these actions, the perpetrators play at sovereigns. At the very least, they display their power to dehumanize.

This strand of interpretation—corpse mutilation as a claim to political power, an act of misogyny, a form of sexual terrorism—is convincing to me. And though it pertains to the present, there are elements of it that ring true for the year 1800. But we are still trying to understand how these events would have been understood by contemporaries, and it's certain that Esparragosa, the fiscal, and the clerics would not have inter-preted "sexual crime" in this way. With some of our own ideas about "sexual crimes" aired out, let's try to find our way back to their moment.

It requires taking a deeper dive into the connection be-tween sex and death. Remember the anatomical Venuses? Death agony? Ecstasy and intestines? We're headed back in that di-rection.

First, let's clarify where we stand in the twenty-first cen-tury. Death is not beautiful. And death is definitely not sexy.

Death is wretched and disempowering and too often unfair. It can be laden with pain and bodily fluids. What could possibly be sexy about it?

But the moment the words are out, they become problematic. Sex is no stranger to bodily fluids. Love, it must be admitted, can also be wretched, disempowering, painful, and too often unfair. It can also be tender and humbling and profound. Just like death. So why do we reject the connection so vigorously?

We reject the connection because we have practiced, through a thousand gestures and cultural habits, seeing sex and death as unrelated. But we haven't always, and it takes only a slight stretch of the imagination to see that the connections are there. "The omnipotence of nature," writes Philippe Ariès, in his renowned cultural history of death, "asserts itself in two areas: sex and death." This observation forms the foundation for Ariès's thesis about how we changed our minds regarding death. To oversimplify his complex and subtly illustrated thesis, sex and death were strangers in the European imagination until the end of the Middle Ages. (He claims this goes beyond Europe, though his evidence is largely drawn from there.) But after the sixteenth century, "love and death came closer together, until by the end of the eighteenth century they formed a veritable corpus of macabre eroticism."[46]

A veritable corpus! He's talking, for example, about how religious paintings change, so that scenes depicting death as "chaste" or "serene" in the Middle Ages depict it with violence and eroticism in the sixteenth century. He describes a 1517 painting by Niklaus Manuel-Deutsch in which death, a rotting skeleton, takes a young woman by force: "He violates her, he plunges his hand into her vagina. Death is no longer the instrument of necessity but is driven by a desire for pleasure;

death has become sensuality."[47] And, what do you know, he mentions our friend Saint Agatha, in a seventeenth-century painting by Cavallino, which shows her "plunged into an ecstasy that is both amorous and mystical. Swooning with pleasure, she holds her hands over a bleeding bosom from which her breasts have been severed."[48] *Pleasure?* How? She feels pleasure because "the little death of sexual pleasure is confounded with the final death of the body."

And then Ariès tells us that the corpse itself becomes an object of desire. In both literature and art, corpses or near corpses—bodies that seem dead—are swooned over, made love to, and held up to the viewer as paragons of erotic beauty.[49] Writing of necrophilia in the eighteenth century, Ariès says that by this period the hesitant suggestions of earlier centuries had become overt and unfettered declarations: "The first signs of death will no longer inspire horror and flight, but love and desire." Indeed, in one example after another, "the dead body and the beautiful victim" are presented so that they arouse the emotions of the reader, the viewer.[50] Which brings us to the Marquis de Sade, who in this context begins to seem less like an aberration and more like a man excessively addicted to the typical pleasures of his day. Sade's characters end up in churchyards after dark and simply can't contain themselves in the presence of beautiful corpses. Sade claimed that he knew of men in real life who bought corpses for their own nonmedical purposes. Ariès cites at least one piece of supporting evidence from 1781, a complaint that "certain persons . . . also steal dead bodies from cemeteries and commit on them everything that impiety and debauchery might inspire."[51]

The dead body and the beautiful victim. Victims of violence, in some cases. But there are also other victims. Of disease. Of punishment. Of neglect. Think back a few chapters to the words of Dr. Flores, the man who made the anatomical wax models in Guatemala: he desperately wanted to get his hands on the "beautiful husband-poisoner" who was about to be hanged and would make such a perfect subject for dissection. What is he describing? A dead body, a beautiful victim.

These are dark waters. I'm not denying it. But I think these dark waters were more familiar to people in 1800 in Guatemala than they are to us. They had not yet acquired the air of taboo that hovered over them (as Ariès also points out) in the later nineteenth and twentieth centuries. The actions taken by the perpetrator were surely disrespectful, inconvenient, and audacious. Sade's contemporaries in France didn't just roll their eyes at the treatment of newly buried bodies; they considered such acts impious and debauched. Similarly, Guatemalans could view these actions as distasteful, even horrid, but nonetheless familiar.

Spanish Americans, Guatemalans included, were accustomed to thinking about sexuality as something that could easily veer into the unnatural. Indeed, this category was capacious. For centuries, ecclesiastical (and sometimes civil) authorities had prosecuted crimes against nature—sodomy, bestiality, masturbation, and "unnatural" sexual positions, along with crimes that "bordered on the unnatural, such as incest, solicitation in the confessional, sex with the Devil, abortion and infanticide, erotic desecration of holy images, and suicide." (Perhaps even we, enlightened as we are, can agree that sex with the Devil is a bit beyond the pale.) The fact of these crimes belies the slipperiness of the categories "natural" and "unnatural." Sure, these seem pretty clear-cut, in the sense that "natural" sex was understood to be about a single, legitimate purpose—procreation. But the clarity of this is confounded by how colonial thinkers understood nature itself to create aberrations; in treatises of the period, "nature and the unnatural intimately commingle, in a process that strips these categories of their assumed oppositional values."[52]

This isn't to say that the categories lack meaning, but the choices made—about which behaviors belong where—can be surprising. Consider the case of María Mejicana, which coincidentally took place during July and August 1800 (so the court was hearing this case alongside our case). Mejicana, thirty-five years old, had a long-standing relationship with José Ignacio Flores, a forty-year-old man with whom she had a six-year-old boy. On the night of July 28, Flores sneaked in to the room Mejicana shared with a friend and crept into bed with her. Startled at first, Mejicana came around sufficiently to have carnal relations with her lover. But afterward, she found herself in excruciating pain—both her *partes pudendas* and her face were swollen and covered with blisters. Esparragosa examined her the next day and described in overwhelming detail the blisters ("about to pop") on her vagina and face. What had caused this? A powerful garlic ointment, which Flores had intentionally brought with him and contrived to spread on his lover's genitals.

Here's where our views and the colonial views on deviance diverge. To us, the most troubling elements here are probably the sneaking in at night (was this normal? consensual?) and, of course, the malicious application of an ointment that made Mejicana break out in painful blisters. But what did the colonial court care about? The illicit relationship. In one witness testimony after another, the officials hammered away at the conditions of this illicit "friendship," how long it had been going on, and so on. In the end, the fiscal determined that the garlic maneuver had been *sucio*—dirty—but the injuries did not warrant punishment of any kind. The illicit friendship, on the other hand, earned José two years of public works and María six months' seclusion![53]

This case brings the limits of colonial toleration into relief. There is probably some overlap in the things that cause us to recoil. We are disgusted by the treatment of Padilla's body (and Mejicana's, in a different way), and Guatemalans probably were too. But they had more important categories of transgression. Illicit friendship was a bigger deal than the sadistic use of toxic ointments.[54] In the case of María Rosa Padilla, they were probably less disturbed by a sense of sexual deviance evident in Padilla's mutilation than by the fact that this had happened in a chapel, on sacred ground, to a woman whose place in family memory would now be marred by this act.

The campo santo was not public in the same way that the windowsills were public, but this crime nonetheless reflected upon the city and its inhabitants. It made a mockery of the chapel; it brought attention to the laughable conditions of Esparragosa's dissection corridor; it flaunted the perpetrator's sense of impunity and spit in the eye of the criminal justice system. Where would these crimes stop? Would there be no end?

8

Bourbon Justice
In Which Liberata Returns

*Accumulating an infinite number of precise details about thou-
sands of unknown people who have been invisible for so long can
be a source of such happiness that you can begin to forget that
writing history is actually a different kind of intellectual exercise, one in which fascinated recollection is just not enough. . . .
The trap is nothing more than this: you can become so absorbed
by the archives to the point that you no longer know how to interrogate them.*

—ARLETTE FARGE, *THE ALLURE OF THE ARCHIVES*

On September 13, 1800, Liberata Bejarano was found
in the doorway of a house in La Candelaria, a
neighborhood at the northeast edge of Guatemala
City. She was placed in the *casa de recogidas,* the

women's jail. At the same time, the remaining suspects who had been jailed to investigate her disappearance were released.

I would have expected the court to be interested in where she had been for the previous two and a half months, but if the officials asked her any questions, they don't appear in the record. Nevertheless, we know that Liberata wasn't kept in the casa de recogidas for long. The logbooks of San Juan de Dios show that she was admitted on September 15 with a fever, and she stayed at the hospital for nearly two months. These records also identify her as sixteen years old and "castiza," naming her mother and father, so there can be no doubt that it's the same Liberata Bejarano.

Then we lose sight of her. And the investigation peters out.

On the one hand, the dossier reads like a spectacular failure for Guatemalan justice officials. They were utterly baffled. They never got their man, and not for lack of trying. The fiscal who assessed the case in August of 1800 admitted that "no matter how much I study this case and discuss [with others] the strange events described in it, I cannot find the necessary thread to find my way satisfactorily out of the labyrinth created by these proceedings." This was so, he noted, "despite the exactitude and diligence" of the alcaldes and other officials involved.[1]

On the other hand, maybe this case wasn't such a failure. There's another way to read these long, insistent police proceedings. Sure, they didn't get their man. But the justice system evinced a remarkable degree of creativity and flexibility when confronted with a baffling crime. And, critically, it demonstrated the breadth of its resources: manpower, political muscle, and financial stability. When the alcaldes had a lead, they arrested dozens of people. When the fiscal wished it, he arranged for extra policing. When the city's high-ranking clerics

pushed back, the fiscal effectively put an end to their meddling. When the perpetrator continued to elude the alcaldes,
the fiscal announced a one hundred–peso reward. Four soldiers stood in attendance while the announcement was read
aloud in a public place and posted in writing by an escribano.

So was the Guatemalan police a force to be reckoned
with in 1800? Or not?

As it turns out, this is a loaded question. It's loaded because so
many authors have considered it, looking at different regions
and approaching it from different angles. And it's loaded because the answer to the question connects with other loaded
questions. If the police were at the height of their powers, was
that because of the Bourbon reforms? Can we then say that the
Bourbon reforms were, broadly speaking, effective? If we acknowledge that they were effective, what actual effect did they
have? Did they truly benefit the poor and the general public, as
their proponents claimed? Or were they oppressive? Is it fair
to see them as "top-down" impositions, and, if so, are they an
example of the "enlightened despotism" that writers have observed elsewhere in the eighteenth century? What exactly does
enlightened despotism *mean?* Is it just that the enlightenment
had despotic elements, or was the enlightenment, as a whole,
entirely despotic? It was the eighteenth century, after all, a period known less for the advancement of human rights than for
the advancement of imperial wars, a period in which slavery
was in its heyday, and monarchical powers reached an apogee.
Perhaps the naked pursuit of profit and state control were less
covert and more self-aware than before, but surely a glimmer
of self-awareness is not enough to qualify as enlightenment.
Why do we call it enlightenment anyway?

And so, pulling on this one bit of yarn, we've managed to

unravel the whole sweater. Scholars have debated for years—
in some cases, decades—all of the questions I've raised in the
previous paragraph. They have argued that the reforms were
effective, ineffective, oppressive, retrograde, modernizing, despotic, and enlightened. You may remember from Chapter 3
the passage from Pamela Voekel that compared the reforms
to "social engineering," seeing them as a particularly devious
method of preserving elite status for the elite. Scholars have
belabored this for so long and so energetically because there's
so much at stake for ourselves and for our own moment.

We put a lot of weight on the eighteenth century, or,
more specifically, on the "long" eighteenth century: from the
late seventeenth to the early nineteenth, that period in which
we imagine that enlightenment(s) emerged and something like
modernity began to take shape. And we put so much weight
on it because, for better or worse, we see ourselves as belonging still to that era. Think about the aggressive endeavors in
the past half-century to "modernize" regions seen as techno-
logically challenged, the enduring and unironic calls for "progress," both economic and social.[2] Calls for "progress" might
even come from opposite ends of today's political spectrum,
with one person calling for economic investment in languish-
ing fossil fuel industries while another calls for social change
on transgender rights.

Even the ways in which we resist and criticize these cur-
rents acknowledge our membership in this era. As Bianca
Premo points out in her lucid discussion of "enlightenment"
as concept, twentieth-century scholars forcefully explained
how "the Enlightenment's promotion of universal values were
linked to modern atrocities, including genocide, fascism, im-
perialism, and capitalist underdevelopment."[3] But despite such
critiques, and postmodernism notwithstanding, we have not

really moved on. The criticisms have such heat because they acknowledge that we are still *in it*. And instead of replacing the old comfortable confidence in enlightened thought, critiques have in some cases yielded to surprising vindications. Some scholars have "recovered an Enlightenment that could not be portrayed only as the dark harbinger of imperial inequality or fascist homogenization. Some have found gender inclusive, anti-imperial, and even anti-racist strains of Enlightenment thought."[4] We have a kind of ongoing, overlapping critique and defense; which is only to be expected, since it often feels that in describing the Enlightenment we are describing ourselves.

The way we write about this period is political. That is, motivated and influenced by our political beliefs. It's true for all authors (and arguably for all subjects, too, though I believe this one is a particular flashpoint). It's impossible to read Voekel's argument about social engineering without perceiving a lateral critique of present-day inequalities. An elite that protects itself with social stratification; a state campaign against the poor rather than against poverty; a lower class desperate to fight back with their bodies. She's writing about eighteenth-century Mexico, but it could just as well be about the United States in the 1980s (or now).

Similarly, Bianca Premo's effort to "get closer to something like a 'lived' or 'practiced' Enlightenment among ordinary people, even those who could not read and write," reflects a decades-long commitment among historians to amplify the voices of the underrepresented, to bring them actively into the historical conversation as masters of their own destinies in opposition to what historian E. P. Thompson famously called "the enormous condescension of posterity."[5] (Of course, some scholars of a more recent generation might flinch at Thompson's self-avowed wish to "rescue" the working class from this

fate, seeing such an effort as its own form of condescension.)
Even an author's framing, the choice of focus, is political. Victor Uribe-Uran's study of spousal homicide in the Bourbon era
examines "the 'female condition'—the situation of women living in familial milieus under the relative control of patriarchs
. . . whose power over the household was generally sanctioned
by the dominant legal regime."[6] Without a foundational conviction that legal structures can be patriarchal, itself a political
position, such an interpretation would be inconceivable.

In light of all this, you might wonder: where is the line
between interpretation informed by political position and distortion created by political position? It's hard to say. It's another version of the time-worn problem of subjectivity and
historical analysis. There are those who would argue that there
is *only* distortion. From this point of view, there's nothing to be
gleaned from the documents I've studied that *isn't* skewed by a
reader's perspective (time period, age, gender, political leanings,
and so on). Why did I find it worthwhile to focus on a single
case about the butchering of women's bodies? Surely I wasn't
the first to read it. Something about my own convictions—
the importance of telling stories about obscure people, about
women, about forgotten injuries—led me to choose this case
and frame it as I have. Other scholars, with different convictions, might see this case as an enigmatic but ultimately unin-
formative dead end. (Let's hope they are wrong.)

At the other end of the spectrum are those who shudder
at the very mention of "distortion," sensing in that word the
resurgence of old ghosts: the linguistic turn, debates about
truth and fiction, and ultimately the frustrating conclusion
that historical methods—always subjective somehow—are incapable of telling the truth. From such a perspective, there is
absolutely something to be gleaned from the documents, and

it is the historian's task to use every tool at her disposal (re-gardless of political leanings) to analyze them correctly. It goes without saying, for such a reader, that there is such a thing as "correct."

Most historians fall somewhere in the middle, as do I. It seems delusional to ignore the influence of my cultural mo-ment, my politics, my own background; of course they influ-ence what I see and how I interpret the historical record. Can any historian reasonably deny that? But it seems just as silly to throw up my hands and claim that, because of these in-fluences, I can say nothing of value about the past. To borrow the excellent conception from a colleague who pressed on this question, there is a difference between neutrality and objectiv-ity.[7] I'm certainly not neutral on any of the matters discussed in this book, let alone on the enlightenment and its despo-tisms, but I *can* pursue objectivity. Historians, and the public at large, can agree on the criteria that make things true, the criteria that make things questionable or false. We can agree that claims, whether or not they pose as neutral, cannot be pulled out of thin air. We can agree that evidence matters, and can agree on what evidence consists of. We can agree that some material substantiates a point well, and other material does not. And we can agree that good interpretations do certain things. In my view, they consider as much context as possible; they take leaps, but measured leaps; they rely responsibly on imagination; they take into account the interpreter's starting point and tendencies. It's not a matter of reading "correctly," because I don't think such a paradigm exists, but it's a matter of reading with awareness.

Arlette Farge's apposite reminder, that we cannot simply gape in awe at the documents, we must interrogate them, serves to remind us that how we interrogate matters. I certainly don't

want to be the narrow-minded inquisitor, who asks only leading questions and already has an answer in mind. (Do these
cases prove that Guatemalan women were powerful agents in
their own right who fought back against the system? I know
already the answer and it is "yes"! Do these cases prove that
mixed-race women were woefully oppressed in colonial Guatemala? Obviously, yes!) So I've tried to interrogate with an
open mind, ready to be surprised. I acknowledge that I can't
think of every question, and that my questions are shaped by
my presumptions, but a genuine effort has been made to be
open to possibilities. My approach to loaded questions, you
might say, is to approach armed with more questions.

Here are some of the questions I had in mind as I was
reading one criminal case after another, trying to get a sense
of whether the behavior of the justice system in this case was
typical or not. That is, trying to get a sense of whether (remember that length of yarn) the police were at the height of
their powers. What kinds of crimes were brought to the court?
Who brought them to the court—alcaldes or other officials or
ordinary people? What techniques were used to identify and
investigate crimes? What did people consider "violent" crime,
and did such considerations vary from one group of people
to another? Once the complaint was made, how did the court
respond? Which cases were dropped and which were prosecuted? What kinds of crimes received harsh sentences? What
effect did these proceedings have, collectively, on Guatemalans
and their experience of city life?

There are more, but these are some of the essentials. And
here's what I concluded.

The Guatemalan justice system in 1800 *was* at the height
of its powers. It was not a perfect system, nor a wholly effective
one, even by its own standards. People got away with crimes.

But through the deliberate expansion of police presence and power, the priorities of the criminal justice system were expressed and felt. They made a tangible difference in the texture of urban life. These priorities were as follows: first, to sharply constrain the ability of ordinary Guatemalans to commit public acts of disorder, including but not limited to violence; second, to model and enforce strict codes of behavior conducive to good governance; third, to assert as uncontested the criminal justice system's power to implement these enforcements.

Guatemala was not a police state in the twentieth-century use of the term. The police did not squirrel people away in secret torture chambers. The justice system's control was neither total nor totally repressive. It did not extend to most places within the kingdom. But within the confines of Guatemala City, the colonial government operated as an early modern police state.[8]

By calling Guatemala in 1800 a police state, I'm not arguing that this is a starting point for a twentieth-century police state. So many of the critical institutions transform or fall apart in the nineteenth century that more work would be needed to understand how and whether any connecting threads make their way from one period into the next.[9] Rather, my intention is to highlight how policing in 1800 reflected and in some ways epitomized the transformation envisioned by Bourbon reformers: Guatemala, transformed into a place that was an efficient, orderly, productive, civilized, and modern component of the Spanish state. Policing wasn't just helpful for accomplishing this transformation. Policing was critical to it.

Unpacking the term "police" is a key first step to making this claim.

In 1800, it was a term in transition. During the nineteenth

century and consolidating in the twentieth, it would come to have its familiar meaning: a tool of law enforcement; a civil force, of a local or national government, responsible for crime prevention and detection. But before 1800, and still recognizably in that moment, the term meant something more complex.[10]

Both in English and in Spanish (*policía*), "police" derives from the Greek word *polis*—the polity, or city state, a unit as much political as physical. In the Spanish colonial world, the meanings go beyond this straightforward etymology. As Richard Kagan elucidates in his classic study of Hispanic urban spaces, the notion of *policía* was at the heart of the Spanish colonial project. It was built on the Aristotelian idea of the city as the "locus of civilized life." Cities were meant to be bulwarks against the *un*civilized wilderness: the areas *out there* where lawlessness and barbarism reigned. For this reason, *policía* was about much more than following the law, though lawfulness was an essential component. *Policía* "implied the subordination of individual desires and interests to those of the community, a subordination guaranteed by ordinances and laws. *Policía* in this sense amounted to good government, especially the order, peace, and prosperity that government supposedly engendered." It also had cultural connotations, intertwined with these political meanings. To live with policía was to behave with decorum, to be urbane; in other words, to police *oneself* in the same way that the government policed the community. As Kagan emphasizes, *policía* "thus represented a combination of two concepts: one public, linked to citizenship in an organized polity, the other connected to personal comportment and private life, both inseparable from urban life."[11] Put simply, it was synonymous with being civilized.

These centuries-long meanings, still alive and influential in 1800, cast a somewhat different light on what the Guatemalan police were supposed to be doing. They were not—yet— simply in the business of preventing and detecting crimes. Yes, they were headed in that direction. But they were still understood to be the responsible caretakers for this broader quality of policía—for maintaining civility, urbanity, and good governance.[12] They were responsible for maintaining *moral* order.

This is starkly evident in the guidelines set out in 1791 for the policing of the newly designated Guatemalan barrios. The *Description of Districts and Neighborhoods and Instructions for Their Magistrates,* written by Don Francisco Robledo and approved by both the Guatemalan president and the criminal court, did three striking things at the same time. First, the document asserted the privileges and obligations of new alcaldes de barrios: neighborhood magistrates, or police. Second, it divided the city into neighborhoods, that is, spatial and community units: there would be six cuarteles, or districts, and two barrios, neighborhoods, in each zone.[13] And third, it itemized a whole host of activities that the magistrates were supposed to police in their designated neighborhoods. As Jordana Dym has explored in her study of the dispute surrounding their formation, the alcaldes de barrio were created in Guatemala City because of local demand. This is noteworthy, because there's a temptation to see the alcaldes de barrio as something implemented across Spanish America by central administrators. This may be true—elsewhere. In Guatemala, city elites were alarmed by what they perceived as escalating crime rates and devised their own plan for policing bad behavior.[14] According to longstanding tradition, the city already counted on two *alcaldes ordinarios*—city magistrates. But they wanted more. In fact,

Guatemalan officials initially requested twenty-one alcaldes de barrio, a change that would have resulted in a tenfold increase in the police force. They were granted twelve.[15]

The 1791 publication outlining their duties and powers is a remarkable window onto a moment when the old policía and the new policing converged. The responsibilities of policing, as they would come to be understood in later decades, are fully laid out. Alcaldes were to apprehend criminals suspected of violent or other serious crimes; they were to document the cases (through a scribe) and bring them to the appropriate judge; they were to assist one another, as they could, across neighborhood lines; they were to do this as impersonally as possible, and as representatives of the state. All of these requirements seem foundational to modern policing. But a great number of the enumerated instructions touch upon aspects of life that have more to do with the old notion of policía. Number 21: the alcaldes were responsible for making sure that *vecinos* (neighbors) kept the streets clean, free of "filth, dead animals, or any other thing that might pollute them." Pigs were not allowed to roam free, nor were horses and mules to be tied up at doors and windows. The alcaldes were responsible for ensuring that every person swept his or her sidewalk and cut the grass (seriously!), and that everything was generally kept tidy. Number 31: residents were not permitted to accept servants in their household who did not arrive with a letter of reference, and they were to notify the alcalde whenever a servant was hired or dismissed. Number 33: the alcalde had the right to move someone forcibly to the hospital, even if that person (or his or her parents) did not want to go. As the instructions reasoned, people were irrationally afraid of that noble institution, and would rather die in the misery of their homes than seek the help they clearly needed. The examples go on. A change of residence had to be reported to the alcalde. Lighting candles in the street was forbidden. Needless to say, being drunk and causing a ruckus were absolutely not okay.[16]

As these instructions make evident, the document was as much about providing residents with rules for good behavior (policía) as it was about providing alcaldes a list of duties (policing). The *Description* offers a vision: an argument about how Guatemala City ought to look. And it falls to the alcaldes to make it happen. In this vision, vecinos are orderly and respectful. They live moderately. They do not indulge in drink or gambling or other forms of vice. They keep themselves, their homes, and their city clean. They are productive people. They don't waste themselves or their time in idle pursuits. And, also important, they keep an eye on their neighbors to make sure that they, too, are living according to these guidelines. It's a community effort. The *Description* asserts that where this vision is not being fulfilled in reality, the alcalde is allowed and expected to intervene. If people are "lazy" and do not find a profession in which to engage themselves productively, the alcalde can ask them to find work within two weeks. If they don't oblige, they can be drafted for military service or public work. If people do not live quietly at home, fighting with spouses or parents or children, causing escándalo and offering a "bad example," they must be reported to the alcalde. And if people don't respect the authority of the alcalde, who carries a distinguishing ceremonial baton for the explicit purpose of being respected, they will face criminal charges.[17]

So this is what "policing" meant in 1800. Something that drew on long-standing ideas about civility and order, but that also offered some novel twists on how to enforce it. To my mind, there are three elements of these guidelines that stand out. They are not entirely innovations; more exactly, they are old techniques with new applications or new resources. And their implementation resulted in a tangibly different atmosphere in Guatemala City: a new kind of policing.

First, the use of paper records to monitor vecinos. Second, the heavy reliance on the *rondas,* or neighborhood patrols. Third, the enhanced bureaucratic method of finding suspects.[18]

Let's consider these in turn.

Monitoring. The 1791 *Description* outlined carefully how each magistrate would keep track of what occurred in his neighborhood. Below, an abbreviated translation of the most relevant clauses:

> 9. Each Neighborhood Magistrate will receive a notebook, to serve as a logbook, bound in fine leather and with 200 pages. The pages will be common paper, numbered and with the neighborhood escribano's rubric. And on these pages he will make note of cases that come up, complaints that are made, and the measures taken. With this notebook he will report every month to the Chief of the District . . .
>
> 10. At the end of his year of service, the Magistrate will hand over his logbook to the Chief of his district, so that it may be given to his successor, and he will do the same when the notebook is completed, so that it may be placed in the Archive . . .
>
> 11. These logbooks will be taken as evidence [*han de hacer fé*]; the Neighborhood Magistrate should use them in writing reports and testifying . . .
>
> 12. The Magistrate will form in his neighborhood a *Padrón* (census) of all the neighbors and residents,

making note of the names and *estado* of their wives,
children, servants or dependents, the age of each,
their sex, their employment, their profession and
if they practice it, specifying the street or block
where they live. The *Padrón* will be located in the
logbook with a space four fingers wide in the margin and with ten or twelve blank pages at the end.
This will be passed to the Chief of the District, who
will make a comprehensive census based on all the
neighborhoods, and this will in turn be given to
the President, so that he has a general report on the
whole City.[19]

Paper was not a new technology in 1800. Nor was the use
of a census new. (It had been used for centuries as a way of
collecting tribute taxes.) But the use of a logbook to combine
census data with observations of behavior, a logbook that would
be taken as legal fact and live in the archive (as evidence) and
circulate to higher authorities? This was new to Guatemala
City. As the instructions go on to detail, these were the logbooks that would hold all the magistrate's notes on who had a
new maid, who was gambling, who had not been working, and
who was fighting with his parents.

These are the logbooks I consulted when I was looking
for Manuela Trujillo, and they can be quite thorough, giving
an immediate snapshot of a family's situation. The 1796 padrón for the neighborhood of La Habana details that in number 44 of block 8 lived Bartolo Herrarte, a castizo tailor, fifty
years old, married to the fifty-year-old mestiza María Melchora
Azeytuno, and their son—Don Manuel José Herrarte, a single,
twenty-five-year-old scribe. Folded into the entry is a story of
upward mobility, for the son has a "Don" and a writing profes-

sion. Compare it with the portrait of number 50 on the same block, where Paubino Rubayo, a thirty-eight-year-old mulato coach driver, lived with his large family: his wife, Ygnacia Obando, a thirty-six-year-old mulata; Ana Josefa, eighteen and *soltera;* Ana Josefa, seven and a *doncella;* Miguel José, eighteen; Venancio, ten; and Dolores, four. With all its attendant unfairness and sexism, the *soltera* even gives us (and the magistrate who inscribed it) an immediate gauge of social standing: only young women who were chaste could claim doncella status, whereas *soltera* meant unmarried and no longer chaste. And, of course, a young woman's sexual status worked indirectly to place her family's status.

Given the broad range of perceived misbehaviors and the broad discretion of the magistrate, it is no surprise that the newly appointed alcaldes de barrio used these monitoring practices in ways that resulted in many more inquiries into the doings of city dwellers and, ultimately, many more arrests. The notebook and its intended demographic data imply the right to know the background, status, location, and business of every resident, even if they could not guarantee the feasibility of acquiring this knowledge. And the magistrates used their privileges to stop and ask people their business with frequency after 1791. In many cases, the mere suggestion of something being off was enough to trigger the magistrate to action.

Consider the intriguing case of José María Juárez and Vicenta García, who were stopped in 1803 by the magistrate of El Perú (where much of our action took place), Don Antonio Cesar. It's unclear what, exactly, caught the magistrate's eye, but he approached the pair and asked them to explain themselves. Both Juárez and his wife, García, were dressed as men. Cesar demanded to know who they were and where they lived and why García was dressed like a man. Juárez explained repeatedly (first to the magistrate and then in jail, several times), that they had been walking through a dangerous neighborhood, and Juárez had worried about his wife's safety. He had dressed her in his own clothes as a means of protecting her, of deflecting the possible attention of rowdy men in the street. Cesar was not convinced. He didn't like the explanation, and he wasn't sure that they were really married. He thought they might be involved in something shady, like making *pulque*. Part of the problem was that they were from Ciudad Vieja, a town on the edges of the old capital, and for that reason were unfamiliar to the magistrate in his own neighborhood. The couple was finally released, for it was proven that they were who they claimed to be, but they nonetheless spent more than two weeks in jail on account of the magistrate's suspicion.[20]

The magistrate's ability to monitor the population was made easier not only by the paper technologies he employed—the logbook and the related legal tools—but also by the rondas established in 1791: neighborhood watch patrols. The patrols were described this way in the instructions:

> 50. It will be their particular duty to patrol the Neighborhoods of their District, on those days and hours that they consider appropriate. . . . For this purpose the patrol will be formed by district [not by neighborhood], and if the [officials] are too few they will call upon four or six vecinos to accompany them. No one shall be permitted to refuse this duty, unless he is legitimately incapable of fulfilling it, and in order not to cause an undue burden, the duty will rotate among vecinos, so that those who serve one week will not do so again until others have done so.

These patrols had a notable effect on daily life in the city, and especially on night life. It was Don Antonio Cesar's patrol that picked up the suspicious Juárez and García. And patrols like it went out nightly, pacing the streets and looking for trouble-makers.

"Trouble" took many different forms, as the 1791 *Description* anticipated. The city in darkness was an auditory landscape, and often the first signs of trouble were screams or voices raised in anger. Sometimes, a witnessing vecino would be out on the street, looking for the patrol and calling for it to approach. In one 1791 case, the patrol was out at night and heard a commotion. As they drew near, they were accosted by a man who raced through on horseback, waving a sword. One of the officials of the patrol responded with his own sword. The man got away, but when they reached the site of the initial "escándalo," they found a crowd of men, one of them wounded. To their frustration, they were unable to learn anything more about the man on horseback, who went by "Garnica."[21]

At other times, "trouble" took a more mundane guise, as it did in an 1803 case against José Domingo González and Susana Espinosa. The patrol had come across them walking together at nine in the evening, and they were placed in jail on suspicion of being unmarried. It was true. They were soon to be married, but not yet, and errands had kept Espinosa out late at night (as she claimed) before González arrived to walk her home. They were released, but only on the condition that they fulfill the marriage immediately. González paid four pesos and two reales in court fees after he and his fiancée were released from jail.[22]

As this case and others suggest, sometimes it looks very much as though the patrol was looking for trouble. Maybe even *making* trouble.

Heading out for their patrol one evening in August 1804, an alcalde and an escribano heard a ruckus at the home of Micaela Vivar. They arrived, found the door closed, and demanded entry. They found Vivar in the company of four men, all of whom were drunk. Vivar was also drunk and, according to the report, scantily clad—*casi desnuda*. The two officials proceeded to forcibly drag Vivar out into the street, which, not surprisingly, provoked her to shout insults and obscenities. The officials considered her so unruly that they tied her up. Vivar, for her part, responded by calling the magistrate a "cochino alcagüete amancebado." Translated literally, a cheating pig and a pimp; rendered closer to its current value, a fucking bastard.

The magistrate was not pleased. Vivar was placed in the women's prison, and the four men were jailed as well. But what were the charges? Strikingly, the criminal case that followed was not about anything that occurred inside the house before the patrol's arrival. Instead, the criminal case revolved around the violent insults "suffered" by the magistrate during his confrontation with Vivar and the four men. The case proceeded swiftly. The four men, found guilty of nothing more than drunkenness, were punished lightly. Vivar, on the other hand, was sentenced to six months seclusion and advised "severely that in future she should treat magistrates with the accommodation and respect that they deserve."[23]

There are many interesting elements to this case. A first, painfully obvious, is the gender dynamic between Vivar and the magistrate. Cases of insults were not uncommon (there were many in this late colonial period), and officials were quick to arrest people of all kinds who did not show them the proper respect. But in this case it's hard to ignore the power imbalance between Vivar—barely clothed, tied up, and dragged out into the street by a pack of men—and the magistrate—clothed, bearing a weapon, and surrounded by backup. Vivar's only weapons were her words, and she knew it. After calling him a pimp, she screamed, "Tomorrow I'll prove it to you." To me, that sounds like an ominous prediction of what will happen to her in jail. Am I reading too much into her bitter insult? Maybe. Either way, the encounter and the sentence provide a clear reminder of how women deemed indecent fared against the criminal justice system.

A second point of interest is how Vivar's case shines a light on the issue of privacy—or lack thereof. I've said that the "police state," as I'm imagining it in 1800, was not like twentieth-century police states, and I do think that the ornate invasions of everyday privacy typical of recent police states were not enacted in Guatemala in 1800. But that's not necessarily because privacy was respected. It's because "privacy" didn't look the way we imagine it. It was a gray area, ill-defined and ill-articulated, something more like "nonpublic" than strictly "private." It was also variable, in the sense that some people were understood to deserve greater respect for their persons and space than others. The ambiguity about privacy is nowhere more evident than in the 1791 instructions on domestic disputes, which state the following:

> 29. Magistrates will know of domestic disputes among spouses, parents, children, servants, slaves, and vecinos, mediating these amicably, even when the people in question have a privileged *fuero* [legal status]. And if mediation is not enough, the case shall be referred to the court . . .
>
> 30. Without intruding [*mesclarse*] on the internal governance of the Home, the magistrates will attend

> to disputes in their neighborhoods, if they come to
> his attention by chance or if they have been made
> public through scandal and bad example. He will
> urge the head of the family to remedy the situation
> and, if this is insufficient, legal recourse will be taken.

On the one hand, clause §30 recognizes that the "Home"
must have its internal governance. And if disputes sometimes
are made "public," that must mean they are sometimes *not*
made public. But on the other hand, the right to know and,
ultimately, intervene is clearly established in the preceding
clause. This seeming contradiction evidences what Victor
Uribe-Uran has called the "organizing fiction" of the public/
domestic divide.[24] That is, historians look for this divide in the
past because we understand it to exist now; but in doing so, we
risk interpreting through anachronism. In Guatemala City of
1800, some places were clearly more public than others: the
cathedral plaza was more public than the bedroom. But "the
world of the home was in reality closely linked to the world of
the street," as Uribe-Uran writes of the Spanish Atlantic more
broadly. It would seem that the real distinction was not between private and public but between *secret* and public. A thing
done at home became public the moment it was known. Notice
the line in §30 about disputes that "come to [the magistrate's]
attention by chance." If a thing was known, it was fair game.
   Perhaps the right way to think about "public" is not as
a dichotomy but as a quality on a spectrum, similar to and
tracking closely with "escándalo."[25] Some behaviors could cause
almost no escándalo at all—done in secret, at home, and especially if they were trivial. Maybe a little blasphemous outburst
when you hit your thumb with a hammer. Surely not so bad,
and not public. But some actions could cause greater escán-

dalo, even inside the home. If, for example, a spousal argument got loud, and the neighbors could hear—more public.
And even worse escándalo could be caused when someone did
something big and attention-grabbing and intentional in a
very trafficked place. Like insulting a magistrate in front of
his patrol. Or brandishing weapons in a drunken street brawl.
Or, say, I don't know—leaving severed body parts lying around.
Extremely public. If we think of "public" as something on a
spectrum, the magistrate was already intervening in something rather public when he banged on Vivar's door. She was
causing a disturbance. The fact that she made it more public
by getting louder and hurling insults was just one more count
against her.

    Nevertheless, and related, a third interesting aspect of the
Vivar case is that—to our eyes—it seems such a clear instance
of overreaction. Could we even say police brutality? I've been
alert to the possibility as I've read these criminal cases. There
are instances, but it's hard to see patterns. This may very well
be because of who is generating the cases (magistrates) and who
is writing down the testimony (escribanos). If they wanted to,
they could hide almost anything. Yet given a magistrate's willingness to tie up a near-naked woman after dragging her from
her house, and given his willingness to testify about it in court,
I rather suspect that officials in general felt that they had little
to hide. If behavior of this kind didn't have to be concealed, what
would?[26] It seems more likely to me that where "brutality"—as
we would see it—occurred, it was omitted because it seemed
unimportant. When we do see brutality documented, it's reported as a matter of course, and always in the context of explaining a series of events related to the misdeeds of the
accused.

    So, for example, when the prison warden Don Antonio

Sánchez was called to the women's prison to respond to a "riot"—a fight between two women—he immediately applied his whip to the women in question. One of them responded with florid insults. Enraged, Sánchez applied the whip more liberally to every woman within reach. The only reason we know of these events at all is that one of the women, Manuela Agatona, a prisoner who seems to have had some greater freedoms and administrative responsibilities, complained of being lumped together with the others. She had been the one to call the warden in the first place, and then she was cruelly whipped for her trouble![27]

In another instance, when Don Manuel Sánchez and his patrol apprehended Manuel Silvestre Rodríguez in 1800, Sánchez reported that Rodríguez had launched into heated insults and "obliged me to hit him [*hechar la mano*] but his imprudent mother and daughter threw themselves upon me, pulling me by the hair and giving voice to such injuries against me that . . . I gave one of them a shove that threw her to the ground." While he fought the two women, the members of his patrol tied up Rodríguez, and they took him to jail. Later, reported Sánchez, the young man's father came to Sánchez's house at ten in the evening, "insulting me with great escándalo to which the entire neighborhood was witness . . . for which I had him tied up in my own living room and taken to jail."[28] If any sense of transgression is observed in these descriptions, it's clearly the sense of injury suffered by Sánchez—the insults—and not the injury of being shoved and tied up by an official. These actions were reported by Sánchez as the necessary actions taken in his own defense, in the apprehension of such unruly characters.

We get these details only when people pushed back, and such instances are surprisingly rare. That's probably because people knew that resisting arrest, as Vivar and Rodríguez did, could result in a stiff sentence. It took daring and confidence to stand up to the patrol, as is evident in a fascinating case from 1800. Tensions must have been high, because the confrontation occurred on July 20 in the neighborhood of San Juan de Dios—right in the middle of our mutilations case. Nearing the Laguna de San Francisco (bottom right of Figure 29 in Chapter 6) at 8:30 P.M., the patrol approached a group of six or seven men who were gathered there, drinking and talking. They were told to go home. The patrol continued on its way, but it observed that two of the men were especially drunk, and that one of these, a black man, was carrying an unsheathed sword. (Yes, the gender/race subtext here is hard to miss.) The patrol tried to confiscate the sword, and then things got complicated. Another party was going on nearby, so part of the patrol moved off to deal with it while the remaining members tried to arrest the two drunks. They resisted. The black man's hands were bound, and he fought back, causing "grande escándalo" and threatening the escribano's life. He protested the entire way as he was dragged to the jail, shouting out provocations and resisting physically. Two soldiers had to help in order to get him into the jail.

In the proceedings that follow, we get some rare insights into the makeup of a patrol. Each of its members testified in the case to support the accusations against José Justo Lima, a thirty-three-year-old free mulato, who strenuously argued against charges of misconduct and rallied the supporting testimony of a high-ranking español. The members of the patrol all said that Lima fought back, insulted the officials, and resisted arrest. Through their depositions, we learn that the patrol consisted of eight men. The oldest one was thirty. Most were in their early twenties. Three were Indios. All but one, including the magistrate, were illiterate and could not sign their depositions. Lima—older, literate, and a member of a reputable household—might be forgiven for seeing the patrol as a gang of young thugs. They were not far from it.[29]

These were, no doubt, the vecinos mentioned in the 1791 instructions: people recruited by the magistrate to man the patrol. There isn't enough in the case of José Justo Lima to determine how the members of the patrol knew one another. They might have been a close group of friends; they might have had the familiarity of colleagues; they might have been near strangers. Whatever their history, the presence of these unofficial recruits highlights a key feature of Guatemalan policing: the community's role in supporting the work of the magistrate. They were ordinary men—neighbors. But they carried the authority of the ronda.

This is the last "police state–ish" element, and it has to do with how crimes were identified, how suspects were found and tracked. It wasn't just the city magistrates doing the work. The web expanded, relying on secret police and officials in other towns.

In 1799, eight years after the instructions were put in place, city officials lamented how recognizable alcaldes had become. On the one hand, their markers of authority made them visibly respectable, and it could be assumed that their presence deterred crime. On the other hand, their easy recognition made it difficult to catch people who were deliberately concealing their misdeeds. As a result, Guatemalan officials took the astonishing step of authorizing alcaldes to deputize agents of their choosing who would walk the city in plainclothes and arrest people at will. Lamenting in particular that "individuals of the plebeian class of this city continue to carry weapons at every hour," officials determined that these deputized individuals would operate independently of the patrols, and could thereby make arrests without being encumbered by the presence of others. In effect, the law created a secret police of limitless numbers.[30]

Sometimes crimes and criminals spilled beyond the city's limits, and in those cases law enforcement agencies in different regions were expected to collaborate with one another. Previously, such an endeavor would have been laughably difficult to execute, given the impediments of distance and communication, but the improvement of postal schedules and archival practices in the late eighteenth century made it newly possible.[31] Indeed, the police could actually pursue suspects—or people of interest—across long distances. The long-winded case against Josef Gregorio Barrientos (first mentioned in Chapter 5) is a good example. Barrientos injured his wife severely in January 1800 and immediately fled the city. Officials took notice of the crime not only because Josefa Anastasia Tortola, his wife, was four months pregnant and had three other children, but also because she died of her injuries in the San Juan de Dios Hospital.

The magistrate sent notice of Barrientos's flight to Sacatepéquez, Chimaltenango, Sololá, Quezaltenango, and Escuintla, including a detailed physical description: "short, thick-bodied, round-faced, dark-skinned, a sparse and pointy beard like an Indio."[32] The case files show that the notice duly made its rounds, arriving in Antigua on February 19; in Parramos on September 15; in Sololá on September 20; in Quezaltenango on September 25; and in Escuintla on October 12, 1800. He was not found all that year, nor for many years afterward. Not until October 12, 1811, was he apprehended in Guatemala City.

To us, such a long pursuit may seem ordinary; at the time, it was remarkable. Think of the coordination, institutional memory, and administrative logistics required to make it happen: the creation of a document that could describe him to people who had never met him, the development of a mail system that could convey that document widely and rapidly through Guatemala, and the archival coherence that allowed the case to survive in officials' hands for a decade, so that when Barrientos finally reappeared, the accusations written years earlier were there, waiting for him. And, perhaps most important, his arrest required the *engagement* of the criminal justice system: officials had to care enough to put all these pieces on the board, to play the long game. Barrientos was caught by a fairly sophisticated bureaucracy.

Paper is what made it all work. The census data, the logbooks, the legal depositions, the arrest warrants, the police archive, the correspondence among officials. It was the crucial crime-fighting tool of the 1791 reform.

In earlier chapters, I mentioned the incredible increase in the number of criminal cases heard by the Guatemalan secular courts: a few per year in the early 1700s, then more than a hundred per year in the early 1800s. As noted, there must be multiple explanations for this rise, and archival loss is surely a factor. But the amount of paper amassed in the late eighteenth century tells us a clearer story when we focus more closely on the period before and after the 1791 instructions. In the 1780s, there were, on average, 22.5 cases of violent crime per year. In the 1790s, with and after the implementation of the instructions, there were 79.1 cases per year. A 250 percent increase. In the next decade (1800–1809) there were 161 cases per year.

Archival loss might account for missing papers from the seventeenth century, and it might even explain the fewer cases per decade in the early eighteenth. But there's no reason why papers from 1791 would be better preserved than papers from

1789. Indeed, given their priorities, court officials would have been zealously preserving and organizing what documents they could as part of their efforts to keep track of criminals.[33] Whatever they had, they wanted to keep. These three decades tell a clear story of intentional growth; a heightened focus on crime fighting, spelled out explicitly in the instructions to the alcaldes de barrio. The purpose was certainly to combat the perceived increase in crimes. But in relation to violent crime, the purpose was more specific: to limit the ability of the population to engage in public violence and thereby to create a state monopoly over violence.

This observation, which I came to independently based on this collection of criminal cases, resonates with a long line of interpretation. Max Weber famously posited that a state is defined by how it "successfully claims the monopoly of the legitimate use of physical and symbolic violence over a definite territory and over the totality of the corresponding population." As recast here by Pierre Bourdieu, the symbolic violence is important because it "makes us forget" its origins in institutions and instead becomes an unquestioned, natural aspect of experience.[34] It becomes normalized. For Bourdieu, "symbolic violence" means how the dominant class legitimizes and naturalizes the status quo, imposing it on subordinated groups. Others have theorized symbolic violence as a demonstration of power showing "who can get away with what against whom."[35] To give an example for Guatemala in 1800, symbolic violence was manifested in women's and Indians' ineligibility for official positions. It wasn't really questioned by contemporaries—it just *was*.

But physical violence matters, too. Bourdieu credits Norbert Elias, an early-twentieth-century sociologist, with "showing that the state could not have succeeded in progressively establishing its monopoly over violence without dispossessing its domestic competitors of instruments of physical violence and the right to use them."[36] This is one way to read the increase in the number of cases relating to violent crime: not just a wish to make the city safe; rather, an effort to limit the population's ability to act violently, leaving the state as the only body that could legitimately use force. Who was entitled to use force? Certainly magistrates, as we saw previously in the cases against Michaela, Manuel, and José Justo, and other state actors, too. Officials placed people in the stocks and whipped them. On occasion, they performed executions. In prison, as far as I can tell, the use of violence was routine and expected.[37]

The effect of these entitlements was amplified by the growth of the policing corp. As historian Ana Margarita Gómez has demonstrated, Guatemala City was both more policed and more militarized at the end of the colonial period. Increased troops were initially necessitated by the foreign wars, but they were gradually relied upon more for domestic policing. Their duties in transferring the Guatemalan population from Antigua to Nueva Guatemala after the 1773 earthquake segued easily into urban patrolling, so that by the late colonial period troops in urban areas worked hand in hand with officials to monitor and disarm the population.[38]

The most vivid evidence that the state wished to monopolize violence comes from the body of cases around illicit weapons. Remember José Justo Lima's unsheathed sword? His drunkenness might have gone unnoticed had it not been for the sword he was carrying. Nor were civilians allowed to carry short knives that could be easily concealed. The laws prohibiting sharp steel weapons had been around for a while,[39] but once again we see a remarkable increase in enforcement at the end of the colonial period.[40] Until 1780, there's a scant case

31. A tracing of the weapon allegedly used by "Pistonero" in 1800

every few years. Then there's an average of 3.4 cases per year for the 1780s and an average of 12.5 per year for the 1790s. A 260 percent increase.

Fittingly enough, paper plays an important part in the prosecution of these crimes. When confiscated, the knives were *traced* onto the page, as they were in the case of Josef Pantaleón González, aka "Pistonero" (Figure 31).

Pistonero's story would be humorous if its implications weren't so grim. In February 1800, he tried to steal two roosters in the neighborhood of La Habana, and he made the mistake of threatening one of the rooster's owners, Isabel Flores, with a knife. At that point, the whole neighborhood got involved. The thief was chased, the alcalde was called, Pistonero was apprehended, and his misguided adventure came to an

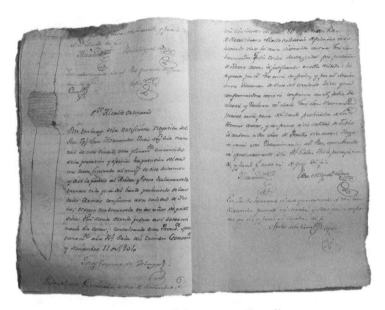

32. A tracing of the weapon allegedly
used by José León Hernández in 1801

abrupt end. It's notable that once Pistonero sobered up, he denied that the knife was his. Nevertheless, he was sentenced to six months of prison in the presidio.[41]

The fascinating case of José León Hernández brings several of these elements together: the power of the ronda, the use of paper to improve surveillance, the reliance on neighbors to help monitor, and the costs of challenging the state's monopoly over instruments of violence. In August 1801, Hernández was apprehended by the patrol, and though he was doing nothing wrong at the time, he was searched. They discovered a knife in the pockets of his pants (Figure 32). Hernández was arrested. At his first interrogation, he protested that he was too drunk to testify. The next time, he admitted that he had been out and about (*paseando*) for a few days in the neighborhood of La Ha-bana. He assumed that he'd been arrested because his mother had given the alcalde a written notice—presumably a physical description—to search for him. Asked what he'd been doing immediately before his arrest, Hernández said he'd been jok-ing around with a friend named Ambrosio. He'd run into him on the street and nabbed the cigarette Ambrosio was smoking. In the ensuing chase, the patrol got hold of him. Confronted in court with the knife, Hernández denied ever having seen it. He went even farther, saying the pants he'd had on that day didn't even have pockets. (This would have been easy to prove or disprove, so it's interesting that he made the claim.) The court didn't believe him. But the judges did care about giving him the appropriate sentence according to his *calidad* (race and class), so the court scribe went to search the parish archives, looking for baptism records that would answer the question of whether Hernández was mestizo or Indian. In the end, he was sentenced to two years of public works.[42]

Hernández doesn't sound like much of a criminal, but he was exactly the kind of man the patrols targeted: wandering around, not doing much of anything, wasting time instead of working. The patrols probably approached many such young men every day, searching for telltale weapons or other pretexts for imprisonment.

Does the use of a drawing in the margin of a case look dif-ferent now than it did when we started this investigation? It does to me. It speaks of how paper and ink could create evidence, of how the judiciary could transform a three-dimensional ob-ject into a two-dimensional legal instrument, of how officials wielded forces of surveillance on and off the page. It speaks to me about the dark magic of documentation and the power of the state.

Epilogue
In Which the Window Is Closed

We cannot bring back to life those whom we find cast ashore in the archives. But this is not a reason to make them suffer a second death. There is only a narrow space in which to develop a story that will neither cancel out nor dissolve these lives, but leave them available so that another day, and elsewhere, another narrative can be built from their enigmatic presence.

—ARLETTE FARGE, *THE ALLURE OF THE ARCHIVES*

For all their instruments of power, the alcaldes could not apprehend every wastrel, find every concealed weapon, document every misdeed, eliminate every threat to their control. They simply couldn't. The goal was too lofty to begin with. It would have been impossible to eradicate public crimes and keep the city perfectly clean and orderly and to establish once and for all that only the authorities had the right to wield force. The window crimes were a reminder of how unattainable these goals were. They pointed out to everyone that the Guatemalan police were fallible. It was still possible to do something really nasty in the public eye and get away with it.

Because that's what they did. Whoever took apart women's bodies in the summer of 1800 did get away with it. It's possible they got away with even more.

There's a note tucked into the middle of the mutilations case, a letter written by alcalde José Mariano Roma:

> In 1800 this court pursued an investigation into who had left a pair of women's breasts on the window of Don Cayetano Díaz, a pair of ears at the same house, a pair of hands on the window of the house diagonal to it, and a pair of human buttocks I know not where. I have before me now a case with similarities to this one, and since they are so similar it seems likely that whoever was a suspect in the last case could again be in this one. As such I need to see the described documents, which I ask you to send me with the greatest possible alacrity, with the understanding that they will be returned to the court. May 7, 1804.

May 1804. Just shy of four years later, it looks like our perpetrator struck again. It's the only mention I've found of these follow-up crimes, and as far as I know there's no legal case surrounding them. Was the case lost? Was it never pursued? Did the crimes just stop?

I don't know. It's frustrating, because cliffhangers aren't as fun in real life as they are in fiction. And it's frustrating because the judiciary's failure is the historian's failure, just as its successes are my successes. When the powers of the state succeeded, the crime was documented, and we get to read about it. When the powers of the state failed, a paper was misfiled or lost, or an official never did the paperwork, or the case eluded officials altogether. With those failures, we also lose. We don't get to learn what happened. Herein lies one of the strange contradictions of working with the documents of an overzealous criminal justice system: the more intrusive they were, the more we benefit. The dark magic of documentation is also the magic that enables historians to do what we do. We learn little from lazy alcaldes.

Where the alcaldes have failed, there's some temptation to speculate. Let's be honest—I've been speculating all along. So have you.

Having learned what I have about the demographics of Guatemala City, contemporary conceptions of death and sexuality, patterns of violence against women, the workings of enlightened medicine, the salient iconography of the period, the space of the city, and the balance of power between officials and vecinos, I do have a profile in mind. It seems likely to me that the perpetrator of this crime is a man. More likely younger than older. I imagine someone at the edges of colonial institutions, but not entirely outside of them. Maybe someone who spent time in the hospital as a prisoner. Or someone who worked in the hospital before some relationship soured. Perhaps someone who lost a relative in the San Juan de Dios. Or someone who suffered firsthand the strictures of Bourbon punishment and nurtured a creative vengeance. There must be some combination of engagement and disaffection: enough engagement to care, enough disaffection to lash out with hostility.

But speculation only goes so far, and then I reach a juncture where I'm compelled to either invent or leave the unknown to stand for itself.

I'm not averse to invention, on principle. In my other life, I'm a fiction writer, and I believe without a whisper of doubt that fiction and literature have truths to offer that are inaccessible to history. Moreover, I like conjecture in historical works. I appreciate it when historians go out on a limb. But with this project, I have found myself more bound to the "evidence," such as it is, than I ever imagined I would be. I find that I don't want to make things up about Manuela Trujillo, or Simona Villagrán, or María Rosa Padilla. Why is this? I find myself humbled by the realities of these women's lives. My inventions about them feel like liberties. I am chastened by a sense of respect, and at the same time I'm troubled that a narrative form I believe in so strongly—fiction—is thereby construed in my own thinking as a form of disrespect.

Yet that's how it is. There are details about these people that bring me up short and that forbid me from going further. Remember that Simona Villagrán was in her thirties when she died. Remember that she had an infant who died a couple of weeks before she did. Remember, her sister described Simona as utterly broken after this, succumbing to death with little resistance. And remember that she was survived by another child, a ten-year-old daughter, who gave testimony in the case about the state of her mother's corpse. These are formidable circumstances: brief on the page, excruciating in real life. I feel equal to the task of observing the moment, even trying to imagine the perplexity and grief Simona's daughter must have felt. But I don't care to elaborate it. The shape and limits of that grief, the weight of it, are hers alone.

And the silence matters. It's significant—painfully significant—that we don't know more about these women and their "ordinary" lives. Whether we know about them makes no difference to their importance in their own moment, but knowing or not knowing makes quite a difference for us. The characters who people the past matter to how we see it. It's significant that the most substantial archival record on Simona's life was the result of an energetic police inquiry, and that she left no mark elsewhere. It's significant that I can't find another written word about Manuela Trujillo. It's significant that I can learn a great deal about Doctor Don Narciso Esparragosa, even some about Don Cayetano Díaz, and very little about Liberata Bejarano. It communicates a truth about the conditions of colonial life. To invent their lives would be, somehow, to deny the violence of their erasure.[1] That erasure is genuine; I would not wish to lessen it or, worse, to ignore it. We can look into their lives, catching glimpses through the muddled pane. But we also have to accept that these are only glimpses. And then we draw back, and move on, and the shutters close.

Notes

Introduction

1. AGCA, Signatura A2, Legajo 195, Expediente 3982. 1800. "Se me demostró la ventana donde encontré los pechos de mujer uno sobre otro con la diferencia de que el uno que cubre al otro se halla . . . cortado en redondo pendiente el otro de un pellejo y este solo el circulo de la tetilla, y otro nervio muy corto . . . advirtiendose que este pellejo tiene una mancha renegrida y ambas tetillas en circulo otra mancha cada una en circulo: por cuyas señas parese que el dueño de el se halla embarasado."

2. In Chapter 8 I will discuss the images of weapons used in criminal cases. Apart from this genre of traced weapons, I've seen only a handful of illustrations. One other is by Narciso Esparragosa, a drawing of a fetus (AGCA, Sig. A2, Leg. 173, Exp. 3444); yet another is a drawing of an injured hand (AGCA, Sig. A2, Leg. 191, Exp. 3892).

3. AGCA, Sig. A2, Leg. 195, Exp. 3982. 1800.

4. More about this in Chapter 3, but the example that always comes to mind for me is drawn from Anthony Lane's review of the film *Irreversible*. Lane recounts watching the film in the theater and seeing a man show up a few minutes before and then leave a few minutes after the brutal, nine-minute rape scene for which the movie became infamous. Anthony Lane, "Culture Shocks," *New Yorker,* March 3, 2003, https://www.newyorker.com /magazine/2003/03/10/culture-shocks.

5. For a treatment of political violence that similarly understands violence as language, see Jeremy Adelman, "The Rites of Statehood: Violence and Sovereignty in Spanish America, 1789–1821," *Hispanic American Historical Review* 90, no. 3 (2010): 391–422.

6. These cases include everything from unprocessed complaints to completed cases with convictions. They are drawn from some five thousand documents relating to violent crime in this period between 1500 and 1811, when Guatemalan governance changed. José de Bustamante was appointed captain of Guatemala in 1810, and the removal of King Ferdinand VII during the Peninsular War in Spain began the long, fragmented process for independence. All of the documents for this analysis are held at the Archivo General de Centroamérica (AGCA).

7. While there are trends applicable to Spanish America as a whole, the manifestations of control in Guatemala were decidedly local.

8. An extensive literature exists on not just the drug trade across the Americas but the violence particular to that drug trade. See, for examples of recent scholarly articles: Howard Campbell and Tobin Hansen, "Is Narco-Violence in Mexico Terrorism?" *Bulletin of Latin American Research* 33, no. 2 (2014): 158–73; Howard Campbell, "No End in Sight: Violence in Ciudad Juárez," *NACLA Report on the Americas* 44, no. 3 (2011): 19–22; Angélica Durán-Martínez, "To Kill and Tell? State Power, Criminal Competition, and Drug Violence," *Journal of Conflict Resolution* 59, no. 8 (2015): 1377–1402; Cory Molzahn, Viridiana Ríos, and David A. Shirk, "Drug Violence in Mexico: Data and Analysis through 2011," Trans-Border Institute, University of San Diego, San Diego, 2012.

9. For discussion of the atrocious crime against Cruz, see Mary Jane Treacy, "Killing the Queen: The Display and Disappearance of Rogelia Cruz," *Latin American Literary Review* 29, no. 57 (2001): 40–51; Juan Carlos Vázquez Medeles, "El olvido en la memoria de Rogelia Cruz Martínez," *Tzintzun,* no. 56 (2012): 169–210.

10. The approach I'm taking here is different from but modeled on the work of other scholars. This approach is more deliberately self-conscious: I attempt to "show my work" in a way that departs from the models I'm emulating. Nevertheless, I've taken my guidance and inspiration from several works written in the 1980s and 1990s. Natalie Zemon Davis's classic book, *The Return of Martin Guerre,* was an early eye-opener. Her manner of telling a story while insisting on high standards of scholarly work continues to be a much-imitated ideal. I've also patterned some of my methods on works by Carlo Ginzburg and Richard Kagan, whose *Lucrecia's Dreams* may be the closest to what I'm attempting. All of these are to some degree "microhistories," and while this book isn't, strictly speaking, a true microhistory, it has borrowed liberally from the form. For an excellent discussion of microhistory and what it does, see the introduction to Steven Bednarski, *A Poisoned*

Past: The Life and Times of Margarida de Portu, a Fourteenth-Century Accused Poisoner (Toronto: University of Toronto Press, 2014). See also the nuanced discussion by John Brewer: John Brewer, "Microhistory and the Histories of Everyday Life," *Cultural and Social History* 7, no. 1 (2010): 87–109.

The three works mentioned above are Carlo Ginzburg, *The Cheese and the Worms: The Cosmos of a Sixteenth-Century Miller* (New York: Penguin, 1982); Richard L. Kagan, *Lucrecia's Dreams: Politics and Prophecy in Sixteenth-Century Spain* (Berkeley: University of California Press, 1990); Natalie Zemon Davis, *The Return of Martin Guerre* (Cambridge: Harvard University Press, 1984).

1

Strangers in the Valley

1. The barranco even today carries some of these connotations. Bodies are occasionally dumped there by criminals, despite the settlements and houses that cling to the ravine's steep edges.

2. AGCA, Signatura A2, Legajo 159, Expediente 3128.

3. AGCA, Sig. A1, Leg. 53, Exp. 1340.

4. AGCA, Sig. A2, Leg. 234, Exp. 4986.

5. I've explored some of this Guatemalan archival history in *Distance and Documents at the Spanish Empire's Periphery* (Stanford: Stanford University Press, 2013). Increasingly, historians are paying attention to archives as a historical subject in their own right. This "archival turn," as historians know it, has prompted scholars to think differently about the structures, institutions, and people who house historical sources. Put (over-) simply, the premise of these studies is that archives are not neutral. They don't simply convey information (whatever that is) to the willing researcher. They also select, omit, group, modify, and do much more to these sources, inserting themselves into the nature of the source and what it conveys. Some of the scholarly pieces (besides Arlette Farge's, below) that take up the approach in interesting ways are Antoinette M. Burton, *Archive Stories: Facts, Fictions, and the Writing of History* (Durham, N.C.: Duke University Press, 2005); E. Ketelaar, "Tacit Narratives: The Meanings of Archives," *Archival Science* 1, no. 2 (2001): 131–41; Kirsten Weld, *Paper Cadavers: The Archives of Dictatorship in Guatemala* (Durham, N.C.: Duke University Press, 2014); Carlos Aguirre and Javier Villa-Flores, "Los archivos y la construcción de la verdad histórica en América Latina," *Jahrbuch für Geschichte Lateinamerikas,* no. 46 (2009).

242 Notes to Pages 20–26

For essays that cover a range of approaches and arguments, see: F. X. Blouin and W. G. Rosenberg, *Archives, Documentation, and Institutions of Social Memory: Essays from the Sawyer Seminar* (Ann Arbor: University of Michigan Press, 2007); Francis X. Blouin and William G. Rosenberg, *Processing the Past: Contesting Authority in History and the Archives*, rpt. ed. (2011; New York: Oxford University Press, 2013).

6. Arlette Farge, *The Allure of the Archives*, trans. Thomas Scott-Railton (New Haven: Yale University Press, 2013), 30.

7. Oakah L. Jones, *Guatemala in the Spanish Colonial Period* (Norman: University of Oklahoma Press, 1994), 164.

8. W. George Lovell et al., *"Strange Lands and Different Peoples": Spaniards and Indians in Colonial Guatemala* (Norman: University of Oklahoma Press, 2013), 83. The population climbed and then crested by the end of the eighteenth century. As Catherine Komisaruk has shown, much of this labor influx was female—in particular, for domestic service—skewing the city's population heavily toward women; *Labor and Love in Guatemala: The Eve of Independence* (Stanford: Stanford University Press, 2013). The colonial demography of Guatemala is comparatively well developed in English-language sources, thanks to early work by scholars that laid the groundwork for future studies. Demography has thereby become, for many who focus on colonial Central America, a reliable starting point. See W. George Lovell and Christopher Lutz, *Demography and Empire: A Guide to the Population History of Spanish Central America, 1500–1821*, Dellplain Latin American Studies, no. 33 (Boulder, Colo.: Westview, 1995); Murdo J. MacLeod, *Spanish Central America: A Socioeconomic History, 1520–1720* (Berkeley: University of California Press, 1973); Adriaan C. Van Oss, *Catholic Colonialism: A Parish History of Guatemala, 1524–1821* (Cambridge: Cambridge University Press, 1986); Adriaan C. Van Oss, "La población de América Central hacia 1800," *Anales de la Academia de Geografía e Historia de Guatemala* 55 (1981): 291–312.

9. In colonial Spanish America, the term often used for outsiders and migrants, sometimes overlapping with "foreigners," is *forastero*. The term varies in meaning across time and space, but it does appear in late-colonial Guatemalan documents, and in such cases it is meant to designate a "stranger" who is also an "outsider": someone who is both unfamiliar and understood to be "from elsewhere." For discussions of the term and its meanings in other regions, see Isabel Castro Olañeta et al., "Originarios y forasteros del Sur Andino en el período colonial," *América Latina en la Historia Económica* 23, no. 3 (2016): 37–79; Judith Farberman, "Las márgenes de los pueblos de indios. Agregados, arrendatarios y soldados en el Tucumán colonial. Siglos

XVIII y XIX.," *Nuevo Mundo Mundos Nuevos. Nouveaux mondes mondes nouveaux—Novo Mundo Mundos Novos—New World New Worlds,* November 9, 2009; Raúl Fradkin, "Vecinos, forasteros y extranjeros: las élites locales coloniales y su identidad social (Buenos Aires a Fines de La Era Colonial)," in *El otro en la historia: el extranjero: compilación de trabajos presentados en el VII Congreso Internacional de ALADAA (Asociación Latinoamericana de Estudios Afroasiáticos) México, noviembre de 1992,* ed. Susana Murphy, 123–47 (Buenos Aires: Facultad de Filosofía y Letras, Universidad de Buenos Aires, 1995); Romina Zamora, "Forasteros y migrantes. Un acercamiento a la construcción de la trama social en la ciudad de San Miguel de Tucumán en las últimas décadas coloniales," *Anuario del Instituto de Historia Argentina* 7 (2007): 59–84.

10. For a lively treatment of the preconquest period, see Charles C. Mann, *1491: New Revelations of the Americas before Columbus* (New York: Vintage, 2006).

11. Tellings and retellings of the conquest abound. These two are especially readable: Matthew Restall, *Seven Myths of the Spanish Conquest* (Oxford: Oxford University Press, 2004); Inga Clendinnen, *Ambivalent Conquests: Maya and Spaniard in Yucatan, 1517–1570* (Cambridge: Cambridge University Press, 1989). For Guatemala in particular, see W. George Lovell, *Conquest and Survival in Colonial Guatemala: A Historical Geography of the Cuchumatan Highlands, 1500–1821,* 3rd ed. (Montreal: McGill–Queen's University Press, 2005); Laura E. Matthew, *Memories of Conquest: Becoming Mexicano in Colonial Guatemala* (Chapel Hill: University of North Carolina Press, 2012). Matthew's book describes the legacy of the Mexican conquistadors in Guatemala.

12. Inga Clendinnen, "'Fierce and Unnatural Cruelty': Cortés and the Conquest of Mexico," *Representations,* no. 33 (1991): 72; on Alvarado see, for example, Lovell et al., *"Strange Lands and Different Peoples."*

13. Lovell et al., *"Strange Lands and Different Peoples."*

2
History of Violence

1. Titled either *asesor* or *fiscal,* both legal advisers to the court. For an excellent introduction to these roles and the legal system of Spanish America in which they functioned, see chapter 1 of Matthew C. Mirow, *Latin American Law: A History of Private Law and Institutions in Spanish America* (Austin: University of Texas Press, 2004).

2. "Lo que no tiene duda es, que son de mujer, y que cualquiera que haya sido ver o similarmente ha muerto a mano de unos cruelísimos verdugos"; AGCA, Signatura A2, Legajo 195, Expediente 3982.

3. The literature on violence in Latin America is voluminous. The vast majority of these studies have focused on political violence. There are also several works on social violence—fewer on domestic violence specifically. This holds true for Guatemala as well; while the literature on twentieth-century political violence is enormous, the literature on colonial social violence is scant. Over the past fifty years, the historiography on violence has changed in interesting ways. In the last decades of the twentieth century, social historians focused on patterns of social violence as a way of understanding society, race, and gender. Excellent studies of this kind are still being written. But scholars have also begun to question what "violence" is and how it is constructed, scrutinizing the cultural (and legal) practices that created the category. My approach falls in this last direction, and my reading of criminal cases has been driven by the wish to understand how the very term "violence" was deployed as a category. A foundational assumption of this approach is that all conceptions of violence are constructed culturally, and that ours in the present is therefore not necessarily the same as theirs in the past. A good example is the categorization of verbal insults in colonial Guatemala—attacks clearly classified as violence by contemporaries but understood by us now differently. We come closer to a colonial understanding of violence with our cultural-psychological definitions of "abuse," which do encompass the verbal and emotional in addition to the physical. For groundbreaking examples of social histories of violence, see Gabriel Haslip-Viera, *Crime and Punishment in Late Colonial Mexico City, 1692–1810* (Albuquerque: University of New Mexico Press, 1999); Mary Elizabeth Perry, *Crime and Society in Early Modern Seville* (Hanover, N.H.: University Press of New England, 1980); William B. Taylor, *Drinking, Homicide, and Rebellion in Colonial Mexican Villages* (Stanford: Stanford University Press, 1979).

More recent studies that combine the social-historical approach with others (cultural, political, or legal) include Ana Margarita Gómez and Sajid Alfredo Herrera Mena, *Los rostros de la violencia: Guatemala y El Salvador, siglos XVIII y XIX*, vol. 1 (San Salvador, El Salvador: UCA Editores, 2007); Pablo Piccato, *City of Suspects: Crime in Mexico City, 1900–1931* (Durham, N.C.: Duke University Press, 2001); Scott K. Taylor, *Honor and Violence in Golden Age Spain* (New Haven: Yale University Press, 2008); Victor Uribe-Uran, *Fatal Love: Spousal Killers, Law, and Punishment in the Late Colonial Spanish Atlantic* (Stanford: Stanford University Press, 2016).

I've also learned a great deal from studies focusing on regions beyond

Latin America, particularly Arlette Farge's study of violence in eighteenth-century France. Farge collaborated in other publications with Michel Foucault, whose influential work continues to shape our understanding of crime, criminal justice, violence, and power. Arlette Farge, *Fragile Lives: Violence, Power, and Solidarity in Eighteenth-Century Paris* (Cambridge, Mass.: Harvard University Press, 1993); Michel Foucault, *Discipline and Punish: The Birth of the Prison*, 2nd ed. (New York: Vintage, 1995); Michel Foucault, *Security, Territory, Population: Lectures at the Collège de France, 1977–1978*, ed. Michel Senellart, trans. Graham Burchell (London: Palgrave Macmillan UK, 2009).

4. Victor Uribe-Uran, whose incisive study of spousal homicide in the Spanish Atlantic benefits from the author's expertise in Spanish law, writes this of (spousal) domestic violence: "The law was quite casual in addressing cases of *malos tratos* or *sevicia* (battery). The criminal legislation of the time did not deal specifically or in any detail with the problem. Beyond acknowledging that it was 'unfortunately quite frequent' (*demasiado frecuente, por desgracia*), contemporary legal manuals did not discuss battery, except in passing. In general, this conduct was not subject to automatic prosecution; rather, it was considered a *delito privado* (private crime) and as such required the injured party to file charges"; Uribe-Uran, *Fatal Love*, 66.

5. AGCA, Sig. A2, Leg. 148, Exp. 2774. Some scholars have engaged the ideas of Frantz Fanon to explain how seemingly mundane circumstances give way to "violent explosions" that result in a pattern of "autodestruction." In colonized societies, Fanon argues, structural inequalities create a sense of constant powerlessness that finally erupts in crimes of this nature. This is a compelling approach that continues to find traction in the work of some scholars (looking at both present and past societies). In the case examined here and many others like it, I see something rather different. What appears on the surface as sudden or disproportionate violence is, I would argue, often both gradual and proportionate: court cases capture only the final act of long, drawn out conflicts, giving an illusion of "out-of-nowhere-ness." In a society where the legal system frequently failed to satisfactorily resolve conflicts among people of low class, an avoidance of that system seems both logical and, to a certain degree, constructive. Frantz Fanon, *The Wretched of the Earth* (New York: Grove, 1963).

6. For the relationship between the two, see the classic study by William Taylor on colonial Mexico, *Drinking, Homicide, and Rebellion*. See also these recent studies that focus on alcohol in colonial Mexico: Rebecca Earle, "Indians and Drunkenness in Spanish America," *Past and Present* 222, suppl. no. 9 (2014): 81–99; Daniel Nemser, "'To Avoid This Mixture': Rethinking

Pulque in Colonial Mexico City," *Food and Foodways: History and Culture of Human Nourishment* 19, nos. 1–2 (2011): 98–121.

7. AGCA, Sig. A2, Leg. 146, Exp. 2705.

8. There is no systematic study of homicide in Guatemala City for this period, though the 1999 dissertation by Leonardo Hernández considers a large portion of these cases in conjunction with others. Hernández's thesis is one of several invaluable studies written mostly in the late 1990s and framed around "crime and punishment"; Leonardo Fabricio Hernández, "Implicated Spaces, Daily Struggles: Home and Street Life in Late Colonial Guatemala City, 1750–1824," Ph.D. diss., Brown University, 1999. Perry's study of Seville, Haslip-Viera's study of Mexico, and Farge's study of France offered the kind of big-picture social-historical analysis essential for understanding patterns of crime and homicide. For similar studies farther afield, see Daniel V. Botsman, *Punishment and Power in the Making of Modern Japan* (Princeton: Princeton University Press, 2013); Richard van Dülmen, *Theatre of Horror: Crime and Punishment in Early Modern Germany* (Cambridge: Blackwell, 1990); Nancy Kollmann, *Crime and Punishment in Early Modern Russia* (Cambridge: Cambridge University Press, 2012); F. J. McLynn, *Crime and Punishment in Eighteenth-Century England* (London: Routledge, 1989).

9. AGCA, Sig. A2, Leg. 201, Exp. 4107; AGCA, Sig. A1, Leg. 4364, Exp. 35466; AGCA, Sig. A2, Leg. 189, Exp. 3837.

10. AGCA, Sig. A2, Leg. 159, Exp. 3128.

11. Document loss is worth considering, particularly for the sixteenth and seventeenth centuries. However, record-keeping practices were fairly consistent as of 1750, suggesting that the increase after this date cannot be reasonably ascribed to document loss and destruction. Another consideration worth highlighting is the argument presented by Bianca Premo in her interesting study of civil cases from this same period, *The Enlightenment on Trial: Ordinary Litigants and Colonialism in the Spanish Empire* (New York: Oxford University Press, 2017). Premo finds an animating enlightenment sensibility among litigants of Spanish America, individuals who used the courts for their own purposes, making the dockets swell. This argument holds water for civil cases but not for criminal cases, as considered here. The vast majority of criminal cases in Guatemala were brought to the court not by the injured party but by alcaldes. This is not to say that victims in criminal cases were without agency—a separate question altogether. It is to say that the explanation Premo finds in civil cases cannot effectively explain the surge of criminal cases.

12. Catherine Komisaruk's invaluable studies on women in colonial Guatemala offer a more social-scientific approach to these cases: *Labor and Love*

in *Guatemala: The Eve of Independence* (Stanford: Stanford University Press, 2013); "Rape Narratives, Rape Silences: Sexual Violence and Judicial Testimony in Colonial Guatemala," *Biography* 31, no. 3 (2008): 369–96. Studies on other regions signal similar patterns: Carmen Castañeda García, *Violación, estupro y sexualidad: Nueva Galicia, 1790–1821* (Guadalajara, México: Editorial Hexágono, 1989); Sonya Lipsett-Rivera, "The Intersection of Rape and Marriage in Late-Colonial and Early-National Mexico," *Colonial Latin American Historical Review* 6, no. 4 (1997): 559–90; Lee Michael Penyak, "Criminal Sexuality in Central Mexico, 1750–1850," Ph.D. diss., University of Connecticut, 1993; Nicholas A. Robins, *Of Love and Loathing: Marital Life, Strife, and Intimacy in the Colonial Andes, 1750–1825* (Lincoln: University of Nebraska Press, 2015); Zeb Tortorici, "Sexual Violence, Predatory Masculinity, and Medical Testimony in New Spain," *Osiris* 30, no. 1 (2015): 272–94.

13. AGCA, Sig. A2, Leg. 194, Exp. 3975.

14. AGCA, Sig. A1, Leg. 4273, Exp. 34079.

15. For a discussion of these reforms and related social changes, see Lipsett-Rivera, "Intersection of Rape and Marriage"; Gary M. Miller, "Bourbon Social Engineering: Women and Conditions of Marriage in Eighteenth-Century Venezuela," *The Americas* 46, no. 3 (1990): 261–90; Steinar A. Saether, "Bourbon Absolutism and Marriage Reform in Late Colonial Spanish America," *The Americas* 59, no. 4 (April 2003): 475–509; Patricia Seed, *To Love, Honor, and Obey in Colonial Mexico: Conflicts over Marriage Choice, 1574–1821* (Stanford: Stanford University Press, 1992); Kathryn A. Sloan, *Runaway Daughters: Seduction, Elopement, and Honor in Nineteenth-Century Mexico* (Albuquerque: University of New Mexico Press, 2008).

16. " 'Que como hombre fragil lo había cometido: que nadie estaba libre de ser tentado, ni de una mala hora' y otras de igual significación dirigidas no a negar, ni a modificar el delito, si no a disculparlo con generalidad"; AGCA, Sig. A2, Leg. 197, Exp. 4014.

17. AGCA, Sig. A2, Leg. 188, Exp. 3798. Komisaruk also discusses this case in *Labor and Love in Guatemala*, 137.

18. Catherine Komisaruk further clarifies this (non-) distinction: "Many sexual acts that modern expectations would categorize as rape were not clearly defined as criminal, either in Spanish law or in popular understandings in late colonial Guatemala. There was no word with the meaning equivalent to today's concept of 'rape' (or *violación*). The term *estupro*—defloration—applied only if the woman was assumed to have been virginal before the act in question. Further, 'estupro' did not involve any consideration of whether the woman had consented to have sex; the concept was not concerned with women's right to refuse. In practice, the Guatemalan courts limited criminal

investigation for estupro to cases of victims under age thirteen. For men accused of sexual 'force' against teenage and adult women, early modern Spanish laws distinguished the crimes, prescribing differing punishments, according to the woman's socioeconomic status. The punishments were lesser for sexual assaults on women of low social status"; Komisaruk, *Labor and Love in Guatemala*, 137.

19. Spain, *Novísima recopilacion de las leyes de España: dividida en 12 libros, en que se reforma la recopilacion publicada por el Señor Don Felipe II en el Año 1567, reimpresa últimamente en el de 1775, y se incorporan las pragmáticas, cédulas, decretos, órdenes y resoluciones reales y otras providencias no recopiladas y expedidas hasta el de 1804 / Mandada formar por el Señor Don Carlos IV* (Madrid: Spain, 1804), Libro X, tit. 29. Also cited in AGCA, Sig. A1, Leg. 1536, folio 184, 1801.

20. AGCA, Sig. A2, Leg. 188, Exp. 3798.

21. AGCA, Sig. A2, Leg. 151, Exp. 2855. Note also that this case occurred in 1771, before the 1796 law stating that men should not be "bothered" with arrest in cases of estupro. This allowed the asesor to use the term and still consider a punitive sentence.

22. AGCA, Sig. A2, Leg. 150, Exp. 2820.

23. AGCA, Sig. A2, Leg. 157, Exp. 3078.

24. AGCA, Sig. A2, Leg. 188, Exp. 3804.

25. AGCA, Sig. A2, Leg. 157, Exp. 3804. This case is an excellent (if rare) example of an agentive woman creatively using the legal system for her own purposes. Lucía had clearly hit a wall with repeated attempts to punish her husband's domestic abuse. Now, instead, she exploited the court's increasing strictness on drinking and unemployment, and it worked. See also Bianca Premo, "Before the Law: Women's Petitions in the Eighteenth-Century Spanish Empire," *Comparative Studies in Society and History* 53, no. 2 (2011): 261–89.

26. Even legislation from the period targets acts deemed to cause escándalo, identifying these as primary sources of social disruption. See, for example, legislation from 1766; AGCA, Sig. A1, Leg. 1509, folio 45. The term is also used in criminal cases to describe the transgressions of unruly criminals, for example, AGCA, Sig. A2, Leg. 195, Exp. 3989; Sig. A2, Leg. 168, Exp. 3346; Sig. A2, Leg. 196, Exp. 4009.

27. Jessica Delgado, "Virtuous Women and the Contagion of Sin: Race, Poverty, and Status in Colonial Mexico," in Race and Religion in the Spanish Imperial World, Boston College Conference on the History of Religion, Boston College, Chestnut Hill, Mass., 2012.

28. Uribe-Uran, *Fatal Love*, 66.

3
Iconography

1. AGCA, Signatura A2, Legajo 195, Expediente 3982, 1800.

2. Ibid.

3. One of the most influential works to address the starting point of this genre is Judith R. Walkowitz, *City of Dreadful Delight: Narratives of Sexual Danger in Late-Victorian London* (Chicago: University of Chicago Press, 1992). For a general approach to the issue of violence against women in media, see Karen Boyle, *Media and Violence: Gendering the Debates* (London: SAGE, 2005). There's also a fair amount of writing about this in the mainstream press. A particularly striking intervention in the conversation was the 2018 announcement of a prize dedicated to thrillers that avoid violence against women. Alison Flood, "Prize Launched for Thrillers That Avoid Sexual Violence against Women," *Guardian,* January 26, 2018, http://www.theguardian.com/books/2018/jan/26/staunch-prize-launched-for-thrillers-that-avoid-sexual-violence-against-women.

4. There's some debate as to whether complete hands or only thumbs were cut off. Cortés himself boasts of cutting off hands, though it is hard to imagine that the mutilated messengers would have made it far after such violence. Hernán Cortés, *Letters from Mexico,* trans. and ed. Anthony Pagden (1971; New Haven: Yale University Press, 2001), 61.

5. Bartolome de Las Casas, *A Short Account of the Destruction of the Indies* (London: Penguin Classics, 1999).

6. See Michiel van Groesen, *The Representations of the Overseas World in the De Bry Collection of Voyages (1590–1634)* (Leiden: Brill, 2008).

7. Theodori de Bry, *[Spanish Amputate Natives' Limbs]—JCB Archive of Early American Images,* 1598, 0683-10, John Carter Brown Library.

8. See Gómez's article on the military presence in Guatemala City at the turn of the century: Ana Margarita Gómez and Sajid Alfredo Herrera Mena, *Los Rostros de la Violencia: Guatemala y El Salvador, Siglos XVIII y XIX,* vol. 1 (San Salvador, El Salvador: UCA Editores, 2007).

9. The eminent historians of Spanish America, David Brading and John Lynch, have both described this period as a reconquest. D. A. Brading, *Miners and Merchants in Bourbon Mexico, 1763–1810* (Cambridge: Cambridge University Press, 1971); John Lynch, *The Spanish American Revolutions, 1808–1826* (New York: Norton, 1986).

10. AGCA, Sig. A2, Leg. 189, Exp. 3844.

11. Andrea Smith and Luana Ross, "Introduction: Native Women and State Violence," *Social Justice* 31, no. 4 (2004): 1–7.

12. This genre has received growing scholarly attention in the past two decades. Ilona Katzew's 2004 book offers both a broad overview and incisive analysis. Magali Marie Carrera, *Imagining Identity in New Spain: Race, Lineage, and the Colonial Body in Portraiture and Casta Paintings* (Austin: University of Texas Press, 2003); Carolyn Dean and Dana Leibsohn, "Hybridity and Its Discontents: Considering Visual Culture in Colonial Spanish America," *Colonial Latin American Review* 12, no. 1 (2003): 5–35; Susan Deans-Smith, "Creating the Colonial Subject: Casta Paintings, Collectors, and Critics in Eighteenth-Century Mexico and Spain," *Colonial Latin American Review* 14, no. 2 (2005): 169–204; Evelina Guzauskyte, "Fragmented Borders, Fallen Men, Bestial Women: Violence in the Casta Paintings of Eighteenth-Century New Spain," *Bulletin of Spanish Studies* 86, no. 2 (2009): 175–204; Nasheli Jiménez del Val, "Pinturas de Casta: Mexican Caste Paintings, a Foucauldian Reading," *New Readings* 10 (2009): 1–17; Ilona Katzew, *Casta Painting: Images of Race in Eighteenth-Century Mexico* (New Haven: Yale University Press, 2004); Christa Olson, "Casta Painting and the Rhetorical Body," *Rhetoric Society Quarterly* 39, no. 4 (2009): 307–30.

13. Guatemala was its own place and yet deeply connected to Mexico—politically, culturally, and economically a part of New Spain. For this reason (at least partly) scholars of Central America rely on the rich historiography of Mexico to complement what we know about the isthmus.

14. Carrera, *Imagining Identity in New Spain,* 36–37.

15. In Chapter 5 I discuss the racial "reality," in the form of demographic studies for this period. But it should be noted here that demographic statistics are not categorically different from the paintings. Statistics rely on self-identification, which in the colonial period, as now, relies on both subjective interpretation and cultural constructions. To this extent, statistics and paintings are both racial depictions—both snapshots of mindsets primarily. It should also be noted here that most of the casta paintings were produced in Mexico. Racial categories were similar in Guatemala, though not identical—the category "indio," for example, though used in both Mexico and Guatemala, obviously encompassed (erased?) distinct indigenous ethnic groups.

16. Deans-Smith cites Ken Arnold ("Trade, Travel, and Treasure: Seventeenth-century Artificial Curiosities," in *Transports: Travel, Pleasure, and Imaginative Geography, 1600–1830,* ed. Chloe Chard and Helen Langdon [New Haven: Yale University Press, 1996], 266) on the culture of curiosity. Deans-Smith, "Creating the Colonial Subject," 170. On the culture of curiosity and the pursuit of natural history for this period, see Antonio Barrera-Osorio, *Experiencing Nature: The Spanish American Empire and the Early Scientific Revolution* (Austin: University of Texas Press, 2006); Daniela Bleichmar et al.,

eds., *Science in the Spanish and Portuguese Empires, 1500–1800* (Stanford: Stanford University Press, 2009); D. Bleichmar, "Visible Empire: Scientific Expeditions and Visual Culture in the Hispanic Enlightenment," *Postcolonial Studies* 12, no. 4 (2009): 441–66; Sophie Brockmann, "Sumatran Rice and 'Miracle' Herbs: Local and International Natural Knowledge in Late-Colonial Guatemala," *Colonial Latin American Review* 24, no. 1 (2015): 84–106; James Delbourgo and Nicholas Dew, eds., *Science and Empire in the Atlantic World* (New York: Routledge, 2008); Neil Safier, *Measuring the New World: Enlightenment Science and South America* (Chicago: University of Chicago Press, 2008); Paula De Vos, "Natural History and the Pursuit of Empire in Eighteenth-Century Spain," *Eighteenth-Century Studies* 40, no. 2 (2007): 209–39.

17. Deans-Smith, "Creating the Colonial Subject," 177.

18. Pamela Voekel, "Peeing on the Palace: Bodily Resistance to Bourbon Reforms in Mexico City," *Journal of Historical Sociology* 5, no. 2 (1992): 183. For studies of poverty and social engineering specifically, see also Silvia Marina Arrom, *Containing the Poor: The Mexico City Poor House, 1774–1871* (Durham, N.C.: Duke University Press, 2000); Cynthia E. Milton, *The Many Meanings of Poverty: Colonialism, Social Compacts, and Assistance in Eighteenth-Century Ecuador* (Stanford: Stanford University Press, 2007); Sergio Serulnikov, "Customs and Rules: Bourbon Rationalizing Projects and Social Conflicts in Northern Potosi during the 1770s," *Colonial Latin American Review* 8, no. 2 (1999): 245–74; Sergio Serulnikov, *Subverting Colonial Authority: Challenges to Spanish Rule in Eighteenth-Century Southern Andes* (Durham, N.C.: Duke University Press, 2003).

19. Voekel, "Peeing on the Palace," 184.

20. Ibid., 201.

21. For studies of race in Guatemala, some classic and some recent, see Greg Grandin, *The Blood of Guatemala: A History of Race and Nation,* Latin America Otherwise (Durham, N.C.: Duke University Press, 2000); Lowell Gudmundson and Justin Wolfe, *Blacks and Blackness in Central America: Between Race and Place* (Durham, N.C.: Duke University Press, 2010); Christopher Lutz, *Santiago de Guatemala, 1541–1773: City, Caste, and the Colonial Experience* (Norman: University of Oklahoma Press, 1994); Laura Matthew, "Mexicanos and the Meanings of Ladino in Colonial Guatemala," *Journal of Colonialism and Colonial History* 7, no. 1 (2006); Carol A. Smith and Marilyn M. Moors, eds., *Guatemalan Indians and the State, 1540 to 1988* (Austin: University of Texas Press, 1990).

22. See Aaron Pollack, ed., *La época de las independencias en Centroamérica y Chiapas: procesos políticos y sociales* (Mexico City: Instituto Mora,

2013), in particular the chapters by Sajid Alfredo Herrera Mena ("Representaciones de la soberanía en las ceremonias de juramentación: el reino de Guatemala, 1790–1812," 97–122) and Xiomara Avendaño Rojas ("Los escenarios del poder en 1821: la juramentación del Acta de Independencia en la provincia de Guatemala," 225–50), who emphasize the degree to which visual symbolism was effectively employed (by officials) in Guatemala. Both also highlight how the visual vocabulary referenced the sacred.

The complex symbolism of the breast is both long and current. In the past several years, debates over whether breastfeeding mothers should be obliged to cover up have placed our unease with the breast in the spotlight. On the one hand, the female breast is a ubiquitous sex symbol. On the other hand, healthcare and popular culture frame breastfeeding as natural, empowering (for moms), and healthful. For a history of the breast aimed at general readers, see Marilyn Yalom, *A History of the Breast* (New York: Knopf, 1997). Margaret Miles's beautiful book considers an earlier history: Margaret R. Miles, *A Complex Delight: The Secularization of the Breast, 1350–1750* (Berkeley: University of California Press, 2008). For one study (among many) of breast symbolism during the eighteenth century in Europe, see Simon Richter, *Missing the Breast: Gender, Fantasy, and the Body in the German Enlightenment* (Seattle: University of Washington Press, 2012).

23. I am grateful to William B. Taylor for confirming that Guatemalans in 1800 would have been familiar with Saint Agatha.

24. Liana De Girolami Cheney, "The Cult of Saint Agatha," *Woman's Art Journal* 17, no. 1 (1996): 3–9. For other treatments of Saint Agatha, see Nina Corazzo, "Dismembering the Female Body: The Breast of Saint Agatha," in *Semiotics*, 1995, 321–31; Beth Hodgett, "Mysticism, Martyrdom, and Ecstasy: The Body as Boundary in the Martyrdom of St. Agnes," *Journal of the LUCAS Graduate Conference*, 2017, 48–62; Kirsten Wolf, "The Severed Breast: A Topos in the Legends of Female Virgin Martyr Saints," *Arkiv för Nordisk Filologi* 112 (1997): 96–112.

25. Quoted in Cheney, "The Cult of Saint Agatha."

26. For a starting point on the vast topic of sanctity, death, and the erotic, see part II, chapters 5 and 6 in Georges Bataille, *Erotism: Death and Sensuality* (San Francisco: City Lights Books, 1962). For analysis that is more recent and more specific to this topic, see Louis Cardaillac, "Erotismo y santidad," *Intersticios sociales*, no. 3 (2012): 31; Hodgett, "Mysticism, Martyrdom, and Ecstasy."

27. Martha Easton, "Saint Agatha and the Sanctification of Sexual Violence," *Studies in Iconography* 16 (1994): 83–118.

28. Ibid., 93.

29. The breasts on a plate are themselves a meme, reproduced as pastries in some Italian towns (known as St. Agatha's Nipple or Virgin's Breast cookies) and in contemporary artwork. See, for example, George Stoll, *Untitled (Saint Agatha)*, 2008, sculpture, plaster, cheesecloth, spackle, gesso, alkyd, B72 on painted wooden shelf, 5.5 × 10 × 10 in. (14 × 25.4 × 25.4 cm.), 2008, http://www.artnet.com/artists/george-stoll/untitled-saint-agatha-a-3S6y NaVmEV2jixmKqpbJfg2.

30. J. Andrew McDonald and Brian Stross, "Water Lily and Cosmic Serpent: Equivalent Conduits of the Maya Spirit Realm," *Journal of Ethnobiology* 32, no. 1 (2012): 75.

31. Ibid., 75.

32. Ibid., 101.

33. Jessica Delgado, "Virtuous Women and the Contagion of Sin: Race, Poverty, and Status in Colonial Mexico," in Race and Religion in the Spanish Imperial World, Boston College Conference on the History of Religion, Boston College, Chestnut Hill, Mass., 2012.

34. William B. Taylor, *Theater of a Thousand Wonders: A History of Miraculous Images and Shrines in New Spain* (New York: Cambridge University Press, 2016), 8.

35. Ibid., 9.

36. The hate mail is shocking, but the backlash against the inquisition is not too surprising. Napoleon's invasion of Spain in 1808 resulted in the abolition of the Spanish Inquisition, which the Cortes de Cádiz reiterated in 1813. However, when King Ferdinand was restored to the crown in 1814, he reinstated the inquisition. It went through several further death throes, and was not definitely abolished until 1834. The brief reinstatement provoked strong reactions, as one might imagine, and the documents sent here are part (however extreme) of a broader sentiment. They also reflect—in an exaggerated or distorted way—enlightenment principles that had been by now shaping anti-inquisition thought for decades. For two introductions to the inquisition, one classic and one more recent, see Henry Kamen, *The Spanish Inquisition: A Historical Revision* (New Haven: Yale University Press, 1998); Irene Marsha Silverblatt, *Modern Inquisitions: Peru and the Colonial Origins of the Civilized World* (Durham, N.C.: Duke University Press, 2004).

37. AGCA, Sig. A4, Leg. 1, Exp. 25, 1817.

38. There's an element to both of these—more the severed body parts than the poison pen letters—that resonates with what Stuart Clark and others have described as the Renaissance discourse of inversion and misrule. Clark's focus is on demonology, and he persuasively demonstrates that witches and demons exist in the Renaissance imagination because they are part of a world

in which opposites validate and even necessitate one another. The gruesome inversions that witches indulge in, the world turned upside down, rely upon and assert the goodness of the world right-side up; Stuart Clark, "Inversion, Misrule and the Meaning of Witchcraft," *Past and Present*, no. 87 (1980): 98–127. Here there are echoes of that mindset, that sensibility: these deliberate profanities and inversions gain their meaning from the correctness and sanctity of their opposites. But it's a different moment. Different things are happening in 1800, so while there may be some echoes of this sensibility, I suspect that the mindset here is more like what Robert Darnton writes about in *Poetry and the Police*, which focuses on subversive song and verse in eighteenth-century France. Inversion has its place here, too, but with the intent of creating satire, of showing how the real world is just as hypocritical, twisted, and wrong as the world turned upside down; Robert Darnton, *Poetry and the Police* (Cambridge: Harvard University Press, 2011). Writing of Guatemala specifically, Timothy Hawkins recounts criminal cases against subversives who were, precisely in this period (1808) lampooning the authorities; *José de Bustamante and Central American Independence: Colonial Administration in an Age of Imperial Crisis* (Tuscaloosa: University of Alabama Press, 2004), 51.

4
Enlightened Medicine

1. AGCA, Signatura A2, Legajo 195, Expediente 3982, 1800.

2. The history of medicine in Guatemala and New Spain is a growing field. Early histories, like John Tate Lanning's and those by Guatemalan historians, tend to focus on individuals and institutions. More recent works approach the field thematically, complementing similar studies of other regions. For early histories of particular relevance, see Michael E. Burke, *The Royal College of San Carlos: Surgery and Spanish Medical Reform in the Late Eighteenth Century* (Durham, N.C.: Duke University Press, 1977); Lynda deForest Craig, "Patients and Disease in an Enlightenment Hospital: San Juan de Dios in Guatemala City, 1788–1808," Ph.D. diss., University of Ottawa, 1987; John Tate Lanning, *The Royal Protomedicato: The Regulation of the Medical Professions in the Spanish Empire* (Durham, N.C.: Duke University Press, 1985); John Tate Lanning, *Dr. Narciso Esparragosa y Gallardo* (Caracas: Vargas, 1953); John Tate Lanning, *The Eighteenth-Century Enlightenment in the University of San Carlos de Guatemala* (Ithaca, N.Y.: Cornell University Press, 1956); Ramiro Rivera Álvarez, *Hospital de los hermanos de San*

Juan de Dios (Guatemala: [Ministerio de Salud Publica y Asistencia Social], 1982).

For representative recent studies on Guatemala and Spanish America, see Martha Few, *For All of Humanity: Mesoamerican and Colonial Medicine in Enlightenment Guatemala* (Tucson: University of Arizona Press, 2015); Sherry Lee Fields, *Pestilence and Headcolds: Encountering Illness in Colonial Mexico* (New York: Columbia University Press, 2008); Ryan Amir Kashanipour, "A World of Cures: Magic and Medicine in Colonial Yucatán," Ph.D. diss., University of Arizona, 2012; Paul Ramírez, " 'Like Herod's Massacre': Quarantines, Bourbon Reform, and Popular Protest in Oaxaca's Smallpox Epidemic, 1796–1797," *The Americas* 69, no. 2 (2012): 203–35; Adam Warren, *Medicine and Politics in Colonial Peru: Population Growth and the Bourbon Reforms* (Pittsburgh: University of Pittsburgh Press, 2010); Pablo Fernando Gómez Zuluaga, *Bodies of Encounter: Health, Illness and Death in the Early Modern African-Spanish Caribbean* (Nashville: Vanderbilt University, 2010).

3. Tate Lanning, whose work on the university and enlightenment thinkers in Guatemala was groundbreaking, also wrote the most detailed biographical account of Esparragosa. Lanning, *Dr. Narciso Esparragosa y Gallardo*, 13.

4. Ibid., 24–25.

5. AGCA, Sig. A1, Leg. 2522, Exp. 20062.

6. "The historical evidence shows that men and women in the bottom ranks of society were very much concerned with their social positions and commonly differentiated among themselves on the basis of income, gender, race, occupation, and family status. These differences often served as proxies for honor, arranging both individuals and families of the plebeian class in a hierarchy of presumed merit"; Lyman L. Johnson and Sonya Lipsett-Rivera, *The Faces of Honor: Sex, Shame, and Violence in Colonial Latin America* (Albuquerque: University of New Mexico Press, 1998), 10.

7. William Ian Miller, *Humiliation: And Other Essays on Honor, Social Discomfort, and Violence* (Ithaca, N.Y.: Cornell University Press, 1995), 116.

8. In their collected essays Lyman Johnson and Sonya Lipsett-Rivera consider many aspects of colonial honor; their introduction is an excellent place to start for the Spanish American particulars; Johnson and Lipsett-Rivera, *The Faces of Honor*.

9. Ibid., 3–4.

10. Ibid., 4.

11. Ibid., 6.

12. AGCA, Sig. A1, Leg. 4334, Exp. 34988. For similar cases and further analysis, see Susan Broomhall and Sarah Finn, *Violence and Emotions in*

Early Modern Europe (London: Routledge, 2016); Carolyn Strange, R. B. Cribb, and Christopher E. Forth, eds., *Honour, Violence, and Emotions in History* (London: Bloomsbury Academic, 2014).

13. Fay Bound Alberti, *Medicine, Emotion, and Disease, 1700–1950* (Houndmills, Basingstoke, Hampshire: Palgrave Macmillan, 2006), 2. There is a much larger literature on early modern emotions and medicine (separately, together) in Europe. For some introductory materials on the history of emotions, see Christian Bailey, "The History of Emotions," *Contemporary European History* 25, no. 1 (2016): 163–75; Peter Burke, "Is There a Cultural History of the Emotions?" in *Representing Emotions: New Connections in the Histories of Art, Music and Medicine,* ed. Penelope Gouk and Helen Hills, 35–47 (Aldershot: Ashgate, 2005); Gail Kern Paster, Katherine Rowe, and Mary Floyd-Wilson, eds., *Reading the Early Modern Passions: Essays in the Cultural History of Emotion* (Philadelphia: University of Pennsylvania Press, 2004); Jan Plamper, "The History of Emotions: An Interview with William Reddy, Barbara Rosenwein, and Peter Stearns," *History and Theory* 49, no. 2 (2010): 237–65; Jan Plamper, *The History of Emotions: An Introduction* (Oxford: Oxford University Press, 2015); William M. Reddy, *The Navigation of Feeling: A Framework for the History of Emotions* (Cambridge: Cambridge University Press, 2001); Barbara H. Rosenwein, "Problems and Methods in the History of Emotions," *Passions in Context* 1, no. 1 (2010): 1–32; Monique Scheer, "Are Emotions a Kind of Practice (and Is That What Makes Them Have a History)? A Bourdieuian Approach to Understanding Emotion," *History and Theory* 51, no. 2 (2012): 193–220.

Some of the texts I've found most helpful on emotion and medicine, besides Alberti's above, are Fay Bound Alberti, *Matters of the Heart: History, Medicine, and Emotion* (Oxford: Oxford University Press, 2010); Thomas Dixon, *From Passions to Emotions: The Creation of a Secular Psychological Category* (Cambridge: Cambridge University Press, 2003); Dylan Evans, *Emotion: The Science of Sentiment* (Oxford: Oxford University Press, 2002); Ulinka Rublack, "Fluxes: The Early Modern Body and the Emotions," in *History Workshop Journal* 53, 1 (2002): 1–16.

14. Alberti, *Medicine, Emotion, and Disease,* 2–3.

15. Ibid., 3, quoting Thomas Wright, c. 1561–1623.

16. Ibid., 5.

17. Ibid., 6.

18. Ibid., 12.

19. Martha Few, "'That Monster of Nature': Gender, Sexuality, and the Medicalization of a 'Hermaphrodite' in Late Colonial Guatemala," *Ethnohistory* 54, no. 1 (2007): 159–306.

20. Ibid., 163.

21. Ibid.

22. AGCA, Sig. A1, Leg. 4376, Exp. 35664.

23. For additional consideration of Juana Aguilar's fascinating case, see María Elena Martínez, "Archives, Bodies, and Imagination: The Case of Juana Aguilar and Queer Approaches to History, Sexuality, and Politics," *Radical History Review* 2014, no. 120 (2014): 159–82; Zeb Tortorici, *Sins against Nature: Sex and Archives in Colonial New Spain* (Durham, N.C.: Duke University Press, 2018).

24. Ramírez, "'Like Herod's Massacre,'" 204. For similar disputes in other regions, see João José Reis, *A morte é uma festa: ritos fúnebres e revolta popular no Brasil do século XIX* (São Paulo: Companhia das Letras, 1991); Pamela Voekel, *Alone before God: The Religious Origins of Modernity in Mexico* (Durham, N.C.: Duke University Press, 2002). Adam Warren, "Medicine and the Dead: Conflicts over Burial Reform and Piety in Lima, 1808–1850," *Death and Dying in Colonial Spanish America,* ed. Martina Will de Chaparro and Miruna Achim, 170–201 (Tucson: University of Arizona Press, 2011).

25. Few, *For All of Humanity,* 9.

26. Ibid., 10.

27. AGCA, Sig. A1, Leg. 1865, Exp. 12182.

28. Based on what I've seen of Esparragosa's handwriting elsewhere, it's clear that this log and its entries were dictated to an assistant. The cover page identifies a "practicante Don Román Portillo," who was the likely scribe.

29. AGCA, Sig. A1, Leg. 1865, Exp. 12182.

30. AGCA, Sig. A1, Leg. 53, Exp. 1340.

31. This conflict also occurred in the context of a dispute over whether the hospital should remain in the hands of a religious order or, instead, be handed over to secular administration; Christophe Belaubre, "El proceso de laicización de los hospitales en la capital del reino de Guatemala (XVI–XIX)," *Cambios y Permanencias,* no. 2 (2016): 252–85.

32. Lanning, *Eighteenth-Century Enlightenment,* 272.

33. Ibid., 270.

34. Ibid., 268.

35. For images from the spectacular collection at La Specola in Florence, see Saulo Bambi's photographs in Monika V. Düring and Museo La Specola Florence, *Encyclopaedia Anatomica: A Selection of Anatomic Wax Models* (Cologne: Taschen, 2001).

36. R. Ballestriero, "Anatomical Models and Wax Venuses: Art Masterpieces or Scientific Craft Works?" *Journal of Anatomy* 216, no. 2 (2010): 223–34.

37. Ibid., 231.

38. Two useful investigations of the intertwining of sex and death are Georges Bataille, *Erotism: Death and Sensuality* (San Francisco: City Lights Books, 1962); and Philippe Ariès, *The Hour of Our Death* (New York: Knopf, 1981).

For other treatments (some more academic than others) of the anatomical Venuses, see Joanna Ebenstein and Morbid Anatomy Museum, *The Anatomical Venus: Wax, God, Death, and the Ecstatic* (New York: Distributed Art Publishers, 2016); Rebecca Messbarger, *The Lady Anatomist: The Life and Work of Anna Morandi Manzolini* (Chicago: University of Chicago Press, 2010); and Elizabeth Stephens, "Venus in the Archive: Anatomical Waxworks of the Pregnant Body," *Australian Feminist Studies* 25, no. 64 (2010): 133–45.

5
In Hospital, at Home

1. Brianna Leavitt-Alcántara's dissertation on laywomen in Guatemala devotes a section to "tending the sick" in the home. Brianna Leavitt-Alcántara, "Practicing Faith: Laywomen and Religion in Central America, 1750–1870," Ph.D. diss., University of California, Berkeley, 2009.

2. Ibid., 143. In recent years scholars of medicine have focused increasingly on two related topics: the role of women as health workers, both at home and outside the home; and the process by which early modern medical practices were gradually masculinized over time with the professionalization of modern medicine. There is more work on Europe than on Latin America to date. For two entry points to these topics, see Montserrat Cabré, "Women or Healers?: Household Practices and the Categories of Health Care in Late Medieval Iberia," *Bulletin of the History of Medicine* 82, no. 1 (2008): 18–51; Mary E. Fissell, "Introduction: Women, Health, and Healing in Early Modern Europe," *Bulletin of the History of Medicine* 82, no. 1 (2008): 1–17.

3. Leavitt-Alcántara, "Practicing Faith," 144.

4. For description and analysis of the case, see Xavier A. López y de la Peña, "The First Mastectomy for Breast Cancer in America: Aguascalientes, México, 1777," *Gaceta Médica de México* 150, no. 5 (2014): 470–77; L. Pon and J. F. Amatruda, "Breast Cancer between Faith and Medicine: The Peres Maldonado Ex-Voto," *Medical Humanities* 36, no. 2 (2010): 112–14; Claire Voon, "The 18th-Century Devotional Painting That Documents a Brutal Mastectomy," *Hyperallergic*, October 28, 2016.

5. AGCA, Signatura A2, Legajo 207, Expediente 4257.

6. Xavier López y de la Peña speculates the same. López y de la Peña, "First Mastectomy," 473.

7. Pon and Amatruda, "Breast Cancer between Faith and Medicine," 112.

8. Ibid., 113. Pon and Amatruda describe the importance of the Virgin of San Juan de los Lagos, to whom ex-votos are still dedicated. "The cult image in the church of Our Lady of San Juan de los Lagos, some 40 miles south of Aguascalientes, was made with a pre-Spanish medium known as 'tatzinqueni,' a mixture of corn pith and glue from the bulbs of a local orchid." They identify the remaining figures as follows: "a small standing figure of St. Anthony of Padua in a brown Franciscan robe, holding the Christ child, and two smaller holy images, one a seated figurine in a high-backed cathedra, and the other a half-length image in an ornate frame. A two-dimensional image of a white-bearded Jesuit in a black biretta, possibly Ignatius of Loyola, Francis Xavier, Aloysius Gonzaga or a conflation of these saints . . . hangs over the open doorway, a decade after the order's expulsion from Mexico."

9. William B. Taylor, *Magistrates of the Sacred: Priests and Parishioners in Eighteenth-Century Mexico* (Stanford: Stanford University Press, 1996), 244.

10. William B. Taylor, *Theater of a Thousand Wonders: A History of Miraculous Images and Shrines in New Spain* (Cambridge: Cambridge University Press, 2016), 97.

11. Ibid, 124.

12. AGCA, Sig. A1, Leg. 1865, Exp. 12181, 1800–1801.

13. For additional studies of the San Juan de Dios, see Christophe Belaubre, "El proceso de laicización de los hospitales en la capital del reino de Guatemala (XVI–XIX)," *Cambios y Permanencias*, no. 2 (2016): 252–85; Ramiro Rivera Álvarez, *Hospital de los hermanos de San Juan de Dios* (Guatemala: [Ministerio de Salud Publica y Asistencia Social], 1982).

14. Oakah L. Jones, *Guatemala in the Spanish Colonial Period* (Norman: University of Oklahoma Press, 1994), 165. Jones cites Ralph Lee Woodward, *Central America: A Nation Divided,* 2nd ed. (New York: Oxford University Press, 1985), 79.

15. Christopher Lutz, *Santiago de Guatemala, 1541–1773: City, Caste, and the Colonial Experience* (Norman: University of Oklahoma Press, 1997), 95.

16. See Catherine Komisaruk's thorough discussion of these shifts in chapter 3 of *Labor and Love in Guatemala: The Eve of Independence* (Stanford: Stanford University Press, 2013).

17. Lutz, *Santiago de Guatemala, 95.*

18. Jones, *Guatemala in the Spanish Colonial Period*, 171.

19. Lynda deForest Craig, "Patients and Disease in an Enlightenment Hospital: San Juan de Dios in Guatemala City, 1788–1808," Ph.D. diss., University of Ottawa, 1987, 90.

20. Ibid., 91.

21. Ibid.

22. AGCA, Sig. A1, Leg. 284, Exp. 6131. The same records tell us a great deal about the hospital's expenditures. The greatest expenses were on food (excluding chocolate, including wine, meat, and bread) and on the salaries of clerics. Other expenses, in addition to chocolate, included candles, bed linens, medicine, and indulgences—the bula de la Santa Cruzada. One of the hospital logbooks for women mentions eight "servants" in 1796 who were "counted daily" as patients so that they might receive meals. These servants could be the nurses and the bed maker (plus one), or they could be cleaning staff that was not paid other than through meals; AGCA, Sig. A1, Leg. 1864, Exp. 12178.

23. Craig, "Patients and Disease in an Enlightenment Hospital," 88.

24. AGCA, Signatura A1, Leg. 4383, Exp. 35799. A case from 1804 recounts the flight of a prisoner from the hospital: Sig. A1, Leg. 4408, Exp. 36319. The cage is also mentioned in Sig. A2, Leg. 226, Exp. 4781, an 1808 case in which a soldier injured in an altercation was taken to the hospital *jaula*.

25. The total number of married women is 223 for this year. This chart shows only the most prevalent reasons for admission, so not every case is accounted for.

26. Komisaruk, *Labor and Love in Guatemala*, 124.

27. Craig, "Patients and Disease in an Enlightenment Hospital," 17–18.

28. AGCA, Sig. A2, Leg. 195, Exp. 3983.

29. Ibid.

30. AGCA, Sig. A1, Leg. 1865, Sig. 12181.

6

An Urban Space

1. AGCA, Signatura A1, Legajo 6059, Expediente 53804.

2. In AGCA, Sig. A1, Leg. 77, documents list Cayetano Díaz having been assigned manzana 31 after the transfer of the city from Santiago.

3. William B. Taylor, *Theater of a Thousand Wonders: A History of Miraculous Images and Shrines in New Spain* (Cambridge: Cambridge University Press, 2016), 3.

4. Yi-Fu Tuan, *Space and Place: The Perspective of Experience* (Minneapolis: University of Minnesota Press, 1977), 33.

5. Gisela Gellert, "Desarrollo de la estructura espacial en la Ciudad de Guatemala: Desde su fundación hasta la revolución de 1944," *Anuario de Estudios Centroamericanos* 16, no. 1 (1990): 33.

6. Tuan, *Space and Place,* 38.

7. Gellert, "Desarrollo de la estructura espacial," 34.

8. Marvin Estuardo Ramírez Cordón, Irina Montepeque, and Manuel Antonio Morales Montenegro, "Origen y desarrollo de los barrios y cantones de Guatemala" (Guatemala: Escuela de Historia Instituto de Investigaciones Históricas, Antropológicas y Arquelógicas, 2003), 34.

9. Henry Dunn, *Guatimala, Or, The United Provinces of Central America in 1827–8: Being Sketches and Memorandums Made during a Twelve Months' Residence in That Republic* (New York: G. and C. Carvill, 1828), 65.

10. Ibid., 65–66.

11. Ibid., 66–67.

12. AGCA, Sig. A2, Leg. 159, Exp. 3128.

13. Mario Alfredo Ubico Calderón, "Cultura material, energía y arqueología: una vista diacrónica de la Guatemala colonial," *Estudios Digital,* no. 11 (2017).

14. AGCA, Sig. A2, Leg. 195, Exp. 3993.

15. Sidney Markman observes in his architectural study of the plaza that while the space was meant to be neatly allotted to twenty stalls on the north and south sides and fourteen stalls on the east and west sides, the reality was much messier. "In time the area was jammed with a jumble of nondescript huts in complete dissarray"; Sidney David Markman, *The Plaza Mayor of Guatemala City* (Philadelphia: Journal of the Society of Architectural Historians, 1966), 188.

16. AGCA, Sig. A2, Leg. 165, Exp. 3284.

17. AGCA, Sig. A2, Leg. 194, Exp. 3975.

18. Dunn, *Guatimala,* 72.

7
Death, Sex, and the City

1. AGCA, Signatura A1, Legajo 4367, Expediente 35512.

2. Thomas W. Laqueur, *The Work of the Dead: A Cultural History of Mortal Remains* (Princeton: Princeton University Press, 2015), 31.

3. Ibid., 4.

4. I am grateful to Virginia Reinburg for pointing out the significance of this date.

5. Martina Will de Chaparro and Miruna Achim, *Death and Dying in Colonial Spanish America* (Tucson: University of Arizona Press, 2011), 1.

6. Laqueur, *The Work of the Dead*, x–xi.

7. There is a growing literature on Spanish American death and "deathways." Patricia Fernández Esquivel and Manuel Chacón Hidalgo, "Ritos funerarios católicos en el Valle Central de la Costa Rica del siglo XIX," *Cuadernos de Antropología* 17 (2013); Gisela von Wobeser and Enriqueta Vila Vilar, *Muerte y vida en el más allá: España y América, siglos XVI–XVIII* (Mexico City: Universidad Nacional Autónoma de México, 2009). For a treatment of French and British North America, see Erik R. Seeman, *Death in the New World: Cross-Cultural Encounters, 1492–1800* (Philadelphia: University of Pennsylvania Press, 2011).

8. Pedro Pérez Herrero, "Evolución demográfica y estructura familiar en México (1730–1850)," *Familias Novohispanas. Siglos XVI al XIX, el Colegio de México*, México, 1991, 352. Leavitt-Alcántara, "Practicing Faith," 142.

9. Leavitt-Alcántara, "Practicing Faith," 142.

10. Will de Chaparro and Achim, *Death and Dying*, 5.

11. Ibid.

12. Carlos M. N. Eire, *From Madrid to Purgatory: The Art and Craft of Dying in Sixteenth-Century Spain* (Cambridge: Cambridge University Press, 1995), 6.

13. Ibid., 258.

14. Ibid., 450.

15. Cited ibid., 24–36.

16. María de los Angeles Rodríguez Alvarez, *Usos y costumbres funerarias en la Nueva España* (Mexico City: El Colegio de Michoacán A.C., 2001), chapter 3.

17. Eire, *From Madrid to Purgatory*, 449–50.

18. Will de Chaparro and Achim, *Death and Dying*, 98–99.

19. AGCA, Sig. A2, Leg. 195, Exp. 3989.

20. Will de Chaparro and Achim, *Death and Dying*, 98–99. For an interesting contrast that considers the dismembered bodies of contemporary political "martyrs" and "saints," see Lyman L. Johnson, *Death, Dismemberment, and Memory: Body Politics in Latin America* (Albuquerque: University of New Mexico Press, 2004).

21. "The crucial difference between the ostensibly horrifying practice of cutting up the bodies of holy people soon after death . . . and such acts on the body of a common sinner rested in the purpose of the dismemberment and

the subsequent veneration of the parts"; Susan C. Lawrence, "Beyond the Grave: The Use and Meaning of Human Body Parts: A Historical Introduction," Faculty Publications, Department of History, University of Nebraska (online), 1998, 116.

22. See, for example, the following cases: Sig. A2, Leg. 173, Exp. 3444, 1793; Sig. A1, Leg. 5447, Exp. 46670, 1805; Sig. A2, Leg. 223, Exp. 4701, 1807; Sig. A1, Leg. 5389, Exp. 45709, 1809. Lyman L. Johnson and Sonya Lipsett-Rivera, *The Faces of Honor: Sex, Shame, and Violence in Colonial Latin America* (Albuquerque: University of New Mexico Press, 1998).

23. Lawrence, "Beyond the Grave," 115. Lawrence references the scholarly work of Caroline Bynum. See Caroline Walker Bynum, *Fragmentation and Redemption: Essays on Gender and the Human Body in Medieval Religion* (New York: Zone, 1992).

24. Douglass Sullivan-González, *Piety, Power, and Politics: Religion and Nation Formation in Guatemala, 1821–1871* (Pittsburgh: University of Pittsburgh Press, 1998), 37.

25. Ibid., 36.

26. Ibid.

27. Quoted ibid.

28. Quoted ibid.

29. Ibid.

30. João José Reis, *A morte é uma festa: ritos fúnebres e revolta popular no Brasil do século XIX* (São Paulo: Companhia das Letras, 1991); Pamela Voekel, *Alone before God: The Religious Origins of Modernity in Mexico* (Durham, N.C.: Duke University Press, 2002); Adam Warren, *Medicine and Politics in Colonial Peru: Population Growth and the Bourbon Reforms* (Pittsburgh: University of Pittsburgh Press, 2010).

31. AGCA, Sig. A1, Leg. 4367, Exp. 35512.

32. AGCA, Sig. A1, Leg. 53, Exp. 1340.

33. Ibid.

34. It surely didn't help that the hospital was in the middle of a prolonged battle between secular and ecclesiastical authorities, as the two groups struggled to determine who would take primary charge of the hospital and, crucially, where Guatemala City clerics would be treated as patients. See Christophe Belaubre, "El proceso de laicización de los hospitales en la capital del reino de Guatemala (XVI–XIX)," *Cambios y Permanencias*, no. 2 (2016): 252–85.

35. Quoted in Deborah Cameron and Elizabeth Frazer, *The Lust to Kill: A Feminist Investigation of Sexual Murder* (New York: New York University Press, 1987), 99.

36. Ibid., 100.

37. Ibid.

38. Ibid., 103, citing Robert J. Stoller, *Perversion: The Erotic Form of Hatred* (New York: Pantheon, 1975).

39. Cameron and Frazer, *The Lust to Kill*, 164.

40. "Or 'feminicide,' when stressing that these women are killed because of their sex, and that not only the male perpetrators but also the state and its judicial structures are responsible for the insecurity of female citizens and the impunity following acts of violence among them." Ninna Nyberg Sørensen writes that "the concept of femicide is attributed to Diane Russell, who initially defined femicide as 'the killing of women because they are women.' She later sharpened the definition to 'the murder of women by men motivated by hatred, contempt, pleasure, or a sense of ownership over women.' In order to recognize that girls and female babies are also among the victims, 'women' was replaced by 'females,' resulting in a definition of femicide as 'the killing of females by males because they are females.' In Russell's view, femicide is on the extreme end of a continuum of misogynist or anti-female terror that includes a wide variety of verbal and physical abuse. Whenever these forms of terrorism result in death, they become femicides"; "Governing through the Mutilated Female Body: Corpse, Body Politics, and Contestation in Contemporary Guatemala," in *Governing the Dead: Sovereignty and the Politics of Dead Bodies*, ed. Finn Stepputat and Elisabeth Anstett, 203–28 (Manchester: Manchester University Press, 2016).

41. I'm indebted to Peter Haskin for pointing out that the importance (perhaps greater importance) of this aspect might make the fact of legal redundancy less significant.

42. Sørensen, "Governing through the Mutilated Female Body," citing María Victoria Uribe, "Dismembering and Expelling: Semantics of Political Terror in Colombia," *Public Culture* 16, no. 1 (2004): 79–95.

43. Sørensen, "Governing through the Mutilated Female Body," 216, referencing, in part, Deborah Posel and Pamila Gupta, "The Life of the Corpse: Framing Reflections and Questions," *African Studies* 68, no. 3 (2009): 299–309.

44. This fits with a more general feminist interpretation of what is happening in this case: women objectified as their bodies are parceled out, *made* into objects. While this reading may spring to mind for us, it surely would not have been visible to Guatemalans in 1800.

45. Sørensen, "Governing through the Mutilated Female Body," 218.

46. Philippe Ariès, *The Hour of Our Death* (New York: Knopf, 1981), 392–93.

47. Ibid., 370.

48. Ibid., 372.

49. Jolene Zigarovich, *Sex and Death in Eighteenth-Century Literature* (New York: Routledge, 2013).

50. Ariès, *The Hour of Our Death,* 374–75.

51. Ibid., 380.

52. Zeb Tortorici, ed., introduction to *Sexuality and the Unnatural in Colonial Latin America* (Oakland: University of California Press, 2016), 3, 7.

53. AGCA, Sig. A1, Leg. 4369, Exp. 35548.

54. And of course the category of the victim here matters, too. In some ways, Mejicana began on poor footing as a low-class woman of mixed race, and she worsened her lot by engaging in an illicit relationship. It's not a stretch to say that in the colonial imagination, she got no worse than she deserved.

8

Bourbon Justice

1. AGCA, Signatura A2, Legajo 4367, Expediente 35523.

2. Here we risk opening something of a Pandora's box with the term "modernity." I am following the lead of authors who have focused on the seventeenth and eighteenth centuries as a long period of transition. For example, Marc Raeff: "For heuristic purposes I would suggest the following as conveying the essence of what we call 'modern,' as opposed to earlier, 'traditional' European and non-European patterns of culture: what may be detected in the second half of the seventeenth century—and what emerged into the open in the eighteenth in most of Western and Central Europe—is society's conscious desire to maximize all its resources and to use this new potential dynamically for the enlargement and improvement of its way of life. The potential of resources includes not merely material products and riches, but intellectual and cultural creations as well"; "The Well-Ordered Police State and the Development of Modernity in Seventeenth- and Eighteenth-Century Europe: An Attempt at a Comparative Approach," *American Historical Review* 80, no. 5 (1975): 1222. I've also drawn on Reinhart Koselleck, *Futures Past: On the Semantics of Historical Time,* trans. Keith Tribe (New York: Columbia University Press, 2004); Michel Foucault, *Security, Territory, Population: Lectures at the Collège de France, 1977–1978,* ed. Michel Senellart, trans. Graham Burchell (London: Palgrave Macmillan UK, 2009).

3. Bianca Premo, *The Enlightenment on Trial: Ordinary Litigants and Colonialism in the Spanish Empire* (New York: Oxford University Press, 2017), 5.

4. Ibid., 6.

5. Ibid, 9. E. P. Thompson, *The Making of the English Working Class* (New York: Vintage, 1966), 12.

6. Victor Uribe-Uran, *Fatal Love: Spousal Killers, Law, and Punishment in the Late Colonial Spanish Atlantic* (Stanford: Stanford University Press, 2016), 271.

7. My earnest thanks to the reviewer of this manuscript who rightly pushed for more here. This is an invaluable distinction, and I hope I've done it justice here in the unfolding.

8. There is a long and lively discussion of the early modern police state that mostly leaves Spain out of the picture and certainly does not comment on Guatemala specifically. Nevertheless, this discussion offers some insights for our time and place. As a starting premise, this literature does not construe "police state" in twentieth-century terms, but relies on early modern meanings and conceptions. Scholars considering early modern European states comparatively build on the use of the term "police state" by contemporaries to describe the science of administration that either (depending on the scholar's view) anticipated modernity or attended it. A classic treatment by Marc Raeff, with a particular eye on the early modern German states, argued that the "well-ordered police state" could be seen as an antecedent and even precondition for modernity, rather than a result of it; Raeff, "The Well-Ordered Police State." Since my focus here is related to but less focused on the question of modernity, I have found most helpful the treatment by Foucault in his 1978 lectures (March 29, April 5) on "Security, Territory, Population." Speaking explicitly about directions given to police magistrates in this period, Foucault says the following: "I think one of the most fundamental and typical elements of what will henceforth be understood by 'police' is this having 'man as the true subject,' and as the true subject of 'something to which he devotes himself,' inasmuch as he has an activity that must characterize his perfection and thus make possible the perfection of the state. Police is directed towards men's activity, but insofar as this activity has a relationship to the state. What interested the sovereign, prince, or republic in the traditional conception was what men were, either in terms of their status, their virtues, or their intrinsic qualities. It was important for them to be virtuous, it was important for them to be obedient, and it was important for them to be workers and not idlers. The good quality of the state depended upon the good quality of its elements. . . . What is characteristic of a police state is its interest in what men do; it is interested in their activity, their 'occupation.' The objective of police is therefore control of and responsibility for men's activity insofar as this activity constitutes a differential element in

the development of the state's forces"; Foucault, *Security, Territory, Population*, 322. Though Foucault is not writing about Bourbon Spanish America, he well could be. In both the 1791 regulations and the collection of criminal cases, this preoccupation with identifying a person's qualities and how they could or could not be turned to the benefit of the state is clearly in evidence. I'm also grateful to Martín Bernales for sharing with me his work in progress on policing the poor in early modern Spain; his research has influenced my approach.

9. Timothy Hawkins's invaluable reassessment of José de Bustamante, the Guatemalan captain general, describes Guatemala in 1812 as a "counterinsurgency state." Here Hawkins is describing the methods undertaken by Bustamante and previous officials in response to the Peninsular War and the threat of insurgency in the isthmus. A critical component of his argument is that Bustamante did not emerge a tyrant out of nowhere, but that many of the "counterinsurgency" methods he utilized were already being employed, in Guatemala and elsewhere. Hawkins does not dwell on the 1790s and urban policing as direct antecedents, but this period and its methods fold easily into practices of the early nineteenth century. See Hawkins, *José de Bustamante and Central American Independence: Colonial Administration in an Age of Imperial Crisis* (Tuscaloosa: University of Alabama Press, 2004). Michael Riekenberg's complementary work on policing in Guatemala focuses on the nineteenth century as well: Michael Riekenberg, "Nachlassende Staatsbildung: Das städtische Polizeiwesen in Guatemala im 19. Jahrhundert," *Ibero-Amerikanisches Archiv* 23, no. 3 (1997): 243–62. For a broader discussion of political change in nineteenth-century Central America, see Justin Wolfe, *The Everyday Nation-State: Community and Ethnicity in Nineteenth-Century Nicaragua* (Lincoln: University of Nebraska Press, 2007); Douglass Sullivan-González, *Piety, Power, and Politics: Religion and Nation Formation in Guatemala, 1821–1871* (Pittsburgh: University of Pittsburgh Press, 1998); Michael Riekenberg, "On Collective Violence in Nineteenth-Century Guatemala," in *Politics and History of Violence and Crime in Central America* (New York: Palgrave Macmillan, 2017), 183–205.

10. For a complementary treatment of policing in the city of Lisbon in this period, see María Alexandre Lousada, "A cidade vigiada: A polícia e a cidade de Lisboa no início do século XIX," *Cadernos de Geografia* 17 (1998): 227–32. Lousada makes a similar argument about the police in Lisbon being less engaged in repressing and more engaged in surveilling. Other authors characterize the Portuguese "police state" in a slightly different way: a half-century of administrative reform in the wake of the Lisbon earthquake that on the one hand shared many of the preoccupations of the Bourbon reforms—

cleanliness, order, modernity—but on the other hand, in contrast to what I describe here, greatly expanded the state bureaucracy at the expense of the judiciary. See José Subtil, "As mudanças em curso na segunda metade do século XVIII: a ciência de polícia e o novo perfil dos funcionários régios," in *Cargos e ofícios nas monarquias ibéricas: Provimento, controlo e venalidade (séculos XVII–XVIII)*, ed. Roberta Stumpf and Nandini Chaturvedula, 65–80 (Lisbon: CHAM, 2012); José Subtil, "O direito de polícia nas véperas do estado liberal em Portugal," in *As formas do direito: ordem, razão e decisão* (Curitiba: Juruá Editora, 2013), 275–332; Airton Cerqueira Leite Seelaender, "A 'polícia' e as funções do estado: notas sobre a 'polícia' do antigo regime," *Revista da Faculdade de Direito UFPR* 49 (2009): 73–87. For the conception of policing in this period in England, France, and Sweden, see F. M. Dodsworth, "The Idea of Police in Eighteenth-Century England: Discipline, Reformation, Superintendence, c. 1780–1800," *Journal of the History of Ideas* 69, no. 4 (2008): 583–604; Peter Hicks, "The Napoleonic 'Police' or 'Security State' in Context," *Napoleonica. La Revue* 4, no. 1 (2009): 2–10; Toomas Kotkas, *Royal Police Ordinances in Early Modern Sweden: The Emergence of Voluntaristic Understanding of Law* (Leiden: Brill, 2013); Michael Sibalis, "The Napoleonic Police State," in *Napoleon and Europe*, ed. Philip Dwyer, 79–94 (London: Longman, 2001).

11. Richard Kagan, *Urban Images of the Hispanic World, 1493–1793* (New Haven: Yale University Press, 2000), 26–27.

12. Jordana Dym, "El poder en la Nueva Guatemala: La disputa sobre los Alcaldes de barrio," *Cuadernos de Literatura* 14, no. 28 (2013): 200–201.

13. Most of the action for our case took place in the cuartel of San Agustín, which had two barrios: El Perú and San Juan de Dios, after the hospital.

14. "A diferencia de las reformas fiscales de los 1760 y de la creación de las intendencias de los 1780, las cuales se originaron con órdenes provenientes de España, la institución de los alcaldes de barrio en América Central empezó como una reacción local a un problema local. En 1761, queriendo la Audiencia enfrentar un alza percibida en las tasas de crimen, ebriedad, vagancia y ociosidad entre la plebe citadina, clamó por la reorganización y la mejora de las funciones municipales de policía"; Dym, "El poder en la Nueva Guatemala," 202. It is likely, to my eye, that Guatemalan authorities were looking at models elsewhere, even if they claimed to be responding purely to local conditions. Similar reforms in 1782 in Mexico City, for example, were surely recognized. See Gabriel Haslip-Viera's description of these reforms in *Crime and Punishment in Late Colonial Mexico City, 1692–1810* (Albuquerque: University of New Mexico Press, 1999), 47.

15. Dym, "El poder en la Nueva Guatemala."

16. Francisco Robledo, "Descripción de Quarteles y Barrios," *Anales de la Sociedad de Geografía e Historia* 3 (1926): 159–78.

17. Ibid.

18. As Foucault's work and other studies of the early modern police state emphasize, the policing approaches described here do not spring from nowhere in the late eighteenth century but, rather, build gradually over the course of more than a century. In Guatemala, rondas had been in use for decades, as had censuses and search warrants. What we see in the eighteenth century is, rather, a culmination of efforts: a greater investment in these tools, a more consistent application of them, and a doubling down on their implicit authority. Foucault, *Security, Territory, Population*.

19. Robledo, "Descripción de Quarteles y Barrios." Another office to rely on surveillance in this fashion was the late eighteenth-century inquisition, though it could do so only in select places. (My thanks to Bill Taylor for making this connection.)

20. AGCA, Sig. A1, Leg. 4400, Exp. 36144.

21. AGCA, Sig. A2, Leg. 168, Exp. 3346.

22. AGCA, Sig. A1, Leg. 4400, Exp. 36164.

23. AGCA, Sig. A2, Leg. 206, Exp. 4238.

24. Uribe-Uran, *Fatal Love*, 207.

25. See Uribe-Uran's discussion of "public" crimes (serious crimes like murder) and "nonpublic" crimes; ibid., 15.

26. In fact, there are probably a lot of crimes that they would want to conceal, including the one Vivar may have been alluding to. There would be no reason for rape to make it into the record, and it's very likely that it happened. I simply haven't found any evidence of it.

27. AGCA, Sig. A2, Leg. 234, Exp. 4983.

28. AGCA, Sig. A2, Leg. 195, Exp. 3989.

29. Indeed, there is support for the idea that they were actually thugs. In an 1804 case, Dionicio López was apprehended after fleeing the public works project he was sentenced to. He had been convicted for carrying a weapon. But instead of being returned to the public works, he was assigned to a *comisionado*, Don Mariano Mora y Roca, who said he could use a man like Dionicio on his ronda. The case suggests that men who could handle weapons were seen as liabilities if they worked outside the law and assets if they worked with the law; AGCA, Sig. A2, Leg. 206, Exp. 4240.

30. AGCA, Sig. A1, Leg. 2598, Exp. 21330.

31. Sylvia Sellers-García, *Distance and Documents at the Spanish Empire's Periphery* (Stanford: Stanford University Press, 2013).

32. AGCA, Sig. A2, Leg. 195, Exp. 3983.

33. Ignacio Guerra y Marchán, a Guatemalan *escribano* for this period, offers an example of how archives and their organization were being taken seriously in this period. See chapter 5 in Sellers-García, *Distance and Documents.*

34. Pierre Bourdieu, Loic J. D. Wacquant, and Samar Farage, "Rethinking the State: Genesis and Structure of the Bureaucratic Field," *Sociological Theory* 12, no. 1 (1994): 3–5.

35. Nancy Signorielli, George Gerbner, and Michael Morgan, "Standpoint: Violence on Television: The Cultural Indicators Project," *Journal of Broadcasting and Electronic Media* 39, no. 2 (1995): 278–83.

36. Bourdieu, Wacquant, and Farage, "Rethinking the State."

37. See, for example, the aforementioned case in which women were whipped in prison; AGCA, Sig. A2, Leg. 234, Exp. 4983.

38. Ana Margarita Gómez and Sajid Alfredo Herrera Mena, *Los Rostros de la Violencia: Guatemala y El Salvador, Siglos XVIII y XIX*, vol. 1 (San Salvador, El Salvador: UCA Editores, 2007), 123–58.

39. The regulations date back to 1480, with several amendments over the centuries. Since the sixteenth century, restrictions were placed on the kinds of blades people could carry and (short) pistols were banned, even to members of the military. Repeated laws in the eighteenth century specified the types of arms that were prohibited and the punishments for carrying them. In 1761, Charles III (repetitively) banned "pistolas, trabucos y carabinas, que no lleguen a la marca de quatro palmos de cañon, puñales, giferos, almaradas, navaja de muelle con golpe o virola, daga sola, cuchillo de punta chico o grande, aunque sea de cocina y de moda de faldriquera, baxo las penas impuestas . . . y son, a los nobles la de seis años de presidio, y a los plebeyos los mismos de minas"; Ley 13 tit. 6, Lib. 6. R. Spain, *Novísima recopilacion de las leyes de España.*

40. For how this plays out in cases of the military fuero, see Ana Margarita Gómez, "The Evolution of Military Justice in Late Colonial Guatemala, 1762–1821," *A Contracorriente* 4, no. 2 (2007): 31–53.

41. AGCA, Sig. A2, Leg. 194, Exp. 3959.

42. AGCA, Sig. A2, Leg. 197, Exp. 4024.

Epilogue

1. I am indebted to Nancy Quintanilla for illuminating this point in her comments to me.

Illustration Credits

Figures 19, 20, 21, 22, 23: Photographs by Saulo Bambi, Sistema Museale dell'Università degli Studi di Firenze

Figure 24: Davis Museum at Wellesley College, Wellesley, MA

Figures 26, 27: Graphs by author

Figure 29: Ministerio de Cultura y Deporte, Archivo General de Indias, MP-Guatemala, 265

Figure 30: Map by Erin Greb

Index